Advising Gay and Lesbian C

GW00362465

Advising Gay and Lesbian Clients

Anne Barlow
Solicitor and Lecturer in Law, University of Wales, Aberystwyth

Martin Bowley QC
Barrister, 36 Bedford Row

Gill Butler
Solicitor, Evans Butler Wade

Laura Cox QC
Barrister, Cloisters

Matthew Davies
Solicitor, Wilson & Co

Wesley Gryk
Solicitor, Wesley Gryk Solicitors

Angus Hamilton
Solicitor, Hamiltons

Peter Smith
Solicitor, Smith Braithwaite

Mark Watson
Stonewall

Butterworths
London Edinburgh & Dublin
1999

United Kingdom	Butterworths, a Division of Reed Elsevier (UK) Ltd, Halsbury House, 35 Chancery Lane, LONDON WC2A 1EL and 4 Hill Street, EDINBURGH EH2 3JZ
Australia	Butterworths, a Division of Reed International Books Australia Pty Ltd, CHATSWOOD, New South Wales
Canada	Butterworths Canada Ltd, MARKHAM, Ontario
Hong Kong	Butterworths Asia (Hong Kong), HONG KONG
India	Butterworths India, NEW DELHI
Ireland	Butterworth (Ireland) Ltd, DUBLIN
Malaysia	Malayan Law Journal Sdn Bhd, KUALA LUMPUR
New Zealand	Butterworths of New Zealand Ltd, WELLINGTON
Singapore	Butterworths Asia, SINGAPORE
South Africa	Butterworths Publishers (Pty) Ltd, DURBAN
USA	Lexis Law Publishing, CHARLOTTESVILLE, Virginia

© Reed Elsevier (UK) Ltd 1999

All rights reserved. No part of this publication may be reproduced in any material form (including photocopying or storing it in any medium by electronic means and whether or not transiently or incidentally to some other use of this publication) without the written permission of the copyright owner except in accordance with the provisions of the Copyright, Designs and Patents Act 1988 or under the terms of a licence issued by the Copyright Licensing Agency Ltd, 90 Tottenham Court Road, London, England W1P 0LP. Applications for the copyright owner's written permission to reproduce any part of this publication should be addressed to the publisher.

Warning: The doing of an unauthorised act in relation to a copyright work may result in both a civil claim for damages and criminal prosecution.

Any Crown copyright material is reproduced with the permission of the Controller of Her Majesty's Stationery Office.

A CIP Catalogue record for this book is available from the British Library.

ISBN 0-406-90303-4

9 780406 903037

Printed by Redwood Books, Trowbridge

Visit us at our website: www.butterworths.co.uk

Foreword

The two chief claims of any system of law are—or ought to be—that it is certain and that it is just. The law affecting gay men and lesbians in Britain at present is neither. It is struggling to keep abreast of radically changing public and private moralities, sometimes accommodating change, sometimes resisting it.

In this labile situation the present volume is not only a handbook of much-needed guidance to lawyers with gay or lesbian clients. It is a living record of how we are coping as a society with a legacy of prejudice and discrimination in a nascent culture of human rights. It makes this book a special kind of practice manual: one which openly sets out to steer the development of law and practice in a humane and non-discriminatory direction.

The authors share a record of professional distinction and commitment which gives the book both breadth and depth. As well as affording practical guidance which cuts helpfully across the traditional categories of legal learning, their book makes an important addition to the legal literature of human rights.

The Rt Hon Lord Justice Sedley
Royal Courts of Justice, London
January 1999

Contents

Chapter 4 The family home

Chapter 5 Inheritance and succession

Chapter 6   Immigration

Chapter 7   Crime

Chapter 8   Equality 2000

Precedents

Table of statutes

References in this Table are to paragraph number. Where a paragraph number is set in **bold** this indicates that the Act is set out in part or in full. References in this Table to *Statutes* are to Halsbury's Statutes of England (Fourth Edition) where the annotated text of the Act may be found.

Table of European legislation

Table of cases

H

I

J

K

Chapter 1

Legislation and litigation

1.01 In England and Wales homosexuality began in 1967 (speaking strictly legally, of course). It was only in the Sexual Offences Act of that year—'an Act to amend the law relating to homosexual acts'—that the word was first allowed to sully the statute book. Until then, all male homosexuality was illegal. The statute decriminalised such activity between men, but only where both parties were over 21 years of age and the act took place 'in private'. It was a groundbreaking reform. It was also very limited. It did not extend to Northern Ireland, to Scotland, to the armed forces or to the merchant navy. It did not legalise homosexuality. As Lord Reid said in *R v Knuller* [1]: 'There is a material difference between merely exempting certain conduct from criminal penalties and making it lawful in the full sense.'

1   [1973] AC 435 at 457.

A   THE ABOMINABLE CRIME

1.02 Originally a matter for the ecclesiastical courts, buggery—or sodomy as it was sometimes called—was brought within the ambit of the criminal law by a 1533 Act [1] 'against buggery, Welshmen vagabonds and other misdemeanours'. It attracted the death penalty, which lasted until the passage of the Offences Against The Person Act 1861. It also attracted an astonishing range of euphemisms. Section 61 of the 1861 Act refers to 'the abominable crime' of buggery. Section 62 deals with attempts to commit what the relevant subtitle calls 'unnatural offences' and the 'abstract of enactments' refers to 'an infamous crime'. 'Unnatural offences' are still to be found in the subtitle to ss 12 and 13 of the Sexual Offences Act 1956 and even in the relevant chapter in the 1998 edition of Archbold: *Criminal Pleading Evidence and Practice*. 'Gross indecency' dates only from the Labouchere amendment, which became s 11 of the Criminal Law Amendment Act 1885 and which was used in the prosecution of Oscar Wilde a decade later. Blackstone's infamous 'crime against nature' links directly with 'the love that dare not speak its name' of Lord Alfred Douglas.

1   25 Hen 8 c 6.

1.03 The consolidating Act of 1861 was just one of seven—covering not only offences against the person, but also malicious damage, larceny, forgery, coinage offences and accessories and abetters—which had emerged from the deliberations of a number of law commissions and even more reports over a period of nearly 30 years and which were intended to 'consolidate and amend the statute law of England and Wales'. They had been introduced on several earlier occasions, but had always failed to make progress because they were introduced too late in the parliamentary session. Ranging as it did from homicide to causing actual bodily harm, from rape to indecent assault, from bigamy to abortion and, pausing only to deal with the making and having of gunpowder to commit a felony and with the power to arrest any person loitering at night and suspected of a felony, it is hardly surprising that the sections in the 1861 Act dealing with 'unnatural offences' received scant—if any—attention in either House.

1   The suppression of brothels

1.04   The 1885 Act was concerned with the 'protection of women and girls and the suppression of brothels'. The justification for using it as a vehicle to criminalise consensual male homosexual activity in public or in private was that:

> 'At present any person on whom an *assault* [emphasis added] of the kind here dealt with was committed must be under the age of 13, and the object with which he had brought forward this clause was to make the law applicable to any person whether under the age of 13 or over that age.'[1]

The logical absurdities involved make it tempting to accept the explanation which Tom Stoppard gives to Labouchere in his play *The Invention of Love*[2]:

> 'Anybody with any sense on the backbenches was pitchforking Amendments in to get the government to admit it had a pig's breakfast on its hands and withdraw it. My Amendment on indecency between male persons went through on the nod. It had nothing to do with the Bill we were supposed to be debating: normally it would have been ruled out of order. I intended to make the Bill absurd to any person left in what by then was a very thin House ... but that one got away, so now a French kiss and what-you-fancy between two chaps safe at home with the door shut is good for two years with or without hard labour.'

The amendment went through the Commons virtually without debate—except to double the penalty from one to two years' imprisonment. It occupies less than a single column in *Hansard* and was never debated in the Lords at all.

1   HC Official Report (3rd series) cols 1397–1398, 6 August 1885.
2   Stoppard, T *The Invention of Love* (1997) p 63, Faber and Faber.

1.05   It was the Vagrancy Act 1898 which first made it an offence for 'a man persistently to solicit or importune in a public place for immoral purposes'. Originally only a summary offence it was upgraded to be indictable with a maximum penalty of two years' imprisonment by the Criminal Law Amendment Act 1912. Both Acts were, essentially, concerned with the control of heterosexual prostitution, prohibiting living off immoral earnings and, once again, the suppression of brothels. The 1912 Act was originally entitled the Criminal Law Amendment (White Slave Traffic) Bill. Both were extensively debated, though honourable members on all sides and in both Houses were mainly concerned with the rights and wrongs of flogging women. Certainly there is no indication that the offence of 'soliciting for an immoral purpose' was to be used—as it has almost exclusively come to be used—against homosexual men 'cottaging' and 'cruising'.

1.06 The current legislation is very largely contained in the Sexual Offences Act 1956, another consolidating measure passed, this time, under the fast track provisions of the Consolidation of Enactments (Procedure) Act 1949. As a consolidating measure it re-enacted, in virtually identical language, provisions of the Offences Against The Person Act 1861, the Criminal Law Amendment Act 1885 and the Vagrancy Act 1898, as amended by the Criminal Law Amendment Act 1912. It was debated in Parliament for fully three minutes [1]! Only Marcus Lipton—then the Labour member for Brixton—sought to argue that it was a singularly inappropriate time to consolidate what he considered to be bad law. He was very firmly put in his place by Mr Speaker Morrison on the grounds that, as there was no Bill before the House to repeal or alter the existing law, it was not in order for a member to criticise that existing law and the House moved on swiftly to a debate on the shortage of teachers in Birmingham!

1   HC Official Report (5th series) cols 1750–1751, 6 July 1956.

2   A quintessential English public servant

1.07 Lipton's point was that less than two years earlier the then Home Secretary, Sir David Maxwell Fyfe, had set up a departmental committee to investigate the whole question of homosexuality and prostitution. Little more than a year later, on 4 September 1957, the Wolfenden Report [1] was published recommending the decriminalisation of gay sex, in private, where both parties were over the age of 21. The government's motives for setting up the inquiry and then pushing through the 1956 Act before it had reported, were accurately pinpointed by a Conservative backbencher—Earl Winterton—in a debate in the House of Lords when he said:

> 'I know of no better method of putting off legislation than by appointing a committee. It usually does not report for a year or so—sometimes two years, and not until the next Parliament. And whenever the government in power are faced with anything which looks like political dynamite they appoint a committee.'[2]

1   Cmnd 247.
2   HL Official Report (5th series) cols 740–741, 19 May 1954.

1.08 This is not the place for a detailed description of the social background to Wolfenden or for any close analysis of the committee's deliberations and the evidence it received or the conclusions it came to. For that I would refer readers to Stephen Jeffery Poulter's *Peers, Queers and Commons* [1], Leslie Moran's *The Homosexual(ity) of Law* [2] and to Patrick Higgins' *Heterosexual Dictatorship* [3]. But Wolfenden was so central to the struggle for lesbian and gay rights that he demands attention even in a brief overview such as this.

1   Jeffery Poulter, S *Peers, Queers and Commons* (1990) Routledge.
2   Moran, L *The Homosexual(ity) of Law* (1996) Routledge.
3   Higgins, P *Heterosexual Dictatorship* (1996) Fourth Estate.

1.09   The early 1950s had seen an increase in the number of people prosecuted for offences of 'indecency between males' culminating in the conviction and imprisonment of Lord Montagu of Beaulieu, Michael Pitt-Rivers and Peter Wildeblood in March 1954. Their trials, with their accompanying prurient publicity, initiated a public discussion on the relationship between the criminal law and private morality. Debates were held in both Houses of Parliament. A report of the Church of England's Moral Welfare Committee concluded that though homosexual behaviour was sinful it should not be treated as a crime.

1.10   Wolfenden was almost the quintessential English public servant. A product of Wakefield Grammar School and The Queen's College, Oxford, he became a Fellow of Magdalen, headmaster of Uppingham at the age of 28 and Vice Chancellor of Reading University. Described by Sebastian Faulks as 'an ascetic, unsophisticated man, with a good mechanical brain but little imaginative flair' [1], he must have seemed the ideal candidate to produce a 'no change' recommendation. No-one—least of all Wolfenden himself—would have seen him as a likely initiator of a revolution in sexual morality.

1   Faulks, S *The Fatal Englishman* (1997) p 214 Vintage.

1.11   The Wolfenden recommendations were certainly ahead of their time, although with hindsight they could hardly be described as revolutionary. The committee took the view on the age of consent that 'a boy is incapable, at the age of 16, of forming a mature judgment about actions of the kind which might have the effect of setting him apart from society' and settled on 21 for the simple—if simplistic—reason 'that this is the age at which a man is capable of entering into legal contracts, including the contract of marriage, on his own responsibility'. In proposing 21—a recommendation which it conceded was based on 'an element of arbitrariness'—the committee ignored its own findings that 'the main sexual pattern is laid down in the early years of life' and 'is usually fixed by the age of 16'.

1.12   Limited though the Wolfenden proposals were it still took ten years, a change of government, a major jurisprudential debate between Herbert Hart [1] and Patrick Devlin [2] and a lengthy lobbying campaign before they were eventually enacted in the Sexual Offences Act 1967. Among the main opponents of the Bill was the former Lord Chancellor, Lord Kilmuir, who in an earlier incarnation had set up the Wolfenden Committee ten years before. Even then, as part of the political price extracted in return for the basic reform, they were substantially watered down—not least by the very limited 'privacy' definition, still enshrined in s 1(2) of the Act, the section which allowed the successful prosecution of the 'Bolton seven' as recently as January 1998. Younger historians of gay history should study the parliamentary contributions to the debate from Lords Dilhorne and Kilmuir in the Lords and Cyril Osborn and Cyril Black in the Commons to estimate the prejudice which permeated the governing classes in the 1960s. They In retrospect it may be arguable that unnecessary concessions were made to ensure the passage of the Bill, but no-one should underestimate the contributions over many years of men like Antony Grey and Alan Horsfall and the Homosexual Law Reform Society (HLRS). Nor should anyone forget the support behind the scenes and in Cabinet of the then Home Secretary—Roy (now Lord) Jenkins. Without his support the necessary and vital parliamentary time would almost certainly not have been made available.

1   See Hart, H *Law Liberty and Morality* (1963) OUP.
2   See Devlin, P *The Enforcement of Morals* (1965) OUP.

3   A wall of silence

1.13   For 27 years thereafter, there was, with one exception, a legislative wall of silence on these issues in England and Wales. It was not until 1980—largely as a result of the parliamentary efforts of Robin Cook, now Foreign Secretary— that the provisions of the 1967 Act were at last extended to Scotland. Northern Ireland had to wait even longer. It was only after the European Court of Human Rights had ruled in favour of Jeff Dudgeon that the United Kingdom was in breach of arts 8 and 14 of the European Convention on Human Rights [1] in refusing to legalise homosexual behaviour in Ulster, that the 1967 provisions were extended to that province. Even then it took almost exactly two years from that decision for the Conservative government to provide time for the necessary order in council to be debated in the Commons in October 1982.

1   [1981 4 EHRR 149.

1.14   Perhaps, at the time, too many lesbians and gay men thought that the 1967 Act was the end of the war, rather than just a preliminary skirmish. The same mistake must not be repeated after the equalisation of the age of consent. Energies and enthusiasms, time and money, were diverted from political and parliamentary campaigns into developing an open culture and community where gay clubs and discos, gay pubs, gay businesses, gay magazines and gay newspapers proliferated. The hardcore activists, however, kept up the fight. The HLRS became the Campaign for Homosexual Equality (CHE) and the Gay Liberation Front (GLF) was formed in 1970. In 1975 CHE, together with the Scottish Minorities Group (SMG) and the Union for Sexual Freedom in Ireland (USFI), published a draft Sexual Offences Reform Bill. The campaign was launched at a Trafalgar Square rally which *Gay Times* described as 'the largest public gathering of homosexuals of all time in this country'. The attendance was reported as 2,500—compare that with the estimated 300,000 who attended Gay Pride twenty-two years later. Once again the issues were referred to a committee— this time the Criminal Law Review Committee—surprisingly enough by the same man who had eight years earlier facilitated the passage of the 1967 Act, Roy Jenkins. On this occasion the committee deliberated for six years before recommending in April 1981 an age of consent for men of 18—though the five women on the committee produced a minority report advocating 16 as the age of consent.

1.15   By then the eighteen years of Conservative government were well established and the chances of radical law reform in these areas decreased as the Thatcher majorities increased. The only exception, if it can be called that, was the passage in May 1988 of s 28 of the Local Government Act 1988 which forbids local authorities from 'promoting homosexuality' and 'the teaching in any maintained school of the acceptability of homosexuality as a pretended family relationship'—whatever that may mean. For a detailed review of the 18 month battle against s 28, see Stephen Jeffery Poulter's *Peers, Queers and Commons* [1].

1   Jeffery Poulter, S *Peers, Queers and Commons* (1990) Routledge.

4   Radicalising the community

1.16   The importance of s 28 is twofold. First, that although it has never in ten years been tested in the courts, it has undoubtedly acted in a negative way by making many teachers fearful of raising homosexual issues in the classroom—even in sex and health education lessons. One local authority is reported to have used the section to prevent schoolchildren attending performances of *Death in Venice*. Second and more importantly, it radicalised the lesbian and gay community in a way that it had never been radicalised before—not even during the passage of the Sexual Offences Act 1967. This time, anti-section 28 rallies attracted attendances of upwards of 30,000 people and within two years both Stonewall and Outrage! had been formed. Unknowingly—and certainly unintentionally—the Thatcher government had unleashed a momentum for reform and a campaign for equality which is now unstoppable.

1.17   One of the first fruits of that campaign was the publication in July 1990 by Stonewall, CHE and the National Council for Civil Liberties of a Homosexual Equality Bill. It was certainly comprehensive. It aimed to include 'the three core areas without which fundamental equality for the lesbian and gay minority cannot really be said to exist: the right to non discrimination in civil law, to equality under the criminal law and the right to legal recognition of lesbian and gay relationships' [1]. The Bill sought to extend the definition of 'hate crimes' to include sexual orientation and tried to deal with the ban on gays in the military. At the time, Peter Ashman wrote that among the criteria against which the Bill had been drafted was that 'it had to be politically practicable'. It was certainly not. The Conservative majority in 1987 had been over 100 and the chances of such legislation making any progress in that Parliament were non-existent. Nonetheless, the Bill put down a number of important markers and as the legislative climate improves it will surely come to be an increasingly valuable research tool.

1   Peter Ashman *Gay Times,* July 1990.

5   The age of consent

1.18   John Major's re-election in April 1992—albeit with a much reduced parliamentary majority—was a further blow to the hopes of lesbian and gay law reformers. Certainly the Criminal Justice and Public Order Act 1994 provided the first legislative breakthrough for 27 years, after a lobbying campaign—masterminded by Angela Mason the Director of Stonewall—which was a model of its kind. In the course of the campaign several influential papers came out in support of an age of consent of 16 years and the British Medical Association approved a report which stated that 'there is no clear justification for a differential age for male homosexual activity and other sexual activity' and concluded 'there is no convincing medical reason against reducing the age of consent for male homosexuals to 16 years and to do so may yield some positive results'.

1.19   Although that view was supported by the Royal College of Psychiatrists, the Health Education Authority, the Terrence Higgins Trust, the Save the Children Fund and Barnardos (among many others) Edwina Currie's amendment was defeated in the Commons by just 27 votes and in the Lords by 174.

Compromise prevailed and the age of consent of 18 was approved by a majority of 265 in the Commons and of 63 in the Lords. The day after the Commons vote *The Guardian* commented 'Rarely can there have been so little committed enthusiasm for a motion so widely supported.'[1] In the same newspaper David McKie wrote 'The 16 age limit will pass next time in a younger and possibly lefter [sic] Commons.'[1] Matthew Parris wrote in *The Times*: 'We are now set to achieve an equal age of consent soon after the next election, whoever wins it.'[2]

1   *The Guardian*, 22 February 1994.
2   *The Times*, 26 February 1994.

1.20   The Criminal Justice and Public Order Act 1994 at last extended the provisions of the Sexual Offences Act 1967 to the armed forces (s 146(1) and (2)) and to the merchant navy (s 146(3)). But as a result of a Lords' amendment—passed only by 82 votes to 61 and against the advice of even the Conservative government—s 146(4) provided that homosexual conduct in both the armed forces and the merchant navy should continue to be a ground for administrative discharge. Of greater significance was the creation of the offence of male rape and the decriminalisation of consensual heterosexual buggery in private where both parties are over the age of 18. But even this reform was less than equal as the restrictive definition of 'in private' which was taken straight from s 1(2) of the 1967 Act, applied only to homosexuals and not to heterosexuals. At least the parliamentary draftsmen had at last stopped referring to 'unnatural offences'!

1.21   Other attempts at legislative reform during the Parliament of 1992 were less successful. Amendments to the Adoption Act 1976 to permit unmarried couples to adopt were not taken up. In May 1996 Lady Turner's Sexual Orientation Discrimination (SOD) Bill, which would have amended both s 3 of the Sex Discrimination Act 1975 and s 1(3) of the Equal Pay Act 1970 to cover sexual orientation, passed through all its stages in the House of Lords, with support from both the Labour and Liberal Democrat front benches. But—perhaps inevitably—it failed to make any progress in the Commons as the Conservative government took the view that it was 'neither necessary nor desirable.'[1] Only nine days later, the whipped Conservative majority in the Commons refused to accept Edwina Currie's amendment to the Armed Forces Bill which had proposed a new code of conduct for the armed forces which would have applied to all inappropriate sexual behaviour, whether heterosexual or homosexual. As recently as 6 June 1998 George Robertson—the new Secretary of State for Defence—was reported as agreeing 'in principle' that the ban should be lifted because 'people should all be treated equally' but adding that there are still 'practical issues of operational effectiveness' in the way of allowing lesbians and gay men to serve in the armed forces.

1   HC Official Report (6th series) col 1235, 1 May 1996.

B   INTO EUROPE: STRASBOURG AND LUXEMBOURG

1.22   In the political context and climate of the 1992 Parliament it was inevitable that reformers should look elsewhere and led by Stonewall—inspired largely by Peter Duffy QC—they looked to the courts and ultimately to Europe. On 5 April 1993, on the 98th anniversary of Oscar Wilde's arrest and in the very hotel where he was arrested, three men, two aged 19, one aged 24—launched an application to the European Court of Human Rights (ECHR) for a ruling that the

UK's age of consent rules breached their rights under arts 8(1) and 4 of the European Convention on Human Rights. It was not entirely coincidental that one of the young men shared his surname with the great playwright. As a result the case was entitled, most appropriately, *Wilde v United Kingdom* [1]. That case was overtaken by the 1994 reduction of the age of consent to 18, but the European baton was taken up by two 16-year-olds—Euan Sutherland and Chris Morris—and in July 1997 by a majority of 14 to 4 the European Commission on Human Rights reported that:

> 'No objective and reasonable justification exists for the maintenance of a higher minimum age of consent to male homosexual than to heterosexual acts and that the application discloses discriminatory treatment in the exercise of the applicant's right to respect for private life under art 8 of the Convention.' [2]

1   (1995) 80 AD & R 132.
2   Application No 25186/94.

1.23   Three months later the Labour government reached an agreement with the parties that it would make available, as soon as practicable, time for a free vote on the reduction of the age of consent to 16. It was agreed that if the opportunity arose, that vote would take place on a proposed amendment to the existing law. The opportunity did come on 22 June 1998 when Ann Keen's amendment to the Crime and Disorder Bill was passed by the Commons by a majority of 207. In the course of the debate Stephen Twigg, one of six openly gay MPs, said:

> 'This debate is about human rights. Prejudice and discrimination scar not only those who face it but our entire society. The new clause will send out a positive unequivocal and tolerant message. I am proud that tonight the House can put itself on the side of decency, openness and justice.' [1]

And Gordon Marsden—another of the six—said:

> 'The new clause is about equality and social justice, not about privileges, special treatment, positive discrimination. It is about ensuring our fellow citizens' equality before the law. The litmus test of a civilised and pluralist society is how it treats its minorities. We all belong to a minority of one sort or another.' [2]

1   HC Official Report (6th series) col 780, 22 June 1998.
2   HC Official Report (6th series) col 801, 22 June 1998.

1.24   Exactly one month later the Lords rejected the Keen amendment by a majority of 290 to 122. Four years earlier the vote on the same issue had been 245 to 71. As in 1994 the debate was a singularly unedifying occasion. It was riddled with prejudice, bigotry and ignorance. It was notable for the total refusal of Lady Young and her elderly supporters to counter the weight of medical and sociological evidence which has built up in favour of lowering the age of consent to 16 in recent years. It did their Lordships no credit at all. But if nothing else it confirmed that the age of consent is essentially a generational issue. The average age of those who spoke in the Commons in favour of lowering the age of consent to 16 was 44—and only one of them was over 60. The average age of those who spoke in the Lords against, was 74—and only one of them was under 60. Time is not on their Lordships' side.

1.25 But among the prejudiced and the ignorant there were powerful speeches in favour of lowering the age of consent to 16 from Lady Mallalieu, Lord Dhokolia, Lord Lester, Earl Russell, Lord Annan and the Bishop of Bath and Wells. Above all the debate was redeemed by the contribution of Lord Williams of Mostyn, from the government front bench, who started by saying: 'There is a world outside. It is inhabited by the young and the different live there. Many of them will read what your Lordships have said with sad incredulity'. He continued:

> 'There is a moral imperative to the law or it has no virtue and it has no place with us. The moral imperative is equality before the law. If that moral imperative fails because the social equation which is contended for tonight does not allow for it, so that equality dies and falls away, the whole purpose and virtue of law is gone and we shall no longer be a civil society.'[1]

And he concluded:

> 'Is it right to discriminate in law against young men aged 16 and 17 for engaging in homosexual acts and to criminalise them? Is it right to look to a conclusion that will be discriminatory and in breach of the European Convention? I cannot see that it can be right. If it cannot be right I for one will not support it. I refuse to abstain. I shall vote against Lady Young's amendment.'[2]

1   HL Official Report (5th series) cols 967–970, 22 July 1998.

1.26 Bearing in mind the major manifesto commitments contained in the rest of the Crime and Disorder Bill it was hardly surprising that they had a higher political priority for the government than the age of consent amendment—even though 20 of the 22 members of the Cabinet had voted to lower the age of consent to 16 in 1994. On 28 July 1988 the movers of the Commons amendment agreed to accept the Lords' rejection, but only on the government's undertaking to introduce its own Bill, in government time, so that it can be implemented before the end of the 1998–99 session. There will still be a free vote, but as the Bill will, this time, start in the Commons, the Parliament Acts of 1911 and 1949 will now apply and their Lordships' powers will be limited to delaying the measure by 12 months. Rejection will not be an option. A bill for an equal age of consent was included in the Queen's speech of 24 November 1998 and must certainly be in force by the end of 1999.

Gay men and lesbians in the military

1.27 The second area where lesbian and gay reformers turned to the litigation route was in their attempts to overturn the ban on homosexuals serving in the armed forces. The first 'gays in the military' case *R v Ministry of Defence, ex p Smith*[1] failed at both Divisional Court and Court of Appeal level. Neither court was prepared to say that the ban—even when adapted to a human rights context—crossed the *Wednesbury* threshold of irrationality (*Associated Provincial Picture Houses Ltd v Wednesbury Corpn*[2]). But it did draw from the most senior judiciary a whole range of positive dicta. At the end of the Court of Appeal hearing, David Pannick QC told the court that the four applicants would be 'on the first plane to Strasbourg' where the government will be faced by the hurdles of 'pressing social need' and 'proportionality'.

1   [1996] QB 517, [1996] 1 All ER 257, CA.
2   [1948] 1 KB 223, [1947] 2 All ER 680, CA.

1.28   In the second 'gays in the military' case—*R v Secretary of State for Defence, ex p Perkins* [1]—Lightman J in referring the case to the Court of Justice of the European Communities at Luxembourg said:

> 'Homosexual orientation is a reality today which the law must recognise and adjust to, and it may well be thought appropriate that the fundamental principle of equality and the irrelevance of a person's sex and sexual identity demand that the court be able to afford protection to them, and ensure that those of homosexual orientation are no longer disadvantaged in terms of employment.'

1   [1997] IRLR 297.

1.29   Until February 1998 there was a real and widespread optimism that either *Smith* at Strasbourg or *Perkins* at Luxembourg would succeed in forcing the British government to remove the ban. That optimism was based first on the decision of the European Court of Justice in the transsexual case *P v S and Cornwall County Council* [1], that the Equal Treatment Directive of 1976 applies to transsexuals. As a result the Labour government is currently preparing regulations, to be made under the European Communities Act 1972, which will amend the Sex Discrimination Act 1975 to protect transsexuals against discrimination in employment. Reformers felt entitled to ask 'if transsexuals why not homosexuals?'

1   Case C-13/94 [1996] IRLR 347.

C   AFTER *GRANT*

1.30   The second cause for optimism was the opinion in September 1997 of Advocate General Elmer in the 'fares fair' case—*Grant v South-West Trains Ltd* [1]— in which he followed the European Court's decision in *P* and argued that in refusing to extend to the applicant and her lesbian partner the travel concessions to which she would have been entitled had they been a heterosexual unmarried couple, the defendant company was discriminating on the basis of gender contrary to art 119, the equal pay article, of the EC Treaty. In his opinion he said:

> 'Equality before the law is a fundamental principle in every community governed by the rule of law and accordingly in the Community as well. The rights and duties which result from Community law apply to all without discrimination and therefore also to the approximately 35 million citizens of the Community, depending on the method of calculation used, who are homosexual.'

1   Case C-249/96, [1998] All ER (EC) 193, ECJ.

1.31   The refusal of the European Court in *Grant* [1] to find that *P* extended Community law to cover discrimination based on sexual orientation and its acceptance of what Cherie Booth QC had described in her oral submissions for the applicant as the 'equal misery submission' dealt what many, though by no means all, lawyers believed was a fatal blow to the litigation strategy which had dominated much of the battle for lesbian and gay law reform for nearly six years. On 6 July 1998 the government went back to Lightman J to ask him, in the light of *Grant*, to reverse his March 1997 decision to refer *Perkins* to Luxembourg. In his judgment on 13 July the judge considered himself bound 'albeit reluctantly' to withdraw the reference, but added that:

> 'Even if there is no change in the policy, its future must in any event be uncertain. The Council acting under powers conferred by the Treaty of Amsterdam and the European Court of Human Rights on references to the Commission currently before the Commission may bring it to an end, and a challenge may be possible in judicial review proceedings once the Human Rights Bill becomes law.'

1   [1998] IRLR 206.

1.32   The fallacy which lies behind *Grant* was best defined by Dr Robert Wintermute:

> 'If a man complains that he has been treated differently because he has a male partner the usual response is that there is no direct sex discrimination because a woman who has a female partner would be treated in the same way. This comparison avoids a finding of direct sex discrimination by changing not only the sex of the man but also the sex of his partner. Yet for a valid sex discrimination analysis, the comparison must change only the sex of the complaining individual and must hold all other circumstances constant.'[1]

1   (1997) 60 MLR 347. See also para **2.70**.

1.33   The litigation strategy had been tested in two other areas, one successful, one—so far—unsuccessful. In *Re W (a minor)* [1] Mr Justice Singer held it was in the best interests of the child concerned to be adopted by a lesbian, in a long term relationship, with whom the child had been placed by the local authority. He rejected submissions that 'it was inconceivable that Parliament in 1976 would have contemplated adoption by one of a homosexual cohabiting couple' or alternatively that such an application was 'contrary to public policy' and he ended by saying 'any other conclusion would be both illogical, arbitrary and inappropriately discriminatory in a context where the court's duty is to give first consideration to the need to safeguard and promote the welfare of the child throughout his childhood'.

1   [1998] Fam 58.

1.34   The strategy was less successful—so far, although leave has been given to take the case to the House of Lords—in *Fitzpatrick v Sterling Housing Association Ltd* [1]. In that case the Court of Appeal found itself unable, as a matter of strict law, to hold that the plaintiff was entitled to succeed to his late partner's Rent Act tenancy, even though they had lived together for 20 years in a relationship described by Lord Justice Ward, in his dissenting judgment, as 'to all intents and purposes a marriage between these partners. They lived a life akin to that of any husband and wife. They were so bound together that they constituted a family.' Although—and obviously reluctantly—Lord Justice Waite held that only Parliament could rectify this obvious wrong he was still moved to say:

> 'To adopt an interpretation of the statute that allowed all partners, whether of the same or opposite sex to enjoy the privilege of succession to tenancies

protected by the Rent Acts would, moreover, be consistent not only with social justice but also with the respect accorded by modern society to those of the same sex who undertake a permanent commitment to a shared life.'

1 [1997] 4 All ER 991, CA.

1 A change of government: Westminster and Whitehall

1.35 These warmly supportive dicta from so many members of the senior judiciary will not be unimportant—especially when the Human Rights Act 1998 comes into effect, possibly in the autumn of 2000. But after the loss of *Grant* and the election in May 1997 of a Labour government with a majority of 179, those fighting for lesbian and gay equality in this country will have to concentrate their attention on Westminster and Whitehall rather than the Royal Courts of Justice, Strasbourg and Luxembourg. The battle will not be easy, even in a Parliament with a substantial radical majority. The Labour Party manifesto in 1997 did not contain a single specific commitment on sexuality discrimination. This was in contrast to the position in 1992—and to the party conference votes in favour of lesbian and gay rights in 1985, 1986, 1988, 1989 and 1994—the last being passed by a majority of 97.6% of those voting.

1.36 Lesbian and gay law reform could certainly not expect a high priority in the legislation log jam of a new government after 18 years in opposition. But, in the first year of office, reformers were entitled to expect more than the very limited change in immigration practice in October 1997—which is dealt with elsewhere—and the promise of a free vote on the age of consent. In the same period the new government instructed lawyers to argue against the concept of equal pay for same-sex partners in *Grant* and was preparing to argue in favour of the military ban in both *Smith* in Strasbourg and *Perkins* in Luxembourg. In the first month of its second year of office the government indicated its opposition both to including sexual orientation as a specific prohibited ground of discrimination in the Human Rights Bill and to recognising 'queerbashing' as a hate crime in the Crime and Disorder Bill. On 5 June 1998 Lady Turner reintroduced her revised SOD Bill into the House of Lords where it received an unopposed second reading. For the government, Lady Blackstone welcomed it in principle but opposed it in practice for reasons of 'scope and timing'[1]. At least in the same speech the minister confirmed the government's intention to repeal s 28 of the Local Government Act 1988 'as soon as a suitable legislative opportunity arises' and to review the 'gays in the military' ban 'in the course of the current Parliament'—a less than wholehearted commitment.

1 HL Official Report (5th series) col 657, 5 June 1998.

1.37 An essential truth which the government should remember is from the late Lord Bonham Carter's first report of the Race Relations Board and was contained in Lord Lester's speech on the second reading of the 1996 SOD Bill [1]:

'A law is an unequivocal declaration of public policy. A law gives support to those who do not wish to discriminate but who feel compelled to do so by social pressure. A law gives protection and redress to minority groups. A law provides for the peaceful and orderly adjustment of grievances and the relief of tensions. A law reduces prejudice by discouraging the behaviour in which prejudice finds expression.'

1 HL Official Report (5th series) col 398, 6 March 1996.

Chapter 2

Discrimination

A INTRODUCTION

2.01 '1997 marks the centenary of Oscar Wilde's liberation from imprisonment at Reading Gaol...most significantly, tolerance of the fundamental right to personal intimacy was this year recognised across all the main political parties, including the Conservatives...On the legal front, 1997 has also been a special year...all in all 1997 has been a quite extraordinary year of progress on equality issues.'[1]

'Homosexual orientation is a reality today which the law must recognise and adjust to and it may well be thought appropriate that the fundamental principle of equality and the irrelevance of a person's sex and sexual identity demand that the court be alert to afford protection to them and ensure that those of homosexual orientation are no longer disadvantaged in terms of employment...After the decision in the *Cornwall* case it is scarcely possible to limit the application of the [Equal Treatment] Directive to gender discrimination...and there must be a real prospect that the European Court will take the further courageous step to extend protection to those of homosexual orientation, if a courageous step is necessary to do so.'[2]

Optimism that existing anti-discrimination legislation would be held to extend to discrimination against men and women on grounds of their sexual orientation reached its peak in 1997. If the European Community Equal Treatment Directive included within its remit discrimination on grounds of sexual orientation, surely so must the UK's own Sex Discrimination Act, which must be construed in conformity with the Directive. Yet 1998 has seen the European Court of Justice in *Grant v South-West Trains Ltd*[3] unable or unwilling to extend protection by means of judicial interpretation, preferring to leave it to the legislators. Further, in July 1998, the Court of Appeal in *Smith v Gardner Merchant*[4] ruled that the Sex Discrimination Act 1975 could apply to discrimination on grounds of sexual orientation but only on the narrow basis that such discrimination was simultaneously discrimination on grounds of sex.

1   A Case for Equality, Peter Duffy QC, European Human Rights Law Review, 1998 Issue 2.
2   *R v Secretary of State for Defence, ex p Perkins* [1997] IRLR 297, Lightman J.
3   [1998] ICR 449.
4   [1998] IRLR 510.

2.02 If 1997 was a year of optimism for those campaigning for equality for lesbians and gay men, 1998 has so far proved such optimism to be premature.

> 'The ECJ in *Grant*...decided that Community law as it stands at present does not cover or render unlawful discrimination based on sexual orientation...I can see no realistic prospect of any change of mind on the part of the ECJ. This view is reinforced by paragraph 48 of the decision where the ECJ makes clear what it considers to be the way forward: "The Treaty of Amsterdam...signed on 2 October 1997 provides for the insertion in the EEC Treaty of an art 6a which, once the Treaty of Amsterdam has entered into force, will allow the Council under certain conditions [a unanimous vote on a proposal from the Commission after consulting the European Parliament] to take appropriate action to eliminate various forms of discrimination, including discrimination based on sexual orientation." It is a matter for the Council to make this extension in Community rights, not the ECJ...Albeit reluctantly I consider that I am bound to withdraw the reference in this case.'[1]

1   *R v Secretary of State for Defence, ex p Perkins (No 2)* [1998] IRLR 508.

2.03 However, as the millennium approaches and as we now adapt, for the first time in the United Kingdom, to the constitutional protection of human rights through the Human Rights Act 1998, there is increasing interest in the subject of equality and the prohibition of discrimination in the sphere of sexual orientation. Discrimination lawyers are familiar with exercising creativity and imagination in presenting arguments to courts or tribunals unfamiliar or unhappy with the concept of discrimination. The advent of human rights protection will add an exciting dimension to the law for those called upon to advise in this area.

B   THE NATURE OF DISCRIMINATION

2.04 The essential characteristic of discriminatory conduct is the failure to treat people as individuals and to assess them on their individual merits according to the criteria which are relevant to the particular situation. Inevitably this failure stems from generalised stereotypical assumptions about the group to which an individual belongs, for example, women, ethnic minorities and the mentally and physically disabled.

2.05 If one accepts that, both intellectually and morally, all human beings have an equal right to respect and dignity, discriminatory treatment, which fails to recognise their worth as individuals, cannot be tolerated on any basis in civilised society. Equality, in this sense, requires that like should be treated with like, unless there are valid and relevant reasons for the application of different treatment. Discrimination occurs when individuals are treated unequally for invalid and irrelevant reasons based on stereotypical assumptions about an individual's characteristics.

2.06 What society regards as invalid and irrelevant reasons naturally depends on the mores applicable at any particular time but discriminatory assumptions are firmly rooted and difficult to eradicate. Sex discrimination provides a classic example. Aristotle considered women to be irrational and inferior human beings, being merely defective or mutilated males, the male being naturally more fitted to command than the female [1]. Over 2000 years later the Sex Discrimination Act 1975 came onto the statute books. Yet in the early 1980s the law reports were full of examples of stereotypical assumptions about women still operating in the employment field and resulting in less favourable treatment. These assumptions were of course more subtly expressed than those of Aristotle but they were just as damaging. Thus, in *Hurley v Mustoe* [2] an employer recruiting staff acted on the assumption that all married women with small children were unreliable. In *Coleman v Skyrail Oceanic* [3] an employer assumed that husbands were always the breadwinners in a family. In *Horsey v Dyfed County Council* [4] an employer assumed that wives were more likely to follow the careers of their husbands than vice versa. In all these examples women suffered less favourable treatment in employment because an employer failed to consider their merits and circumstances as individuals, arriving at a decision based on general assumptions about the female sex.

1   Aristotle *Politics* Book 1, 400 BC.
2   [1981] ICR 490.
3   [1981] IRLR 398.
4   [1982] ICR 755.

2.07   Race discrimination provides similar examples. Despite the existence of legislation prohibiting racial discrimination since 1965, in *Alexander v Home Office* [1] a West Indian prisoner complaining of a discriminatory refusal to allow him to work in the prison kitchens was described in his induction report as showing 'the anti-authoritarian arrogance that seems to be common in most coloured inmates'.

1   [1988] IRLR 190.

2.08   In exactly the same way, discrimination on grounds of sexual orientation rests essentially on stereotypical assumptions as to gender characteristics. Lesbians and gay men are discriminated against because they fail to conform to the gender stereotype of having heterosexual preferences and because fear, ignorance or religious fervour combine to equate sexual orientation with abnormal sexual behaviour or, worse still, with sexual misconduct. Thus in *Saunders v Scottish National Camps Association Ltd* [1] the applicant, a handyman at a charity camp for young people, was dismissed when he was discovered to be gay. Neither the Employment Appeal Tribunal nor the Scottish Court of Session would interfere with the finding of the Industrial Tribunal that the dismissal was fair because a considerable proportion of employers would reasonably take the view that the employment of a homosexual should be restricted, particularly when the work involved proximity to children.

1   [1981] IRLR 277.

2.09   The way in which society treats such stereotypical assumptions about groups of people within it is undoubtedly a litmus test of the extent of its civilisation. That there is a need for laws to guarantee equality of treatment for individual victims of such views is paramount. The late Lord Bonham Carter, writing in the first report of the Race Relations Board, said as follows:

'A law is an unequivocal declaration of public policy. A law gives support to those who do not wish to discriminate but feel compelled to do so by social pressure. A law gives protection and redress to minority groups.

A law provides for the peaceful and orderly adjustment of grievances and the relief of tensions. A law reduces prejudice by discouraging the behaviour in which prejudice finds expression.'

The moral and philosophical case for effective, anti-discrimination legislation could not be more eloquently expressed.

C DOMESTIC DISCRIMINATION LEGISLATION

1 Background

2.10 Anti-discrimination legislation arrived in the UK very late in the twentieth century. The common law, with its central tenets of personal property, freedom of contract and reputation, did not regard 'equality' as having the same priority. Even in the public law sphere equality has had a mixed reception and discriminatory decisions have been required to cross the threshold of irrationality before they can be struck down. Thus in *Roberts v Hopwood* [1] the House of Lords confirmed the opinion of a district auditor that Poplar Borough Council's attempts to give equal pay to men and women doing like work lacked 'rational proportion' and were therefore unlawful. Lord Atkinson concluded that the council would be failing in their duty if in administering funds which did not belong to their members alone they 'allowed themselves to be guided in preference by some eccentric principles of socialist philanthropy or by a feminist ambition to secure the equality of the sexes in the matter of wages in the world of labour.'

1 [1925] AC 578.

2.11 In the following year Poole Corporation decided that the retention of married women teachers in their public elementary schools was inadvisable. The report of the Education Committee contained the following by way of reasoning: 'the duty of the married woman is primarily to look after her domestic concerns…it is impossible for her to do so and to effectively and satisfactorily act as a teacher at the same time'. When Mrs Short, a well respected but married teacher, was dismissed from her post the courts upheld the dismissal and concluded that they could not interfere.

2.12 Even as the Sex Discrimination Act 1975 was coming into force the case of *Morris v Duke-Cohan & Co* [1] demonstrated the extent of the problem. In finding that a firm of solicitors were negligent in proceeding with the sale of a flat owned by a husband and wife without first obtaining the customary 10% deposit from the purchaser, Caulfield J rejected the solicitors' contention that the wife had in fact given them instructions to proceed, observing that: 'Even if she had given instructions to proceed the solicitors should not have taken instructions from her when the husband was available, for a sensible wife did not generally make major decisions.'

1   (1975) 119 Sol J 826.

2.13 Victims fared no better on the racial discrimination front. Sir Leary Constantine's famous challenge to the discriminatory refusal of access to hotel accommodation resulted in the full force of the common law placing inn keepers under a duty only to accept all travellers who were 'in a reasonably fit condition to be received.'[1] In *Applin v Race Relations Board* [2] Lord Simon said:

'The common law before the making of the first Race Relations Act [1965] was that people could discriminate against others on the ground of colour, etc, to their hearts' content. This unbridled capacity to discriminate was the mischief and defect for which the common law did not provide.'

1   *Constantine v Imperial Hotels Ltd* [1944]1 KB 693.
2   [1975] AC 259.

2.14   Sex equality legislation eventually arrived in 1975 (the Sex Discrimination Act and Equal Pay Act 1970 which came into force at the same time). Race equality legislation in essentially the same form followed in 1976 (the Race Relations Act), after earlier attempts at tackling racial discrimination in 1965 and 1968. These three Acts made discrimination on the grounds of sex, marital status and on the grounds of race unlawful in the fields of employment and in the provision of education and of other goods, facilities and services to the public (for example accommodation, banking and insurance, professional services, entertainment and transport). Subsequently Northern Ireland implemented legislation to tackle religious and political discrimination (the Fair Employment (Northern Ireland) Act 1989). 1995 saw the arrival onto the statute books of the Disability Discrimination Act.

2.15   For lesbians and gay men however, the picture has been a much gloomier one. This is not surprising given the background of criminalisation of all sexual activity between men until 1967 and, further, the impassioned debates which still accompany attempts to lower the age of consent for consenting gay men to 16, equal to that for heterosexuals.

2.16   In their extensive survey of lesbians and gay men at work in 1993 the national lobbying organisation, Stonewall, found compelling evidence of large scale discrimination and, in particular, of harassment of gay employees in the workplace because of their sexuality. Two-thirds of respondents to a detailed questionnaire admitted that they concealed their sexuality from people they worked with. A similar study in 1995 by Social and Community Planning Research painted the same picture and included the disturbing finding that one-third of the heterosexuals surveyed said that they would be less likely to recruit a lesbian or gay job applicant.

2.17   The Stonewall Report, in 1993, observed:

'The overall difference between discrimination and harassment on the grounds of sex and race and discrimination and harassment on the grounds of sexuality is that Parliament has legislated that the former are never acceptable, whereas the absence of legislation and the case law on the latter mean that prejudice against lesbians and gay men is, fundamentally, still permissible...This is why in our view only a change in the law to place discrimination on the grounds of sexuality on a par with discrimination on the grounds of sex or race can fully rectify the situation for lesbians and gay men. We believe this could be done relatively quickly and simply by amending the Sex Discrimination Act to extend the prohibition on discrimination based on sex to include discrimination based on sexual orientation. Enforcement would then be brought within the remit of the Equal Opportunities Commission.'

Five years after publication of this report there have been, as yet, no amendments to the Sex Discrimination Act. The Sexual Orientation Discrimination Bill 1996, whilst receiving substantial cross-party support, fell for lack of time before the last election and has not since been revived.

2.18 Nevertheless, given the recent decision of the Court of Appeal in *Smith v Gardner Merchant* [1] that the Sex Discrimination Act can apply in limited circumstances to sexual orientation discrimination and given optimism that legislative reform is likely in the not too distant future it is worth examining what the Sex Discrimination Act can offer in providing protection against discrimination for lesbians and gay men in the fields of employment, education, the provision of goods, facilities and services and housing. A detailed account of this Act is beyond the scope of this chapter and what follows is no more than a summary of its main provisions.

1 [1998] IRLR 510.

2   The Sex Discrimination Act 1975

2.19 Drawing on experience in the United States and the changing views about women's role in society in the 1960s the Act is primarily complaints based and is designed to ensure formal equality for individuals rather than to eradicate underlying social disadvantage through monitoring and affirmative action. The Act was implemented shortly before the European Community Equal Treatment Directive [1] and in fact owes little to it. Its existence is nevertheless the main reason why no specific implementing legislation was considered necessary to fulfil the UK's obligations under that Directive.

1   EC Directive 76/207.

2.20 There are in Pt I of the Act three basic forms of discrimination prohibited: direct, indirect and victimisation, any or all of which can form the basis for individual complaints to an Employment Tribunal in relation to employment matters and to a county court for non-employment matters. Part II sets out the forms of discrimination in employment rendered unlawful. Part III proscribes various forms of discrimination outside the employment sphere.

2.21 The Equal Pay Act 1970, which came into force with the Sex Discrimination Act 1975 is contained in Sch 1 to that Act. It operates by requiring an equality clause to be implied into all contracts of employment. Whilst not including any reference to the word 'discrimination' the anti-discrimination principle of equal treatment is clearly implicit in the Equal Pay Act 1970, which requires men and women doing like work, work rated as equivalent or work of equal value to have equal terms and conditions of employment.

2.22 In deciding whether discrimination under the 1975 Act has occurred like must be compared with like, a complainant must compare herself/himself with an actual or hypothetical comparator of the opposite sex whose circumstances are the same or similar. The intention or motive of the alleged discriminator is irrelevant. Hereafter references to discrimination are to women since they are usually the victims of sex discrimination although the Act applies to both men and women.

2.23 Direct discrimination is defined in SDA 1975, s 1(1)(a): 'a person discriminates against a woman in any circumstances relevant for the purposes of any provision of this Act if…on the ground of her sex he treats her less favourably than he treats or would treat a man.' Direct discrimination against married people is defined in similar terms in s 3(1)(a) as occurring where: 'on the ground of his or her marital status he treats that person less favourably than he treats or would treat an unmarried person of the same sex.'

2.24 Thus where a local education authority provided more places for boys than for girls in selective schools the House of Lords decided that it was not necessary for the complainant to show that selective education was better than non-selective education. It was enough that, by denying the girls the same opportunity as the boys, the council was depriving them of a choice which was valued by them, or at least by their parents and which is a choice obviously valued on reasonable grounds by many others [1].

1   *Birmingham City Council v Equal Opportunities Commission* [1989] IRLR 173.

2.25 The test of direct discrimination is whether or not the applicant would have received the same treatment but for her sex [1]. Motive and intention are irrelevant.

1   *James v Eastleigh Borough Council* [1990] ICR 554.

2.26 One of the most troublesome areas in sex discrimination law over the years was how to deal with pregnancy discrimination. Initially a woman who was discriminated against on grounds of pregnancy or childbirth was held to have no remedy under the Sex Discrimination Act since a man could never be pregnant and there was therefore no man for her to compare herself with [1]. In this way the 'traditional' comparison of treatment of women and men in similar circumstances under the Act prevented pregnant women who had been discriminated against from pursuing any complaint. Later on the Employment Appeal Tribunal accepted that a pregnant woman could bring a claim if she could demonstrate less favourable treatment than that which an employer would mete out to a sick man, who was seen to be the nearest equivalent [2]. The idea that a healthy pregnant woman should compare herself with a sick man was considered by many to be inappropriate and demeaning to women. Europe, meanwhile, had its own agenda. The need for pregnant women and new mothers to be accorded a special, protected status in the workplace was seen as fundamental to the effectiveness of the equal treatment principle. Thus discrimination on the grounds of pregnancy was held by the European Court of Justice, in a number of cases in the early 1990s, to constitute direct sex discrimination, contrary to the Equal Treatment Directive, any comparison with how a man would be treated being unnecessary. In 1995 the House of Lords held that, construing our Act in conformity with the Directive, pregnancy discrimination constitutes direct sex discrimination under the Act [3].

1   *Turley v Allders Department Stores* [1980] IRLR 4.
2   *Hayes v Malleable Working Men's Club and Institute* [1985] ICR 703.
3   *Webb v Emo Air Cargo (UK) (No 2)* [1995] IRLR 645.

2.27 Employers' dress codes have also presented problems in the courts. A woman may object, for example, to an employer's requirement that she should wear a skirt in the workplace. It is unlikely that any male employee will be subject to the same requirement. A man may however be subject to some other dress requirement, for example to wear a tie. In *Schmidt v Austicks Bookshops Ltd* [1] the EAT ruled that there is no discrimination where male and female employees are subject to different but comparable dress requirements. This principle was recently reiterated by the Court of Appeal in *Smith v Safeway plc* [2].

1 [1977] IRLR 3 60.
2 [1996] IRLR 456.

2.28 Indirect discrimination recognises that discrimination is not necessarily the result of direct prejudices but may also arise because women or married people are placed at a disadvantage by apparently neutral practices which impact disproportionately upon them and cannot be objectively justified. It occurs therefore if an employer applies a requirement or condition to a woman or to a married person which he also applies to a man or a single person but which is such that:

'(i) ...the proportion of women [or married persons] who can comply with it is considerably smaller than the proportion of men [or unmarried persons] who can comply with it, and

(ii) ...he cannot show it to be justifiable irrespective of the sex [or marital status] of the person to whom it is applied, and

(iii) ...is to her [or the married person's] detriment because [he or] she cannot comply with it.' [1]

1 Sex Discrimination Act 1975, ss 1(1)(b) and 3(1)(b).

2.29 Examples of such discrimination include the imposition of a maximum age limit of 28 for appointment as an Executive Officer in the Civil Service. In practice, women were less able to comply with this requirement as they were more likely to have had career breaks connected with childbirth and childcare responsibilities [1]. Further, a requirement or condition which results in less favourable treatment of part-time employees is likely to discriminate indirectly against women [2].

1 *Price v Civil Service Commission* [1978] ICR 27.
2 *Clarke and Powell v Eley (IMI) Kynoch Ltd* [1982] IRLR 131.

2.30 Victimisation occurs if a woman is treated less favourably because she brings proceedings, gives evidence or information or takes any action or makes any allegation with reference to the Sex Discrimination Act or the Equal Pay Act or threatens to do any of these things (SDA 1975, s 4(1)).

2.31 The burden of proving discrimination falls, in direct discrimination cases, on the complainant. In an indirect discrimination case it falls on the complainant save as to the question of justification, where it falls on the party attempting to justify the requirement or condition. The standard of proof required is that which is applicable in civil cases generally: on the balance of probabilities. The Court of Appeal in *King v Great Britain China Centre* [1], a race discrimination case, established the approach appropriate for courts or tribunals when faced with an allegation of discrimination. Neill LJ stated the following:

'(1)   It is for the Applicant who complains of racial discrimination to make out his or her case. Thus if the Applicant does not prove the case on the balance of probabilities he or she will fail.

(2)   It is important to bear in mind that it is unusual to find direct evidence of racial discrimination. Few employers will be prepared to admit such discrimination even to themselves. In some cases the discrimination will not be ill-intentioned but merely based on an assumption "he or she would not have fitted in".

(3)   The outcome of the case will therefore usually depend on what inferences it is proper to draw from the primary facts found by the tribunal. These inferences can include, in appropriate cases, any inferences that it is just and equitable to draw in accordance with s 65(2)(b) of the 1976 Act from an evasive or equivocal reply to a questionnaire.

(4)   Though there will be some cases where, for example, the non-selection of the applicant for a post or promotion is clearly not on racial grounds, a finding of discrimination and a finding of different race will often point to the possibility of racial discrimination. In such circumstances the tribunal will look to the employer for an explanation. If no explanation is then put forward, or if the tribunal considers the explanation to be inadequate or unsatisfactory, it will be legitimate for the tribunal to infer that the discrimination was on racial grounds. This is not a matter of law but, as May LJ put it in *Noone*, "almost commonsense".

(5)   It is unnecessary and unhelpful to introduce the concept of a shifting evidential burden of proof. At the conclusion of all the evidence the tribunal should make findings as to the primary facts and draw such inferences as they consider proper from those facts. They should then reach a conclusion on the balance of probabilities, bearing in mind both the difficulties which face a person who complains of unlawful discrimination and the fact that it is for the complainant to prove his or her case.'

These principles apply equally to cases of sex discrimination.

1   [1991] IRLR 513.

2.32   The Act makes provision in s 74 for the service of a questionnaire on a potential or actual respondent with a view to helping a complainant who considers she may have been discriminated against to decide whether to institute proceedings and how to present her case effectively. Procedural rules concerning discovery and the provision of written answers can obviously provide further assistance to a complainant.

3   Discrimination in employment

2.33   The Sex Discrimination Act 1975 proscribes discrimination at every stage of employment from recruitment and selection, including the advertising of vacancies, transfer, training and promotion opportunities or other benefits, facilities and services, to dismissal or other detriment. Unlike claims for unfair dismissal under the employment protection legislation, a person who is discriminated against by being dismissed does not have to have been employed for a qualifying period before being entitled to bring a claim. Further, employment has a wider definition in the 1975 Act than it does in other employment protection legislation. In s 82(1) it is defined as: 'employment under a contract of service or of apprenticeship or a contract personally to execute any work or labour.' It is also unlawful to apply different compulsory retirement ages to men and women and an employer who wishes to contract out of the state pension scheme must provide equal access to pension benefits in his occupational pension scheme. Steps taken by an employer which may amount to a detriment which may be the subject of a claim include, for example, demotion or withdrawal of privileges.

2.34 In addition, of considerable importance in cases of discrimination in employment, is sexual harassment, which the Stonewall survey found to be a particular problem for lesbians and gay men in the workplace, with many examples of verbal abuse and innuendo, malicious gossip, bullying, false accusations of child abuse, abusive phone calls, damage to property, blackmail and, on occasions, physical violence and death threats.

2.35 Although the word 'harassment' does not appear in the legislation the sexual harassment of women in the workplace has long been proscribed by the Act, being held to constitute a species of direct discrimination under s 1(1)(a) and detriment under s 6(2)(b). In the case of *Strathclyde Regional Council v Porcelli* [1] the Scottish Court of Session referred to sexual harassment as a 'particularly degrading and unacceptable form of treatment which it must be taken to be the intention of Parliament to restrain'. It is clearly established that the standard of behaviour which might constitute sexual harassment is to be viewed from the point of view of the victim, rather than the alleged perpetrator [2]; and that a single act, if it is sufficiently serious, may amount to harassment [3].

1   [1986] IRLR 134.
2   *De Souza v Automobile Association* [1986] IRLR 103.
3   See *Insitu Cleaning Company Ltd v Heads* [1995] IRLR 4

2.36 Of real significance in the area of sexual harassment is the European Community Recommendation on the Protection of the Dignity of Men and Women at Work [1]. This Recommendation recognises that such conduct may be in breach of the Equal Treatment Directive and provides a definition of sexual harassment to which the courts and tribunals have regard, declaring such conduct to be unacceptable if it is 'unwanted, unreasonable and offensive to the recipient'; and if it is used as a basis for employment decisions, such as promotion, or is such as to create an intimidating, hostile or humiliating work environment for the recipient. The Recommendation is accompanied by a Code of Practice containing measures to combat sexual harassment, which was issued following a Resolution of the Council of Ministers calling upon the Member States and the institutions and organs of the European Communities to develop positive measures designed to create a climate at work in which women and men respect each other's human integrity.

1   [1992] OJ C27/4.

2.37 In the case of *Grimaldi v Fonds des Maladies Professionelles* [1] the ECJ held that whilst recommendations have no binding force and do not in themselves confer rights on individuals, national courts are nevertheless:

'Bound to take recommendations into consideration in order to decide disputes submitted to them, in particular where they clarify the interpretation of national provisions adopted in order to implement them or where they are designed to supplement Community measures.'

Whilst the 1975 Act was passed 15 years before the Code was adopted, the UK has agreed that the Act represents its obligations under the Equal Treatment Directive and it is thus arguable that both the Recommendation and its associated Code of Practice can be prayed in aid as an interpretative device when considering sexual harassment claims brought under the Sex Discrimination Act.

1   [1990] IRLR 400.

2.38   In sexual harassment cases the Recommendation and Code of Practice are in fact frequently relied upon by Employment Tribunals both as an interpretative aid and as an indication of action employers should be taking both to prevent harassment from occurring and to deal effectively with it if it does. These two EC instruments are of particular interest to those advising lesbians and gay men since in the Recommendation there is express recognition of the vulnerability of particular groups of workers, including lesbians and gay men. Given that the problem has been recognised in this way it is all the more disappointing that in 1998 the European Court of Justice set its face against deciding that discrimination against people on grounds of sexual orientation contravenes existing European legislation (see further s 4 at para 2.93).

2.39   Importantly employers are also liable under the Act for acts done by employees in the course of their employment, whether or not they were done with the employer's knowledge or approval (s 41(1)). If however the employer can prove that he took such steps as were reasonably practicable to prevent the employee from doing that act or from doing acts of that description in the course of his employment he can rely on the statutory defence available to him under s 41(3) [1].

1   See *Balgobin v Tower Hamlets London Borough Council* [1987] ICR 829.

2.40   An employer may also be liable for harassment committed by employees who are acting outside the course of their employment or even by persons not employed by him if the employer had sufficient control over the circumstances in which the harassment occurred to have enabled him to prevent it from happening. See *Burton v De Vere Hotels* [1].

1   [1996] IRLR 596.

2.41   Knowingly aiding another person to commit discrimination or the giving of instructions to discriminate by someone in authority or applying pressure to discriminate directly are also outlawed (ss 42(2), 39 and 40). The Act extends to 'non-employers', that is: users of contract workers (s 9(2)); partnerships (s 11(1)); trade unions and employers' organisations (s 12); bodies conferring qualifications or authorisations (s 13(1)); providers of vocational training (s 14) and employment agencies (s 15). Furthermore, any term of a contract purporting to exclude or limit the provisions of the Act is unenforceable (s 77(3)).

2.42   Finally the Act contains a number of exceptions to the prohibition of sex discrimination in the employment field. Thus if an employer can establish that being a man is a genuine occupational qualification for a job he may discriminate lawfully in certain respects (s 7(1)). If an employer provides communal accommodation for his employees he may discriminate in its provision if the accommodation is managed in a way which is as fair as possible to men and women (s 46(3)). Discrimination for the purposes of safeguarding national security is lawful (s 52(1)). Offering or paying a woman less remuneration than a man is not unlawful discrimination under the 1975 Act (s 6(5), (6)), but if she carries out like work, work rated as equivalent or work of equal value to that of a man, her contract is modified by the Equal Pay Act 1970 so that she is able to claim equal pay under that Act.

2.43   In addition, certain categories of employees are excluded in many respects from the Act's protection, namely: employees working outside Britain (ss 6(1), 10(1)); police officers (s 17(2)) and prison officers and ministers of religion. The Sex Discrimination Act 1975 (Application to Armed Forces) Regulations 1994 [1] brought members of the armed forces within the Sex Discrimination Act 1975. A new exemption, for acts done for the purpose of ensuring the 'combat effectiveness' of the naval, military and air forces of the Crown, raises an interesting issue as to whether the provisions of the Sex Discrimination Act comply with the Equal Treatment Directive.

1   SI 1994/3276.

2.44   In the employment field the only means of enforcement for an individual is by application to an Employment Tribunal. He or she may seek assistance from the Equal Opportunities Commission for this purpose. The EOC has additional powers to hold formal investigations, to issue non-discrimination notices and they may in certain cases apply for an injunction. Where the Act does not confer the rights granted by the Equal Treatment Directive individuals may rely upon that Directive in claims against state authorities. Time limits apply to any proceedings so that, by s 76(1), a complaint must be presented to a tribunal before the end of the period of three months beginning when the act complained of was done unless the Employment Tribunal, in the exercise of its discretion, allows the claim to proceed because it considers it is just and equitable to do so (s 76(5)).

2.45   If an Employment Tribunal finds that a complaint is well founded and succeeds it may make the following orders:
(*a*)   an order declaring the rights of the complainant and the respondent in relation to the act to which the complaint relates;
(*b*)   an order requiring the respondent to pay to the complainant compensation of an amount which corresponds to any damages he could have been ordered by a county court to pay to the complainant; and
(*c*)   a recommendation that the respondent take, within a specified period, action appearing to the tribunal to be practicable for the purpose of obviating or reducing the adverse effect on the complainant of any act of discrimination to which the complaint relates[1].

1   Sex Discrimination Act, s 65(1).

2.46   Until 1993 awards of compensation in cases of sex discrimination were subject to a statutory maximum. However, following the decision of the

European Court of Justice in *Marshall v Southampton and South West Hampshire Regional Health Authority (No 2)* [1] that capping compensation in this way meant that victims of discrimination did not have an 'effective remedy', the upper ceiling on the size of awards was removed by amending regulations.

1   [1993] IRLR 445.

2.47   The measure of loss is based on tort principles. A complainant must therefore be put, so far as possible, into the position that she would have been in had the act of discrimination not occurred. The amount of compensation awarded will include, in appropriate cases, a sum for injury to feelings which results from the knowledge that it was an act of sex discrimination which brought about the employer's action. Aggravated damages may be awarded where the complainant can establish a causal link between 'exceptional or contumelious conduct or motive' on the employer's part and her injury to feelings. Exemplary damages however are not available. There is in addition a right to interest on any sums awarded. See the Sex Discrimination and Equal Pay (Remedies) Regulations 1993 [1].

1   SI 1993/2798.

4   Discrimination outside employment

2.48   Part III of the 1975 Act deals with discrimination in fields other than employment. Section 22 prohibits discrimination by certain bodies in charge of educational establishments. Section 23 imposes a duty on education authorities not to commit any discriminatory act in carrying out their functions under the Education Acts.

2.49   Discrimination is also prohibited in the provision of 'goods, facilities and services' to the public or a section of the public (s 29). This phrase is not defined and the examples given in the legislation are not intended to be exhaustive (access to public places, hotel accommodation, banking, insurance and finance facilities, entertainment, transport, the services of any profession or trade or any local or other public authority).

2.50   Sections 30 and 31 create liability for discrimination in the disposal or management of premises in relation to consent for assignment or subletting. Discrimination by or in respect of barristers and barristers' clerks is prohibited by s 32. Exceptions apply in relation to voluntary bodies (s 34), establishments for persons requiring special care (s 35), charities (s 43), and sports activities (s 44).

2.51   Proceedings relating to discrimination in non-employment matters have to be brought in the county court. The limitation period is generally six months beginning with the date of the act complained of. Remedies are those which would be obtainable in the High Court (s 66). Injunctive relief is available in addition to damages. Judicial statistics reveal that non-employment discrimination litigation initiated by individuals is very rare and there are obvious concerns about the ability of these courts to build up experience and expertise in dealing with discrimination cases.

5   Sexual orientation discrimination under domestic law

2.52   Clearly all this protection from discrimination is only available if an individual victim can prove that he or she has been directly or indirectly discriminated against within the provisions of s 1 of the Act. The traditional view has always been that lesbians and gay men are not protected by the Act, which requires a comparison between the treatment of a man and a woman in any given case. Thus if an employer treats both lesbians and gay men less favourably than he treats heterosexual men and women, sexuality and not sex is the reason for the treatment and that falls outside the scope of the legislation.

2.53   Even under employment protection legislation there is uncertainty as to the extent of protection against unfair, as opposed to discriminatory, dismissal. Generally employers are required under the Employment Rights Act 1996 to conduct fair procedures and to come to reasonable conclusions as to the facts and as to the appropriate disciplinary penalty in any given case. If an employer discovers that an employee is gay and wants to dismiss him or her for that reason, he should give notice to the employee of the reasons why he considers it unsuitable for the employment to continue, conduct a hearing, give the employee the opportunity to rebut the objections and consider reasonably whether dismissal is really appropriate. It will then be for the Employment Tribunal, hearing an unfair dismissal claim, to decide whether or not the employer has acted reasonably in all the circumstances.

2.54   The case of *Saunders v Scottish Camps Association* (see para **2.08**) has already been referred to. In the case of *Boychuk v HJ Symons Holdings Ltd* [1] Ms Boychuk was dismissed for 'wearing five different badges proclaiming her homosexual proclivities'. The Employment Appeal Tribunal held that a reasonable employer was allowed to decide, on reflection and mature consideration, what customers and fellow employees could be expected to find offensive, there being no need to wait and see whether business was actually damaged, or disruption caused, before dismissing the employee. They said:

> 'Although there are limits upon the employer's discretion to dismiss an employee because he will not accept an employer's standards in relation to attire, hair and behaviour, it is for the Employment Tribunal to strike a balance, according to the circumstances of the particular case, between the need of the employer to control the business for which he is responsible in the interest of the business and the reasonable freedom of the employee...there are quite a number of cases reported. They do not enshrine any principle but they are illustrations of the approach of Employment Tribunals to this problem. But what they do clearly indicate, as one would expect, is that such questions are largely ones of fact, not easy to decide, and which had to be decided according to all the circumstances of the particular case.'

1   [1977] IRLR 395.

2.55   In the case of *Bell v Devon and Cornwall Police Authority* [1] the Industrial Tribunal decided that the dismissal of a bisexual cook who worked in the police canteen was unfair. The police personnel department, having discovered that the applicant was gay, asked users of the canteen for their views and the third who replied stated that they were not willing to eat food that he had prepared. The dismissal was held to be unfair because the employer accepted the views submitted without any further investigation, despite the small proportion of canteen users who expressed a view and the fact that the opinions offered were all suspiciously similar.

1   [1978] IRLR 283.

2.56   A problem that recurs and as demonstrated in *Boychuk*[1] is that of employers who are under pressure to dismiss as a result of pressure from their customers or from other workers or who state that they felt obliged to act on assumed prejudices. It is unlawful to dismiss someone because of the racial or sexual prejudices of the workforce. In relation to prejudice against lesbians or gay men however, the tribunal must consider in each case whether the employer acted reasonably or unreasonably in treating someone's sexuality as a sufficient reason for dismissal, a question to be determined in accordance with equity and the substantial merits of the case. It is to be hoped that most tribunals would now expect an employer to take steps to educate his workforce and not simply resort to dismissal as a way out of the problem, finding a dismissal unfair in such circumstances. This however will always turn on the view of the first instance fact-finding tribunal.

1   *Boychuck v HJ Symons Holdings Ltd* [1977] IRLR 395.

2.57   Many cases have concerned the dismissal of gay men for holding criminal convictions for sex offences such as gross indecency. Since many men plead guilty in the hope of avoiding publicity and retaining their employment, employers should be readier to understand these problems and not always take the convictions at face value.

2.58   Generally lesbians and gay men could claim constructive dismissal if the employer has failed to provide them with basic support in the workplace or to protect them from harassment by fellow employees, provided that the individual had complained to the employer and no action had been taken to prevent such conduct.

2.59   However the fact that an unfair dismissal has, so far, offered little hope to applicants in such circumstances is compounded by the requirement that, at present in order to bring a complaint of unfair dismissal, an employee must have two years' service. This is not necessary under the Sex Discrimination Act. The qualifying period is currently the subject of challenge in the case of *R v Secretary of State for Employment, ex p Seymour-Smith and Perez* [1] in which the judgment of the European Court of Justice is awaited.

1   [1997] 2 All ER 273, [1997] 1 WLR 473, HL.

2.60   Clearly, given the difficulties and limitations, the availability of protection under the Sex Discrimination Act, in particular in relation to dismissal or harassment, led to increasing interest in the possibility of using that Act in cases of direct discrimination on grounds of sexual orientation. It is worth re-stating here the relevant statutory provisions.

2.61 In order to make out a complaint of direct discrimination it is necessary to show that the complainant was treated less favourably on grounds of sex. The statutory provisions provide as follows:

'A person discriminates against a woman in any circumstances relevant for the purposes of any provision of this Act if—

(a) on the ground of her sex he treats her less favourably than he treats or would treat a man.'

The comparative exercise required by the 1975 Act is found at s 5(3):

'The comparison of cases of persons of different sex under s 1(1) must be such that the relevant circumstances in the one case are the same, or not materially different, in the other.'

2.62 As we have seen the intention or motive of the discriminator is irrelevant so far as liability is concerned under the test for direct discrimination in s 1(1)(a) [1]. Further the objective and purely causal 'but for' test for establishing direct discrimination was endorsed by the House of Lords in *James v Eastleigh Borough Council* [2].

1 *Birmingham City Council v Equal Opportunities Commission*[1989] IRLR 173.
2 [1990] ICR 554.

2.63 If therefore an essential feature of an individual's sexual orientation is the gender of those with whom he or she forms sexual relationships, the 'but for' test for direct discrimination is fulfilled. If an employer dismisses a gay man for being in a sexual relationship with another man but would not dismiss a woman who was also in a sexual relationship with another man, the only difference between the two situations is the sex of the dismissed employee, suggesting that sex discrimination within the meaning of the Act has occurred.

2.64 Before the case of *Smith v Gardner Merchant* [1] there was some indication that this approach had found favour with a Scottish Industrial Tribunal in the case of *Wallace and O'Rourke v BG Turnkey Services (Scotland) Ltd* [2]. Here, two female applicants alleged that they had been dismissed by the respondent company because they were having a lesbian relationship with each other. They submitted that if a male employee would not have been dismissed after forming a relationship with a female co-worker, then it must be directly discriminatory within s 1(1)(a) for a female employee to be dismissed after so doing. The only difference between the two situations was the gender of the dismissed employee. The tribunal gave an opinion after a preliminary hearing on this issue of law and, as the case settled before a full hearing could occur, no precedent was set. However, while the tribunal's reasoning was not detailed, they did not accept the respondent's contention that the applicants could not bring a complaint of direct discrimination because they were claiming that they had been dismissed on grounds of their sexuality and not because of their sex. The tribunal noted that they were being asked to find 'that there is a rule of law to the effect that the dismissal of a woman, because she is carrying on a lesbian relationship, is never sex discrimination. In the view of the tribunal it is quite impossible to lay down such a categoric rule.'

1 [1998] IRLR 510.
2 Nos S/457 & 458/93 (9 July 1993, unreported).

2.65   In the *Smith* case the facts were as follows. Paul Smith was employed as a barman in August 1992. He was dismissed in April 1994 following a complaint by a fellow employee, Ms Touhy, that he had treated her in a threatening and aggressive manner. Paul Smith claimed that he had been sexually harassed by that employee because he was a gay man. He alleged that she had made offensive remarks to him about his sexuality, including saying 'that he probably had all sorts of diseases and that gay people who spread AIDS should be put on an island'.

2.66   It was argued before the Industrial Tribunal, at a hearing to determine whether they had jurisdiction to determine the claim under the Sex Discrimination Act, that such treatment was contrary to the Act in that the offensive remarks would not have been made to a lesbian and, further, that Ms Touhy's allegations of threatening and aggressive behaviour would not have been made against a lesbian. The tribunal regarded the claim as one of discrimination on grounds of sexual orientation and ruled that it was therefore outside the scope of the 1975 Act. Similarly when the appeal came before the Employment Appeal Tribunal, it was held that less favourable treatment of a gay man was not discrimination on grounds of sex either under the 1975 Act or the EC Equal Treatment Directive, the EAT confirming the traditional view that discrimination against lesbians or gay men is discrimination on the grounds of sexual orientation and not on the grounds of sex. The taunting of a gay man about his sexuality in the workplace does not therefore constitute sexual harassment and falls outside the ambit of the Act.

2.67   The Court of Appeal decision earlier this year[1] allowed Paul Smith's appeal and remitted the case to the Employment Tribunal for it to be determined on its facts. However, for reasons which are explained further below, it was no longer possible to pray in aid the Equal Treatment Directive, the appeal proceeding purely on the basis of the provisions of the Sex Discrimination Act.

1   [1998] IRLR 510.

2.68   The Court of Appeal ruled that discrimination on grounds of sexual orientation is not, per se, discriminatory. However, discrimination stemming from the complainant's orientation may constitute unlawful discrimination on grounds of his or her sex where a comparison is made with a gay person of the other sex in circumstances where that other person would be treated more favourably than the complainant.

2.69   The central issue in the appeal was the need to identify the appropriate comparator for someone like Paul Smith. There were three alternatives, namely that: no comparator was necessary at all; that the comparator was a heterosexual woman, the 'relevant circumstances being the same' that is, their sexual attraction to men, or, finally; a lesbian, the relevant circumstances being their sexual orientation. Ward LJ dealt with these as follows:

> '(a)   *The no-comparator argument*   This is built upon the unique position of the pregnant woman for whom no comparable male can ever be found. It was submitted that a homosexual male is in a similarly unique position. Neither the Employment Tribunal nor the Employment Appeal Tribunal had difficulty in rejecting this argument. Nor do I.

(b)   *The heterosexual comparator*   To establish who the appropriate comparator is in this case must depend upon how one determines what are the relevant circumstances. One can test the matter this way. If an employer is willing to accept female employees without a university degree, but will not accept male employees for the same job without a degree, the proper comparator, when an unsuccessful male applicant for employment makes his complaint under s 1, must be a female employee without a university degree. The lack of qualification is the personal characteristic of the applicant which must be regarded as the relevant circumstances for the purpose of making out the comparison in s 5(3). It can be no different if the relevant personal characteristic of the complainant happens to be homosexuality.

(c)   *The homosexual comparator*   To compare like with like, a male homosexual must be compared with a female homosexual'

Thus only the final alternative succeeded, Ward LJ saying that he saw the force of the heterosexual comparator argument but rejecting it without explanation.

2.70   This was disappointing. Considerable assistance for the heterosexual comparator argument was derived from an article by Dr Robert Wintermute which was referred to in argument and in the Court of Appeal judgments. He writes:

'...for a valid sex discrimination analysis, the comparison must change only the sex of the complaining individual and must hold all other circumstances constant. Otherwise a change in some other circumstance (such as the complaining individual's qualifications) could hide the sex discrimination. If an employer refused to hire a woman with the required university degree she would reply "I have the required degree. You have changed both my sex and my qualification. Change only my sex and compare me with a man with the required degree...". If the sex of the man is changed, but the sex of his male partner is held constant, the man's comparator is a woman with a male partner and the direct discrimination is clear. If the sexes of both the man and his partner are changed, the man's comparator becomes a woman with a female partner and the direct discrimination disappears with a wave of the wand.'[1]

1   (1997) 60 MLR 347. See also para **1.32**.

2.71   Though heralded by some as a victory, the decision in *Smith* does not, in fact make new law and does not afford any further protection to gay men and lesbians. Usually homophobic behaviour will be directed equally towards members of both sexes. With the exception of sex-specific sexual harassment (as the facts in *Smith* itself demonstrate) or prejudices relating to HIV status, there may be few cases where the victim will be able to prove less favourable treatment on the *Smith* test. There are some situations where this might occur, for example a boys' school might be willing to employ a lesbian but not a gay man; or a lesbian woman may be sexually harassed by a man who tries to make her sleep with him to 'cure her' of her lesbianism, a not uncommon situation according to the Stonewall research for their report. It is in any event a wholly unattractive proposition that a gay man subjected to discriminatory treatment can only succeed in a complaint by adducing evidence that a lesbian would have been treated more favourably or vice versa. It will be difficult to find an actual or hypothetical lesbian comparator who is appropriate for the facts under consideration. It is even more unattractive that an employer is permitted to defend a complaint by showing that he would have treated both equally badly, termed the 'equal misery' defence in the case of *Grant v South-West Trains* [1]. There are clear differences in the positions of lesbians and gay men, which are differences of gender. There is not one homosexual experience.

1   [1998] ICR 449.

2.72   However until new or amending legislation arrives on the statute book this is now the only possible route for individuals who suffer discrimination on grounds of their sexual orientation. Each case, inevitably, will turn on its own facts and on the evidence adduced; and 'the nature of the complaint and the factual matrix in which it is made will determine in each case judged on the particular facts what the relevant circumstances are' (Ward LJ in *Smith*). It may well be that many employment tribunals, dissatisfied with the somewhat illogical and unfair results which seem to flow from this test, will be able to decide on the evidence that the harassment or other discriminatory treatment is indeed gender specific and that there is liability. Only time will tell.

D   EUROPE

2.73   Before the Court of Appeal decision in *Smith v Gardner Merchant* [1] and given the uncertainty as to the ability of the Sex Discrimination Act to provide protection against discrimination for lesbians and gay men, lawyers had begun to look at European legislation and international norms to see to what extent these might assist.

1   [1998] IRLR 510.

2.74   The principle of supremacy of European Community law means that, in the case of conflict between rights established under Community law and those arising under national law, it is Community law which must prevail. In *Amministrazione delle Finanze dello Stato v Simmenthal Spa* [1] the ECJ declared that 'direct applicability...means that rules of Community law must be fully and uniformly applied in all the Member States from the date of their entry into force' by the national courts, that is the date from which they are to be implemented. They went on to hold that:

> 'A national court which is called upon, within the limits of its jurisdiction, to apply provisions of Community law is under a duty to give full effect to those provisions, if necessary refusing of its own motion to apply any conflicting provisions of national legislation, even if adopted subsequently and it is not necessary for the court to await a prior setting aside of such provisions by legislative or constitutional means.'

1   [1978] ECR 629.

2.75   In Britain the matter was dealt with by the provisions of the European Communities Act 1972, s 2(1) which provides as follows:

'All such rights, powers, liabilities, obligations and restrictions from time to time created by or arising by or under the Treaties, and all such remedies and procedures from time to time provided for by or under the Treaties, as in accordance with the Treaties are without further enactment to be given legal effect or used in the United Kingdom, shall be recognised and available in law, and be enforced, and allowed accordingly.'

This obligation to disapply domestic law has been accepted in a number of cases involving sex discrimination in the employment sphere, since the relevant Community equality legislation is concerned solely with the rights of workers.

2.76   In *R v Secretary of State for Employment, ex p Equal Opportunities Committee* [1] judicial review was sought of the longer periods of service needed by part-time workers to qualify in respect of redundancy and unfair dismissal rights. It was successfully argued that these requirements were indirectly discriminatory contrary to art 119 and the Equal Treatment Directive. The House of Lords held that it was possible to grant a declaration that the provisions of the Employment Protection (Consolidation) Act 1978 were incompatible with Community law, even though a prerogative order would not apply. Thus a declaration can be sought determining the compatibility of primary legislation with Community law, which in this case led to an amendment of s 64 of the 1978 Act.

1   [1994] IRLR 176.

2.77   The principal European equality provisions are contained in art 119 of the Treaty of Rome, which provides that men and women should receive equal pay for equal work, the Equal Pay Directive [1] (which re-states and amplifies the equal pay principle) and the Equal Treatment Directive [2] which is of particular importance in terms of sex discrimination in the employment field.

1   EC Directive 75/117.
2   EC Directive 76/207.

2.78   The Equal Treatment Directive was adopted under art 235 of the Treaty, which allows for action to be taken by the Community to achieve one of its objectives where the Treaty has not otherwise provided the necessary powers. Its purpose is to put into effect the principle of equal treatment for men and women as regards access to employment, working conditions and social security. Article 2(1) of the Directive provides that the principle of equal treatment means that there 'shall be no discrimination whatsoever on grounds of sex directly or indirectly by reference in particular to marital or family status.' The principle of equal treatment can be excluded from application to situations where 'the sex of the worker constitutes a determining factor' under art 2(2) and under art 2(3) where special provision is made for the protection of women particularly as regards pregnancy and maternity and under art 2(4) when positive action measures are taken to remove existing inequalities which affect women's opportunities. Article 3 applies these requirements to selection and promotion decisions, art 4 provides for vocational guidance and training and art 5 covers discriminatory dismissals. Article 7 deals with victimisation, art 6 provides that Member States must enact a right to a remedy by judicial process. Article 9 requires Member States to inform the Commission about measures taken to implement the Directive, which the UK government considered was not necessary in view of the prior existence of the Sex Discrimination Act 1975.

2.79 Four other directives also relate to sex discrimination. The Sex Discrimination (Social Security) Directive 79/7 deals with matters of state social security, the Sex Discrimination (Occupational Social Security) Directive 86/378 deals with occupational pensions. This was originally implemented in the United Kingdom by the Social Security Act 1989 but the coverage of that Directive is now dealt with in the Pensions Act 1995. The Sex Discrimination (Self-Employed) Directive 86/631 deals with the position of self-employed women, in particular in agriculture and family businesses; and finally Directive 92/85, the Pregnant Workers' Directive, provides for the protection of the health and safety of pregnant and breastfeeding women.

2.80 The Equal Treatment Directive has what is known as direct vertical effect, that is an employee can rely upon it directly only in respect of organs of the state. Otherwise national courts are required to interpret their national law in the light of the wording and purposes of the Directive. In the Employment Appeal Tribunal, in *Smith v Gardner Merchant* [1], reliance had been placed, although to no avail, on the Equal Treatment Directive as providing a wider definition of discrimination than that contained in the Sex Discrimination Act and as requiring the word 'sex' to be read as including sexuality. In the Armed Forces dismissal cases, in addition to the irrationality challenge to the policy of automatic discharge on the grounds of sexual orientation, it was argued that the policy breached the Equal Treatment Directive and was unlawfully discriminatory [2]. Reliance was placed on its legal basis (art 235), on its purpose and on the European Court of Justice's recognition of the principle of equality as a fundamental human right. In *Defrenne* [3] the ECJ noted that respect for fundamental rights was one of the general principles of Community law, the observance of which the court has a duty to ensure; and that 'there can be no doubt that the elimination of discrimination based on sex forms part of those fundamental rights'. Reliance was also placed upon art 26 of the International Covenant on Civil and Political Rights 1966, which covenant has been ratified by the United Kingdom. Article 26 is a free-standing anti-discrimination provision which includes a prohibition on discrimination on grounds of sex. In the case of *Toonen v Australia* [4] the Human Rights Committee decided that the word 'sex' in art 26 includes sexual orientation. It was therefore argued that the EC Equal Treatment Directive should be interpreted broadly, having regard to the international perspective, and in particular having regard to the recognition of vulnerability of lesbians and gay men at work in the EC Recommendation and Code of Practice on the Protection of the Dignity of Women and Men at Work. This has already been referred to in s 3 at para **2.36**.

1   [1998] IRLR 510.
2   *R v Ministry of Defence, ex p Smith* [1996] QB 517.
3   Case 149/77 [1978] ECR 1365.
4   (1994) 1-3 IHRR 97.

2.81 The argument was a powerful one. In the first place discrimination on grounds of sexual orientation, as in the case of sex discrimination against a woman, rests essentially on stereotypical assumptions as to gender characteristics. Lesbians and gay men are discriminated against because they fail to conform to the gender stereotype of having heterosexual preferences. In the workplace the Equal Treatment Directive requires that men and women should be treated equally without any reference to questions of sex. Given the purpose of this Directive this word ought to be held to incorporate sexuality within it. Thus, in this situation, there is sex discrimination per se without having to investigate the actual or hypothetical treatment of a person of the opposite sex. Alternatively, even if it was appropriate to adopt a comparative approach to the treatment of men and women the argument is still sound. The true comparison for a gay man is a heterosexual woman on the basis that if a man with a sexual preference for other men is treated less favourably than a woman with a sexual preference for men sex is the ground for the difference in treatment. But for the fact that he is a man he would not have been discriminated against.

2.82 The argument was nevertheless rejected by both the Divisional Court and the Court of Appeal. The then Master of the Rolls, Sir Thomas Bingham, stated:

> 'I find nothing whatever in the EEC Treaty or in the Equal Treatment Directive which suggests that the draftsmen of those instruments were addressing their minds in any way whatever to problems of discrimination on grounds of sexual orientation. Had it been intended to regulate discrimination on that ground it could easily have been done, but to my mind it plainly was not. It is true that the Commission's Code of Practice, drawn up many years after the Treaty and the Directive, makes reference to sexual orientation but it seems to me quite plain that this Code is directed to banning unacceptable behaviour in the workplace and not to regulating employment policy in relation to sexual orientation. …There is equally, in my opinion, no assistance to be gained from cases decided under the International Covenant on Civil and Political Rights. …It is evident from cursory consideration of [the language of art 26] that its terms extend well beyond anything to be found in the EEC Treaty or the Equal Treatment Directive.'

2.83 The Court of Appeal thereby upheld the view of the Divisional Court that the Equal Treatment Directive was everything to do with discrimination as between men and women but nothing to do with sexual orientation. The House of Lords refused leave to appeal.

2.84 To require protection against discrimination on grounds of sexual orientation to have been in the minds of the legislators is to ignore the purposive interpretation to be applied to European laws. It probably was not in their minds in 1976 but then it is also unlikely that they had in mind at that time pregnancy discrimination or discrimination in relation to pension entitlement. A purposive interpretation requires account to be taken of social changes and of our greater awareness of the problems of discrimination faced by different groups of people, not a rigid adherence to the intentions of the legislators of 20 years ago.

2.85 Shortly after the arguments advanced on behalf of the applicants in *R v Ministry of Defence, ex p Smith*[1] received such short shrift from the domestic courts, the European Court of Justice decided the landmark case of *P v S and*

Somerset County Council[2], which drove a coach and horses through the traditional view that the Equal Treatment Directive, like the Sex Discrimination Act, permitted only a comparison of treatment as between men and women.

1 [1996] QB 517.
2 [1996] IRLR 347.

2.86 P was employed as the general manager of a unit of an educational establishment operated by the county council, with S as the head. When first employed P was a man but, subsequently, she informed S that she intended to undergo gender re-assignment. The governors of the establishment were informed and, whilst she took sick leave in preparation for surgery, she was given notice of dismissal and was not thereafter permitted to return in her female gender role. She complained of unlawful sex discrimination. The Industrial Tribunal held that the Sex Discrimination Act did not apply, on the basis that a woman undergoing gender re-assignment would also have been dismissed and P was therefore not treated less favourably than a woman in such circumstances would have been. However they were uncertain whether the broader wording and purpose of the Equal Treatment Directive meant that P's treatment breached the equal treatment principle contained within it and they referred this question to the European Court under art 177 of the Treaty.

2.87 The ECJ decided in P's favour, holding that discrimination on grounds of gender re-assignment contravenes the equal treatment principle. The court considered that 'the scope of the directive cannot be confined simply to discrimination based on the fact that a person is of one or other sex'. It applies to discrimination arising from gender re-assignment because 'such discrimination is based, essentially if not exclusively, on the sex of the person concerned...To tolerate such discrimination would be tantamount, as regards such a person, to a failure to respect the dignity and freedom to which she or he is entitled and which the court has a duty to safeguard.'

2.88 In so deciding they followed the opinion of Advocate-General Tesauro, who had recommended a:

'rigorous application of the principle of equality so that...any connotations relating to sex and/or sexual identity cannot be in any way relevant...Sex is important as a convention, a social parameter. The discrimination of which women are frequently the victims is not of course due to their physical characteristics, but rather to their role, to the image which society has of women...In the same way it must be recognised that the unfavourable treatment suffered by transsexuals is most often linked to a negative image, a moral judgement which has nothing to do with their abilities in the sphere of employment.'

He added:

'... it is necessary to go beyond the traditional classification and recognise that, in addition to the man/woman dichotomy, there is a range of characteristics, behaviour and roles shared by men and women so that sex itself ought rather to be thought of as a continuum. From that point of view it is clear that it would not be right to continue to treat as unlawful solely acts of discrimination on grounds of sex which are referable to men and women in the traditional sense of those terms, while refusing to protect those who are also treated unfavourably precisely because of their sex and/or sexual identity...The objection is taken too much for granted and has been raised on several occasions in these proceedings that the factor of sex discrimination is missing on the grounds that "female transsexuals" are not treated differently from "male transsexuals". In short both are treated unfavourably, hence there can be no discrimination at all...I am not convinced by that view. It is quite true that even if P had been in the opposite situation that she would have been dismissed anyway. One fact, however, is not just possible, but certain: P would not have been dismissed if she had remained a man.'

2.89 The reasoning behind this important decision led to renewed interest in the Equal Treatment Directive being held to apply to discrimination on grounds of sexual orientation. The 'purposive' interpretation to be applied to European laws, as P's case so clearly illustrates, was thought to be likely to apply in relation to sexual orientation. Since the decision of the European Court of Justice in *P v S* the Employment Appeal Tribunal held that the Sex Discrimination Act also applied to discrimination against transsexuals, construing the Act, as they were required to, so as to conform to the Equal Treatment Directive [1].

1   *Chessington World of Adventures Ltd v Reed* [1997] IRLR 556.

2.90 Further developments took place, encouraged by the ECJ decision in the case of *P v S*. First, an employment tribunal referred to the ECJ a question relating to equal pay for same-sex partners in the case of *Grant v South-West Trains Ltd* [1]. Second, another dismissed gay ex-serviceman mounted a new challenge to the Ministry of Defence policy of automatic discharge from the Armed Forces on grounds of sexual orientation, by way of judicial review. In *R v Secretary of State for Defence, ex p Perkins* [2] the question whether there was a breach of the Equal Treatment Directive was referred to the ECJ.

1   [1998] IRLR 206.
2   [1997] IRLR 297.

2.91 In the first of these cases Lisa Grant, a clerical worker employed by South-West Trains, was refused a travel pass for her female partner with whom she had lived in a stable relationship for some time. Her contract of employment with South-West Trains provided that:

'You will be granted such free and reduced rate travel concessions as are applicable to a member of your grade. Your spouse and dependants will also be granted travel concessions.'

The Staff Travel Privilege Ticket Regulations provide that:

'Privileged tickets are granted to a married member of staff for one legal spouse. Privileged tickets are granted for one common law opposite sex spouse of staff subject to a statutory declaration being made that a meaningful relationship has existed for a period of two years or more.'

Lisa Grant's request for travel concessions for her partner was turned down because she was not of the opposite sex.

2.92 Relying extensively on the decision in *P v S* the opinion of Advocate-General Elmer delivered on 30 September 1997 was that Lisa Grant should succeed, concluding that:

'(1) A provision in an employer's pay regulations under which the employee is granted a pay benefit in the form of travel concessions for a co-habitee of the opposite gender to the employee, but refused such concessions for a co-habitee of the same gender as the employee, constitutes discrimination on the basis of gender, which is contrary to Article 119 of the EC Treaty.

(2) Such discrimination on the basis of gender cannot be justified by reference to the fact that the employer's intention is to confer benefits on heterosexual couples as opposed to homosexual couples.'

2.93 Unusually however, the European Court, giving judgment on 17 February 1998, disagreed with the Advocate-General and held that there was no breach of art 119. They held that European Community law does not cover discrimination based on sexual orientation. Therefore a refusal by the employers to allow travel concessions for a person of the same sex with whom a worker has a stable relationship, where such concessions are allowed to a worker's spouse or to a person of the opposite sex with whom a worker has a stable relationship outside marriage, does not constitute discrimination prohibited by art 119 of the EC Treaty or the Equal Pay Directive. Further, although this case was determined under art 119 of the EC Treaty and the Equal Pay Directive, the court stated that: 'community law as it stands at present does not cover discrimination based on sexual orientation such as that at issue in the main proceedings.'

2.94 Before the European Court had decided the *Grant* case Lightman J had referred the *Perkins* case to the European Court of Justice. When referring to the case of *P v S* he said:

'The entire social policy reasoning of the Advocate-General, as it seems to me is equally applicable to those of homosexual orientation as it is to transsexuals. Homosexual orientation is a reality today which the law must recognise and adjust to and it may well be thought appropriate that the fundamental principle of equality and the irrelevance of a person's sex and sexual identity demand that the court be alert to afford protection to them and ensure that those of homosexual orientation are no longer disadvantaged in terms of employment...After the decision in the *Cornwall* case, it is scarcely possible to limit the application of the Directive to gender discrimination...and there must be a real prospect that the European Court will take the further courageous step to extend protection to those of homosexual orientation, if a courageous step is necessary to do so. I doubt, however, whether any courage is necessary, for all that may be required is working out and applying in a constructive manner the implications of the Advocate-General's opinion and the judgment in the *Cornwall* case.'

2.95 The question referred to the European Court was whether the requirement in art 2(1) of the Equal Treatment Directive, that there shall be no discrimination on grounds of sex either directly or indirectly by reference in particular to marital or family status, should be interpreted as including discrimination based on a person's sexual orientation.

2.96 Following the decision in *Grant* the case of *Perkins* was referred back to the Divisional Court for the appropriateness of the reference to be reconsidered. On 13 July 1998 Lightman J withdrew the reference, stating that 'The answer to the question which I have referred is so obvious as to leave no scope for reasonable doubt…there was no reasonable prospect of any change of mind on the part of the ECJ'. He considered that it must reasonably be inferred that the word 'sex' in both the Equal Pay and the Equal Treatment Directives is intended to have the same meaning. The ECJ in *Grant* had clearly proceeded on the basis that the meaning of the word is the same in both. And it was inconceivable that the ECJ did not appreciate the effect of its decision on the scope of the protection available under the Equal Treatment Directive. He also rejected Mr Perkins' submission that *Grant* is inconsistent with the decision in *P v S*. He said that the decision in *P v S* was clearly limited to cases of discrimination based on an employee's gender reassignment [1].

1   [1998] IRLR 508.

2.97 The decision to withdraw the reference was disappointing since there were sufficient factual and legal differences between *Grant* and *Perkins* for the Divisional Court to decide to continue with the reference. In particular, not only were the cases brought under different European provisions, but Mr Perkins lost his livelihood as a result of the Armed Forces policy. In the *Grant* case it was the partner who lost out on a rail concession. Importantly the European Court is not bound by the doctrine of precedent and has in the past overruled earlier decisions as part of its developing jurisprudence. It is to be noted that in *P v S* the Advocate-General held the view adopted by the court that Community law cannot be confined simply to discrimination based on the fact that a person is of one or other sex. In this respect the decision in *Grant* appears to be a retrospective step.

2.98 It seems clear that, for the present, the European Court of Justice has decided to leave the whole question of discrimination on grounds of sexual orientation to the legislators, ignoring the effect of international human rights instruments (the International Covenant on Civil and Political Rights) and pointing out in the judgment in *Grant* that:

> 'It should be observed, however, that the Treaty of Amsterdam amending the Treaty on European Union, the Treaties establishing the European Communities and certain related Acts, signed on 2 October 1997, provides for the insertion in the EC Treaty of an art 6a which, once the Treaty of Amsterdam has entered into force, will allow the Council under certain conditions (a unanimous vote on a proposal from the Commission after consulting the European Parliament) to take appropriate action to eliminate various forms of discrimination, including the discrimination based on sexual orientation.'

Given the requirement for unanimity European legislation may be difficult to obtain but, for the present, the matter clearly rests there.

E THE FUTURE

2.99 Further legal avenues are worth exploring in appropriate cases. For instance Lisa Grant has a second, High Court claim for breach of contract before the courts, in which she contends that her employers were in breach of their own Equal Opportunities Policy, dealing inter alia with sexual orientation, which is incorporated into her contract of employment. Her claim was dismissed at first instance and awaits the attention of the Court of Appeal. It is unclear how this decision can fit happily with the case of *Secretary of State for Scotland v Taylor* [1] in which it was held that an Equal Opportunities Policy did have contractual effect.

1 [1997] IRLR 608.

2.100 Alternatively all employers owe a duty of care to their employees at common law to provide a safe working environment. Some cases of homosexual harassment could be brought on these grounds. In addition the Protection from Harassment Act 1997, which came into force on 16 June 1998, provides an additional civil remedy by way of an injunction and/or damages against a person who pursues a course of conduct which:
(*a*)   amounts to harassment of another; and
(*b*)   which he knows or ought to know amounts to harassment of the other.

Harassment is defined as conduct that would be judged to be harassment by a reasonable person in possession of the same information.

2.101 Naturally the advent of the Human Rights Act 1998, incorporating the European Convention of Human Rights and Fundamental Freedoms into our law, will enable homosexual victims of discrimination to pursue a complaint, when the Act comes into force in the year 2000, insofar as their enjoyment of other substantive rights under the Convention has been infringed. The applicants in *R v Ministry of Defence, ex p Smith* [1] are currently awaiting determination by the European Court of Human Rights in Strasbourg of their claims for breaches of arts 8 and 14 of the European Convention as a result of their dismissals from the Armed Forces. The Council of Europe meanwhile, being aware that art 14 of the Convention, which is not free-standing, has weaknesses inherent in it which have led to it being under-used, have recently drafted a new free-standing anti-discrimination protocol in order to strengthen the principle.

1 [1996] IRLR 100.

2.102 The search for alternatives however skates around the main problem, which is that adverse treatment of lesbians and gay men occurs because of prejudice and a personal antagonism towards a private lifestyle, which is different from that of the majority. Homosexuality, like sex and race, is a permanent characteristic which is generally irrelevant to the provision of employment, education, housing and other services which are available in any civilised society. As we approach the millennium it is surely only a question of time before discrimination against individuals on grounds of their sexual orientation is outlawed expressly by legislation.

2.103   Various codes of practice, including those for the Bar Council, the Law Society and Legal Executives, now prohibit such discrimination. Within the public sector and increasingly in the private sector a number of employers have included lesbian and gay issues in their human resources policies. The survey conducted by Stonewall found that equal opportunities policies certainly did make a difference. Provisions dealing with harassment, equal benefits, equal leave provisions and pension entitlements are now frequently catered for in equal opportunity policies which include lesbians and gay men within their terms. It is through such policies that the educative and awareness-raising process occurs, at least in part, moving society gradually and inexorably towards general acceptance that discrimination against individuals on grounds of their sexual orientation is unacceptable.

Chapter 3

Family matters

3.01   This chapter looks at how the law regards lesbians and gay men as parents. Traditionally, lawyers have been involved in representing lesbians or gay parents in the context of marital breakdown. Whilst most children continue to be born into heterosexual relationships a growing number are conceived in the context of a lesbian relationship. Whether or not society in general approves of these arrangements, the fact is that a significant number of children are being raised in such relationships. The challenge for lawyers is to identify ways of securing legal protection for these new families and, in the absence of any real legal framework, to deal with problems on family breakdown.

3.02   Despite changing attitudes towards homosexuality, some lesbians and gay men marry in the knowledge of their sexual orientation often in an attempt to live a 'normal' life and, in particular, to have children. Until relatively recently to be a lesbian mother or a gay father was seen as a contradiction in terms. Most of the cases which have come before the courts have involved lesbian mothers in disputes with heterosexual fathers. There are a tiny number of cases concerning gay fathers. The other context in which the courts have considered sexual orientation is that of adoption and as will be seen there have been recent positive decisions in favour of both a lesbian and gay male applicant.

A   REPRESENTING THE LESBIAN MOTHER ON THE BREAKDOWN OF A HETEROSEXUAL RELATIONSHIP

3.03   It is impossible to know the number of cases where sexual orientation has been an issue as few have been reported. Over the last ten years or so there has been a marked decrease in the number of contested cases involving lesbian mothers. This is partly explained by the change in culture following the implementation of the Children Act 1989 and partly by changing social attitudes towards homosexuality. This section aims to give an overview of how judicial attitudes have evolved and the issues currently facing lawyers advising lesbian mothers.

1 The case law

3.04 Since the late 1970s there have been a number of Court of Appeal decisions where the court has looked at the suitability or otherwise of lesbians as mothers. Historically the Court of Appeal has had no difficulty in making general non-discriminatory statements such as by Ormrod LJ in *E v E* [1]:

> 'The mere fact of this homosexual way of life on the part of the mother is not in itself a reason for refusing to give her control of the children. There is no rule or principle that a lesbian mother or homosexual father cannot be granted custody of a child.'

1   (27 November 1980, unreported), CA.

3.05 Historically the Court of Appeal has however showed rather less liberal attitudes in implementing this principle:

> 'This is neither the time nor the place to moralise or philosophise about sexual deviance and its consequences by those who practice it, but the possible effect on a young child living in proximity to that practice is of critical importance to that child and the public's interest.' [1]

1   Watkins LJ *Re P (a minor) (custody)* (1983) 4 FLR 401, CA.

3.06 A review of the Court of Appeal decisions (and reported county court decisions) since the late 1970s shows a gradual liberalisation in the courts' attitudes towards lesbian mothers and although the courts have been extremely concerned about the risk to a child of being raised by a lesbian, this concern seems to be receding. This is due no doubt in part to the findings of independent research into the development of children raised by lesbian mothers such as carried out by Golombok et al (see para **3.32**).

3.07 The Court of Appeal has spent much time considering the relationship between sexual orientation and motherhood. The early decisions in particular should be seen in the context of then social attitudes. In the late 1970s and early 1980s there were very few women living openly as lesbians let alone as lesbian mothers. The early cases show a deep hostility towards lesbianism in general and lesbians as mothers in particular. In *S v S* [1] lesbianism was described as 'deviant', in *Re P (a minor) (custody)* [2] as 'devious', in *E v E* [3] as 'unnatural' and in *G v D* [4] as 'unstable'.

1   (1978) 1 FLR 143.
2   (1983) 4 FLR 401.
3   (27 November 1980, unreported), CA. See para **3.04**.
4   (16 February 1983, unreported), CA.

3.08 The Court of Appeal paid much attention to the potential harm to children of being 'around' lesbianism. In *Re P* [1], Sir John Arnold P categorised the issues of concern to the court as those of corruption and reputation. By 'corruption' he meant:

> 'In the sense that by force of example or by erosion of that instinctive rejection of devious conduct which inevitably resides in the normal mind in one way or another the child is likely to come to harm.'

By 'reputation' (which is still highly relevant) he meant:

> 'It cannot be (as I think) disputed that the observation by, at any rate, some sections of the community of a union enjoyed by the mother... will lead to expressions of ridicule or scorn. That is not to say that such sentiments are worthy or proper but merely to recognise the rejection of, and revulsion at, such a way of life is still a not uncommon phenomenon. However just or unjust such a condemnation may be, if it involves a child living in such a household it must be likely to lead the child to be teased and embarrassed at the least.'

1   [1983] 4 FLR 401. See para **3.07**.

3.09   The question of teasing is one which still concerns the court and which will inevitably have to be addressed, if representing the mother.

3.10   The Court of Appeal decisions make much of the benefits to the child of being brought up in a 'normal' heterosexual environment as against a 'deviant' lesbian household. In *Re P* (see para **3.08**) Watkins LJ went as far as to say:

> 'I accept that it is not right to say that a child should in no circumstances live with a mother who is carrying on a lesbian relationship with a woman who is also living with her, but I venture to suggest that it can only be countenanced by the court when it is driven to the conclusion that there is in the interests of the child no other acceptable form of custody.'

3.11   Even in the later case of *C v C (a minor) (custody: appeal)*[1] Glidewell LJ was able to find:

> 'Despite the vast changes over the past 30 years or so in the attitudes of our society generally to the institution of marriage, to sexual morality, and to homosexual relationships, I regard it as axiomatic that the ideal environment for the upbringing of a child is the home of loving, caring and sensible parents, her father and her mother. When the marriage between father and mother is at an end, that ideal cannot be attained. When the court is called upon to decide which of two possible alternatives is then preferable for the child's welfare, its task is to choose the alternative which comes closest to that ideal. Even taking account of the changes of attitudes to which I have referred, a lesbian relationship between two adult women is an unusual background in which to bring up a child.'

1   [1991] 1 FLR 223.

3.12   Of the reported Court of Appeal decisions the most quoted today is *C v C (a minor) (custody: appeal)* [1]. The decision of Callman HHJ (sitting as a county court judge) in *B v B (minors) (custody, care and control)* [2] also deserves careful consideration.

1   [1991] 1 FLR 223. See para **3.11**.
2   [1991] 1 FLR 402.

3.13   In *C v C* the Court of Appeal was called upon to decide whether a lesbian mother was a 'fit' custodial parent for her six year old daughter. The parties had divorced in 1987 after four years of marriage and the husband had remarried.

The child remained with the mother. The case involved slightly unusual circumstances in that the mother, who became a prison officer, formed a relationship with a woman prisoner who was serving a sentence for unlawful wounding and theft. Upon the woman's release she went to live with the mother and child. In October 1989 the mother and father agreed that the father should look after the child following the mother's and partner's eviction from their flat. The father applied for custody. An interim order was made giving the father care and control. The court welfare officer made no recommendation; instead he said that the child was happy in both homes and that both parents were loving parents.

3.14   The judge at first instance made an order in the mother's favour saying:

> 'If I were being asked here to choose between a child being brought up wholly ignorant to lesbian relationships and untouched on the one hand, and on the other hand in heterosexual relationship, it seems to me there might be an appreciable balance one way in favour of what, unlike the welfare officer, I do see as "the normal" but in the end I have to come to the conclusion that the most important factor in this case, and one which is not outweighed by the advantages the other way, is the strong bond, and the one which until October 1989 was almost untampered with, between the child and her mother.'

3.15   The father appealed. The Court of Appeal was asked to decide whether the disadvantages to the child of living in a lesbian household were outweighed by the benefits of continuing what the judge at first instance described as 'the strong bond' between mother and daughter.

3.16   In allowing the appeal and remitting the case for rehearing, Glidewell and Balcombe LJJ commented on the correct approach to the mother's lesbian relationship. Balcombe LJ stressed that being a lesbian is not an automatic disentitlement to having care and control of a child:

> 'The fact that the mother has a lesbian relationship with Ms A does not of itself render her unfit to have care and control of her child. It is however, an important factor to be taken into account in deciding which of the alternative homes which the parents can offer the child is most likely to advance her welfare.'

3.17   Balcombe LJ made it very clear however that a lesbian household is far from the ideal when he said:

> 'If, because the parents are divorced such an upbringing is no longer possible, then a very material factor in considering where the child's welfare lies is which of the competing parents can offer the nearest approach to that norm. In the present case it is clearly the father.'

3.18   The Court of Appeal held that the judge at first instance had not given proper consideration to the mother's lesbian relationship and the Court of Appeal remitted the case to the High Court for a rehearing where the mother received a much more sympathetic hearing. The official solicitor was appointed to act as the child's guardian ad litem and the matter was reheard by Booth LJ.

(i)   C v C (No 2) [1]

3.19   This case demonstrates the importance of expert evidence. The official solicitor commissioned a report from a consultant psychiatrist, Dr Michael King of the Royal Free Hospital and Dr King's evidence was that the child would not be encouraged into a homosexual lifestyle, although it was said that she would be likely to be teased by living with her mother. There was also no evidence whatsoever that she would be involved in sexual activities in the mother's household.

1   [1992] 1 FCR 206.

3.20   Finding in the mother's favour Booth LJ stated:

'I am satisfied beyond any doubt that the bond between mother and daughter is a strong one, I make that finding first on the basis that the daughter has lived so successfully with her mother for so long as part of her childhood years and secondly because it is also clearly evidenced by the child's own expressed wishes.'

3.21   Booth LJ talked about 'the norm' in child centred terms:

'Children are the most conventional of beings. They do not like being different and they do not like having their lives changed. They like things to be in a settled routine, without problems and anything that is different, abnormal, out of the ordinary or unconventional, poses greater or lesser problems, to children. When problems are posed for a child, that child needs to be able to turn to the adult that the child sees as closest to them and the person that this child wants to turn to is her mother.'

3.22   This illustrates quite a different approach from the Court of Appeal's approach which was to identify the mother's lesbianism as the source of the problem which the child could be protected from by living with the father.

(ii)   B v B (minors) (custody, care and control) [1]

3.23   This case concerned three children aged ten, nine and two. When the youngest child was seven months old the mother left to live with another woman with whom she was having a lesbian relationship. It was agreed that the parents would have joint custody of all three children and that the father would have care and control of the older two but care and control of the youngest child was in dispute.

1   [1991] 1 FLR 402.

3.24   The father argued that if the child lived with his mother there would be a severance from normal society, that he would suffer psychological stress and unhappiness, that he might be scarred for life (as per Lord Wilberforce in *Re D* (see para **3.44**)) and that not only would his son's sexual identity be adversely affected but that he would be stigmatised and his reputation would suffer.

3.25 Callman HHJ described the parents' arguments as raising two specific issues:

> 'The first one is what is best for the welfare of the older boy, the girl and in particular the younger boy, but the welfare of all the children has to be considered; and secondly, the specific issue as to the desirability of bringing up a child in a lesbian household. It is the second issue which has given rise to a considerable amount of time being spent to investigate that aspect of the case.'

In dealing with whether a child as a matter of principle be should brought up in a lesbian household Callman HHJ stated:

> 'The particular issue is that I must ask myself whether the proclivities of the mother and the lady with whom she lives are such as to make it undesirable in the younger boy's interest that he should be brought up in that home.'

3.26 An interesting feature of this case is the division by the judge of lesbians into 'militant' and 'non-militant':

> 'What is so important in these cases is to distinguish between militant lesbians who try to convert others to their way of life, where there may well be risks that counterbalance other aspects of welfare and are damaging to the long-term interests of children either in relation to their sexual identity or corruption, and lesbians in private. In this case, I am dealing with two lesbians who are private persons who do not believe in advertising their lesbianism and acting in the public field in favour of promoting lesbianism.'

3.27 The judge did not elaborate further on why 'militancy' would pose a threat to a child's sexual identity. Although he made no specific reference to feminism and political activity this is presumably what he had in mind when describing 'militant' lesbianism.

3.28 Finding in the mother's favour Callman HHJ stated:

> 'It is quite plain to me that in this case, when I do the balancing exercise, [the child's] welfare demands really that he remains with his mother because her maternal care cannot be faulted and she has to my judgment demonstrated her desire to see that he will be brought up on a heterosexual basis and that he will, as he must, see a good deal of his father.'

3.29 This passage illustrates the continuing anxiety on the part of many judges that children should not grow up to become lesbian or gay.

2 Expert evidence

3.30 As can be seen particularly from *C v C (No 2)* [1] independent expert evidence can be very valuable in representing a lesbian mother. Such evidence can be introduced by either instructing a psychiatrist or psychologist to prepare a report which should also summarise the current psychological evidence or by inviting the court to consider the published research.

1 [1991] 1 FCR 206 and see para **3.19**.

3.31 If there are allegations of mental instability or illness a psychiatric report may be justified but given that homosexuality is no longer regarded as a mental illness a psychiatric report is by no means always appropriate. If the client is legally aided, prior authority should be obtained from the Legal Aid Board before any report is commissioned and it is likely that the Legal Aid Board will require an advice from counsel that the report is in fact necessary. If it is intended that the expert should read the papers then leave of the court is required to disclose them [1]. If the application is with consent of the other party the district judge may still need considerable persuading that an expert is necessary, preferring to leave such matters to be investigated by the court welfare officer.

1 Family Proceedings Rules 1991, SI 1991/1247, r 4.23.

3.32 Many judges dealing with family cases are now familiar with the published research on lesbian mothers, although this should not be assumed and the research should be made available to the trial judge. The most important British research on the effects on children of being raised by a lesbian mother is that published by Professor Susan Golombok et al [1].

1 See Golombok, Spencer and Rutter *Children in lesbian and single parent households: psychosexual and psychiatric appraisal* J of Child Psychology (1983 Vol 24, No 4, pp 551–572) and Golombok and Tasker *Adults raised as children in lesbian families* AJ of Orthopsychiatry (1995 Vol 65, No 2, pp 203–215).

3.33 The first study compared the development of the children of 27 single-parent heterosexual mothers with the development of the children of 27 lesbian mothers. The research shows that the two groups did not differ in terms of their gender identity, sex role behaviour or sexual orientation. The two groups did not differ on most measures of emotion, behaviour and relationships, although there were some indications of more frequent psychiatric problems in the heterosexual single-parent group. The research concluded that rearing in a lesbian household per se does not lead to atypical psychosexual development or constitute a psychiatric risk factor.

3.34 The second study followed 25 of the children raised by lesbians and 21 of the children raised by single heterosexual mothers from the original investigation. The study shows that children brought up by lesbian mothers are no more or less likely as adults to be lesbian or gay. The children raised by lesbian mothers were more able to forge closer relationships with their mother's new female partner than had the children from the heterosexual households with their mother's new male partner. Although children from lesbian families experienced no greater peer stigma they were more likely to be teased about their own sexuality in their teenage years. When asked however about their general experience of being teased or bullied by peers, young adults from lesbian families were no more likely to report victimisation than those from heterosexual single-parent households.

3.35 This research, particularly as it relates to children as young adults, has gone a very considerable way to allaying the court's fears that lesbianism presents a risk to a child's emotional development. It could however be argued that the lesbian mother is still in a no win situation as far as the courts are concerned as the best way of being seen as a fit and suitable parent is to produce a child who is heterosexual. Most judges still do not wish to hear that a lesbian mother would be pleased if her daughter grew up to be a lesbian.

3.36 Other American research has looked at the importance or otherwise of a child knowing about his or her lesbian mother's sexual orientation. One study [1] suggests that a mother's openness with her child can benefit both the mother/child relationship and the child's wellbeing in general. The study found that children who learnt of their mother's lesbianism in childhood had higher self esteem than those who were not informed of her sexual orientation or who found out by accident.

1   Huggins, S and Bozett, F W *Homosexuality and the family: A comparative study of self esteem of adolescent children of divorced lesbian mothers and divorced heterosexual mothers* (1989) Harrington Park Press, New York.

3.37 In some cases it may be appropriate to call evidence as to the mother's general character and place in the community. If she continues to have a close relationship with her own family it may be appropriate for evidence of this to be called. If there are supportive and involved grandparents their evidence may be helpful and the involvement of a concerned grandmother can sometimes be of great reassurance to a troubled judge.

3.38 Evidence that the mother is not living some bizarre and exotic life (if that is indeed the case) can help counter the myths and stereotypes that can still surround lesbianism. The mother may for example be active in the PTA, the brownies, the cubs, the church or the women's institute. To counter the idea that the child will have little contact with men it can sometimes be useful to file statements from some of the mother's male friends or male relatives to whom she is close.

3.39 If the mother has a partner, whether to call the partner as a witness or not can be a difficult decision. Calling the partner may distract from the central issue which should be the mother's parenting abilities. If the mother's partner is called there is a risk that she may be cast as the villain of the piece particularly if she is the mother's first female partner. It is too easy for cases to be sidelined by suggestions that the mother was 'seduced' away from normality by her lesbian lover. If a court welfare officer has been appointed to prepare a report and if the partner is to play any role in the child's life, then she will invariably be seen by the court welfare officer who may then express a view as to her character.

3.40 The days when the lesbian mother was asked in evidence to describe her sexual practices are fortunately past. She will however inevitably be asked whether she is 'discreet'. She may be asked how she behaves with her partner (if she has one) in front of the child. This should be addressed in the mother's statement and she should be prepared to deal with it in cross-examination or in questioning by the judge.

3.41 As we have seen, the possibility of teasing at school concerns some judges. It is always possible that a child will be teased by his or her peers if it becomes known that his or her mother is a lesbian and the mother should be prepared to explain how she would deal with teasing should it occur.

B   REPRESENTING GAY FATHERS

3.42   Despite a growing acceptance of homosexuality in general, gay fathers still face very considerable hostility from the courts. There are far fewer reported cases concerning gay fathers than there are cases concerning lesbian mothers. Such cases as there have been show that the courts have a notion of a gay 'lifestyle' which is perceived as a risk to children. When representing a gay father it is usually necessary to dispel some of the myths that surround gay male sexuality, eg that all gay men are sexually promiscuous, have paedophile tendencies and are a corrupting influence on children. The principal concerns of the courts may be said to be:

(*a*)   the effect on the child's sexual and emotional development of having a gay man as a father;

(*b*)   the social stigma which the child may face from having a gay father;

(*c*)   the risks to the child of being sexually abused by the father and/or his associates; and

(*d*)   the effect of the illness on the child if the father is HIV positive or is living with AIDS.

3.43   One difficulty in representing gay fathers is the lack of research into the effects on a child of having an openly gay father. There is a growing body of research on the effect on children of being raised by lesbian mothers (see para **3.32**) and although some of the findings may apply equally to gay fathers, the existing research on lesbian mothers is gender specific. Lesbian mothers are still in general perceived as presenting less of a risk to children than gay fathers. Most applications brought by gay fathers are in respect of contact.

1   The case law

3.44   The leading case remains the damning House of Lords' decision in *Re D (an infant)* [1]. *Re D* concerned an application by the mother of a seven year old boy and her new husband for an adoption order. The father's contact had ceased nine months before an adoption order was made. The father admitted that he had had a number of partners and had been living with a man aged 19. The father was not willing to consent to the making of an adoption order. He was described as perfectly honest, frank and straightforward by the judge and the father had said that he would guarantee that the boy would not be exposed to homosexual influences.

1   [1977] AC 602.

3.45   The judge at first instance dispensed with the father's consent to the making of the adoption order on the basis that the father would be extremely unlikely to prevent the boy coming into contact with other homosexuals. A reasonable parent would take the view 'I must protect my son even if it means parting with him forever'. Making the order, the judge found 'this father has nothing to offer his son'. The father appealed. The Court of Appeal allowed the appeal and Orr and Stephenson LJJ both found that the risks to the child of coming into contact with other gay men had been exaggerated. Access was to be at the father's parents' home and the Court of Appeal accepted that this provided adequate safeguards. The mother appealed to the House of Lords.

3.46   The mother was successful and by a unanimous decision in the House of Lords the adoption order was reinstated. In a famous passage Lord Wilberforce stated:

> 'Whatever new attitudes Parliament or public tolerance may have chosen to take as regards the behaviour of consenting adults over 21, inter se, these should not entitle the courts to relax, in any degree, the vigilance and severity with which they should regard the risk of children at critical ages being exposed or introduced to ways of life which, as this case illustrates, may lead to severance from normal society, to psychological stresses and unhappiness and possibly even physical experiences which may scar them for life.'

3.47   In the unreported case of *Re G* [1] the father's homosexuality was but one of three factors which the court had to take into account (the other two being cessation of access at an earlier date and the fact that the mother was about to remarry). The father sought an order for access which was refused at first instance. He unsuccessfully appealed to the Court of Appeal. Cummings-Bruce LJ stated that if the father's homosexuality had been the only reason for refusing access, an appeal would have been successful despite

> 'the additional problem of the reaction of the children when they got to know their father had sexual activities or a sexual life, which does not confirm to the statistical norm.'

1   (23 March 1980, unreported), CA.

3.48   Unfortunately despite the fact that *Re D* is now over 20 years old it continues to influence the courts. It was, for example, referred to in the 1996 adoption case of *AMT* (see para **3.160**) and it seems that the onus still rests on the gay father to show that he does not pose a risk to his child.

3.49   On separation where the father has a new female partner it is not uncommon for the mother to be concerned about the role of the new partner. In contested cases concerning gay fathers the involvement of the new partner can be at the heart of the dispute.

3.50   On the whole, the courts are reluctant to impose conditions on contact orders but have the power to do so. The Children Act 1989, s 11(7) provides that:

> 'a section 8 order may—
>   (a)   contain directions about how it is to be carried into effect;
>   (b)   impose conditions which must be complied with by any person—
>   (i)   in whose favour the order is made;
>   (ii)   who is a parent of the child concerned;
>   (iii) who is not a parent of his but who has parental responsibility for him; or
>   (iv)   with whom the child is living;
>   and to whom the conditions are expressed to apply;
>   (c)   be made to have effect for a specified period, or contain provisions which are to have effect for a specified period;
>   (d)   make such incidental, supplemental, or consequential provisions as the court thinks fit.'

3.51 The court therefore has the power, for example, to order that the father should not share a bedroom with his male partner during staying contact. If requested to attach such a condition the court must have regard to the paramountcy of the child's welfare and the welfare checklist.

3.52 Whilst there are no reported cases, it is not uncommon for a gay father to be pressurised into giving an undertaking, for example, that his partner will not be present during contact visits or that they will not sleep together during staying contact. If a gay father refuses to give such an undertaking he may be accused of putting his own feelings before those of the children. From the legal point of view it must however be arguable that conditions should only be attached if they are necessary to give effect to the order (see *Re O (a minor) (contact: imposition of conditions))* [1]. Formal undertakings dealing with such issues should be avoided if at all possible as once recorded they may be extremely difficult to discharge at a later date.

1   [1995] 2 FLR 124.

2   Expert evidence

3.53 Whilst there is some American research into gay men as fathers [1] there is as yet no published British research comparable to that undertaken by Golombok et al (see para **3.32**). When representing a gay father, consideration should be given as to whether a psychiatric report is warranted. The same concerns should be borne in mind as in a lesbian case (see para **3.30**).

1   See Barret, Robert L and Robinson, Bryan E *Gay Fathers* (1990) Lexington Books.

3.54 If the father is HIV positive he may already be receiving counselling of some form and it may be worth considering whether a report could usefully be obtained from that source.

3   Advising gay fathers who are HIV positive or living with AIDS

3.55 If the father is HIV positive or is living with AIDS the mother may not know. The question of whether the father's status should be disclosed during the course of proceedings is a difficult one. It very probably should be disclosed to the court on the basis that it is a material factor to be taken into account by the court. Until relatively recently, the life span of a person with AIDS was fairly limited. Thus, it could be argued that it was even more important for a child to have generous contact with his father if that father had a terminal illness.

3.56 How such information should be disclosed should be very carefully considered. It may not be thought appropriate for the mother to first learn of her former partner's diagnosis when she reads his statements in support of his application. There are various agencies which are able to provide professional guidance on all AIDS-related issues and in some cases the court welfare officer may be willing to assist the mother obtain such support and information as she requires.

3.57 Although public knowledge of the AIDS virus has improved over the years it may still be necessary to satisfy some judges that the father does not pose a health risk to the child. There is a wealth of literature on the causes of the spread of the AIDS virus and it may be useful to have this available. In an unreported case in 1993 involving a gay father it was necessary to call oral evidence from a psychiatrist (who was also an expert in AIDS) to satisfy the judge that the children would not contact the AIDS virus if their father kissed them. Fortunately in the vast majority of cases it is rarely necessary to have to go to these lengths.

C APPLICATIONS BY LESBIAN COUPLES FOR A JOINT RESIDENCE ORDER

3.58 There are an increasing number of applications by same-sex couples (overwhelmingly female) for joint residence orders under the Children Act 1989, s 8 (hereafter CA 1989).

3.59 Some judges seem to have no difficulty with the concept of the 'lesbian family' whereas others find it almost impossible to comprehend. It can be difficult for the advocate to choose the right words to describe such an arrangement. In some courts it would appear that the term 'co-parent' is properly understood, whereas in others such a description can be met with incomprehension or even hostility. For the purpose of this chapter the terms 'birth mother' and 'co-parent' will be used to describe the parties.

3.60 The facts of *Re C (a minor) (residence order: lesbian co-parents)* are fairly typical of such applications. In this case a child was conceived by way of donor insemination and the mother wanted her partner's parenting role to be legally recognised. The official solicitor was appointed to act for the child and despite some initial concerns he eventually consented to the making of a joint residence order.

1   [1994] Fam Law Brief 468.

3.61 Unfortunately there are as yet no reported judgments concerning the making of a joint residence order to a lesbian couple. Judicial attitudes appear to vary, even within the same court, and in practice it can be extremely difficult to predict the outcome of such applications.

3.62 In the context of a lesbian relationship, a lesbian co-parent can only acquire parental responsibility by virtue of a residence order and only an unmarried father is entitled to make a free-standing application for a parental responsibility order under CA 1989, s 4.

The procedure

3.63 Either party can lodge the application. If the co-parent issues the application then unless she satisfies the requirements of CA 1989, s 10(5) (see para **3.82**) a letter from the birth mother (and any other person with parental responsibility) consenting to the application should be filed. This will prevent the court fixing the first appointment as an application for leave. The application is by way of Form C1 and only one party need lodge an application.

3.64   An application may be issued in the Family Proceedings Court, the county court or the High Court but the county court or High Court may be considered the most appropriate forum for the application.

(i)   Parties

3.65   The parties will be the mother and her partner. Details of the child's parentage must be given in Form C1. If the child was conceived by way of donor insemination provided by a licensed clinic the legal position is simple and the child has no legal father (see para **3.98**); therefore there is no father to whom notice of the application should be given.

3.66   If the child was conceived by donor insemination using a known donor or through conventional heterosexual intercourse, this information should be given in Form C1. Whether the court will require that the child's father should be served with notice of the application appears to vary from one district judge to another. Much may depend on whether the father plays any role in the child's life. If the father does play a role and he supports the application for the residence order then it is prudent to obtain a letter from him confirming his position and that he is aware of the application. There may be cases where it is wise to have the father at court when the application is heard just in case the district judge wishes to hear from him.

3.67   If the mother has been married to the father or if she has entered into a parental responsibility agreement with the father or he has been granted a parental responsibility order under CA 1989, s 4 then the father will be a party to the application and will have to be served with notice of the proceedings. There are as yet no reported cases of a joint residence order being granted against the wishes of a father with parental responsibility.

(ii)   The hearing

3.68   The majority of applications are granted at the first hearing. Both parties should attend. Most district judges appear willing to deal with applications without statements and without a court welfare officer's report. Indeed no statements should be filed unless directed by the court [1].

1   FPR 1991, SI 1991/1247, r 4.16.

3.69   Some district judges have refused to deal with applications without a court welfare officer's report and there have been one or two cases where the official solicitor has been invited to act for the child. In most cases court welfare officers' reports are entirely unnecessary. It may be successfully argued that these are no longer 'exceptional cases' justifying the appointment of the official solicitor [1].

1   Practice Note *The Official Solicitor: Appointment in Family Proceedings* 8 September 1995.

3.70 Of the handful of cases where an application for a joint residence order has been refused, it has been refused on the basis of the 'no order principle' (CA 1989, s 1(5)). It is essential to demonstrate each and every example of how the child will benefit from the co-parent heaving parental responsibility. This can range from the co-parent being able to give authority for medical treatment to the child being regarded as the co-parent's dependant for the purpose of her pension scheme. In the case of *Re H (shared residence: parental responsibility)*[1] a shared residence order was made to a mother and the child's stepfather although this order was made in the context of a dispute between the mother and her former husband. Many lesbian couples see the main purpose of a joint residence order as a way of obtaining some recognition of their relationship, and indeed of their family, and it can be difficult to persuade the court of the practical necessity of such an order or indeed that orders were designed for this purpose. Bracewell J made very useful observations in *G v F (contact and shared residence: applications for leave)*[2]. This case concerned not a joint application but a contested application for contact and a shared residence order (see para **3.91**) by a co-parent where the parties were living apart. It is undoubtedly easier to show the need for an order in such circumstances as the child will be away from the birth mother for periods of time during which the co-parent may need to exercise parental responsibility.

1   [1995] 2 FLR 883.
2   [1998] 2 FLR 799. This concerned an application for leave to issue an application for a shared residence order and contact order by a co-parent of a four-year old girl. The birth mother opposed the making of a shared residence order and argued that it was a device in order to obtain parental responsibility. In view of the applicant's close relationship with the child the judge rejected this argument.

(iii)   Effect and duration of joint residence orders

3.71 The co-parent will be able to act in loco parentis but their parental responsibility will be subject to a number of restrictions. They will not have the same rights and responsibilities as the child's mother who will retain:
(*a*)   the right to appoint a guardian (CA 1989, s 12(3)(c));
(*b*)   the right to change the child's surname (CA 1989, s 13(1)(a));
(*c*)   the right to remove the child from the UK for one month or more (CA 1989, s 13(1), (6));
(*d*)   the right to consent to the making of an application to declare the child free for adoption (CA 1989, s 12(3), (9)).

3.72 A residence order ceases to have effect when the child reaches the age of 16 (CA 1989, s 91(10)) but can be extended to the child's 18th birthday (CA 1989, s 10(6)). It is generally worth making an application to extend the duration of the order at the time the residence order is granted.

(iv)   Effect of separation on a joint residence order

3.73 If a couple separate after a joint residence order is made the separation does not in itself discharge the order. In these circumstances the co-parent will continue to have parental responsibility whilst the order remains in force (CA 1989, s 12(2)). If appropriate, an application to discharge the order should be made. If the residence order is discharged and the co-parent granted a contact order, she will lose all parental responsibility. If a residence order is made in the co-parent's favour she will retain parental responsibility which she will share with the child's birth mother.

(v) Independent legal advice

3.74 Although a joint application is by its very nature unopposed, normal professional standards should apply and only one of the couple can be the solicitor's client. The respondent to the application should be treated as any other respondent insofar as service of the proceedings is concerned. She should be advised of the desirability of obtaining independent legal advice. Whilst in most cases it is unnecessary for both parties to incur the costs of being legally represented at the hearing, nevertheless it can be very helpful for the non-represented party to obtain advice from a solicitor who can then confirm by letter that the respondent has been independently advised and understands the nature of the application and how it will affect her position. This letter can either be filed before the hearing or produced to the district judge on the day.

3.75 Whether the respondent to the proceedings is independently advised or not she should still return the acknowledgement of service to the court and the solicitor should file a statement of service in Form C9.

(vi) Legal aid

3.76 Legal aid is available to make an application for a joint residence order although there is evidence of a lack of consistency between the various Legal Aid Area Offices and some applications have been refused on the basis that there is no conflict justifying legal representation.

D DISPUTES BETWEEN SAME-SEX PARENTS

3.77 Just like some heterosexual parents, not all same-sex couples raising children together are able to agree the arrangements for children on their separation. Some female couples who have children together are very clear as to which of them is the mother, whilst others wish to give their children two mothers with equal parenting responsibilities.

3.78 Such arrangements can be difficult to negotiate as a couple and can become even more problematic on separation. Over the last five years or so a growing number of cases concerning disputes between female couples about children have come before the courts. In the absence of reported decisions it is very difficult to say whether there is any consistent approach being adopted by the judiciary.

3.79 The co-parent is almost always bound to be legally at a disadvantage. She has no legal status in the child's life unless she has acquired parental responsibility by virtue of a residence order with the child's mother. She may have played a very significant parenting role in the child's life but in most cases it is unlikely that she will be accorded the status and consideration that would be conferred on an unmarried father who had played a lesser role.

3.80   Most of the cases that have come before the courts concern applications by co-parents for contact. In cases concerning young children, if the birth mother is opposed to contact it can be extremely difficult to persuade a court to impose an order against her wishes.

3.81   On separation the co-parent can apply to the court for a s 8 order. Depending on the circumstances she may be entitled to make the application as of right or may require leave of the court to issue an application.

When leave is not required

3.82   Under CA 1989, s 10 leave is not required (inter alia) by any person:
(*a*)   with whom the child has lived for a period of at least three years; or
(*b*)   if there is a residence order in force with respect to the child, who has the consent of each person in whose favour the order was made; or
(*c*)   who has the consent of those with parental responsibility.

(i)   Carer for three years

3.83   Although the three-year period does not have to be continuous it must have begun not more than five years before the making of the application and it must not have ended more than three months before the making of the application (CA 1989, s 10(5)(b)).

3.84   So as not to miss the three month deadline, care should be taken to establish the precise date of separation if the parties have in fact lived together. Disputes as to fact can arise if the parties continued to maintain separate households during the relationship. It is not uncommon for the couple and child to spend time together at each other's home. In such a situation as a preliminary issue the court may have to hear evidence as to whether the child has 'lived' with the applicant for the requisite period of three years.

(ii)   With consent

3.85   In some cases there will be no need to apply for leave as the mother will consent to the application being made. There is no prescribed form for this consent. In practice the court will accept this in letter form. Care should be taken that the consent is expressed as 'consent' as 'will not object to leave being granted' is not the same as 'will consent to'.

(iii)   Applications for leave—procedure

3.86   An application may be issued in the Family Proceedings Court, the county court (with appropriate jurisdiction), or in the High Court. The county court or High Court is probably the best forum for such applications. The Family Proceedings Court is often quicker and cheaper but may not be considered the best tribunal for dealing with what are still unusual cases. The applicant must file a Form C2 which exhibits a draft application in Form C1. On the issue of the application the court will either grant the application, or fix a date for a hearing.

3.87   In *Re M (prohibited steps order: application for leave)*[1] Johnson J held that an application for leave should normally be on notice other than in genuinely urgent cases. In *Re F and R (section 8 order: grandparents' application)*[2] it was held that in a case where there are issues of fact the court should hear limited evidence from the parties (but not usually others) to form a view on the merits of the application to enable the court to decide whether there is a realistic possibility of the application being successful. In practice in lesbian cases some district judges have ordered welfare reports or even appointed the official solicitor to investigate applications (see para **3.69**).

1   [1993] 1 FLR 275.
2   [1995] 1 FLR 524.

(iv)   The test to be applied in considering whether or not to grant leave

3.88   The CA 1989, s 10(9) sets out the criteria to be applied by the court when considering an application for leave. The court must have particular regard to:
(a)   the nature of the proposed application for the s 8 order;
(b)   the applicant's connection with the child;
(c)   any risk there might be of that proposed application disrupting the child's life to such an extent he would be harmed by it; and
(d)   if the child is being looked after by a local authority the authority's plans for the future, and the wishes and feelings of the child's parents.

3.89   The court is entitled to take into account whether to grant leave is in the overall best interests of the child. The fact that an applicant is successful in an application for leave is no guarantee that she will be successful in the substantive application.

3.90   In *Re M (care: contact: grandmother's application for leave)*[1] the Court of Appeal likened an application for leave to an application for leave to apply for contact to a child in care under CA 1989, s 34 and held:
(a)   if the application is frivolous, vexatious or an abuse of process it must fail;
(b)   if there is no real prospect of the applicant eventually being granted a substantive order it must fail; and
(c)   the applicant must show prima facie a good arguable case.

1   [1995] 2 FLR 86.3.91

3.91   In *G v F (contact and shared residence order: applications for leave)*[1] Bracewell J considered an application for leave in the context of a lesbian relationship. The respondent had conceived by way of donor insemination in 1993, with the applicant acting as co-parent. The parties separated amicably and there appeared to be an agreement that each would play a substantial role in the upbringing of the child. The applicant had regular staying contact with the child until 1997. She issued applications for leave to make applications for contact and shared residence of the child. Allowing the application for leave, Bracewell J held that:
(a)   the issue of welfare was not determinative of the application for leave. The proper approach was to ask whether there was an arguable case. There was no presumption of any kind that if the application for leave was granted that thereafter the substantive orders should be made.

(b)   It was not inappropriate to make an application for shared residence in order to obtain a parental responsibility order.

(c)   The fact that the relationship between the applicant and the respondent was a lesbian relationship was to be seen as background circumstances. There was no basis for discriminating against the applicant in her wish to pursue the proceedings on the basis that she and the respondent lived together in a lesbian relationship.

(d)   For a joint residence order to be granted, persons do not have to be mother and father and neither does there have to be equal periods in respect of the time spent in different households (see para **3.58**).

1   [1998] 2 FLR 799.

3.92   When acting for a birth mother, considerable thought should be given as to whether or not to consent to an application for leave if leave of the court is required. Each case must be judged on its merits but not consenting to leave can result in two potentially lengthy and expensive hearings. On the other hand, if the court refuses leave then the matter is decided at an early stage. In advising a birth mother, matters such as the applicant's connection with the child (was this a genuine co-parenting situation?), the length of time that has elapsed since separation (has contact continued?), the age of the child and whether there is any sibling relationship between the child and any child the applicant may have will all be relevant.

E   CREATING FAMILIES: DONOR INSEMINATION, FERTILITY TREATMENT AND SURROGACY

3.93   As social attitudes have changed more and more lesbians are having children outside of relationships with men. In the past many lesbians married, and no doubt some continue to do, simply in order to have children. There is evidence to show that since the late 1970s the number of lesbians having children through donor insemination has steadily increased. Indeed attempts were made in 1989 during the committee stage of the Human Fertilisation and Embryology Bill to prohibit lesbians and single women having access to clinics providing donor insemination.

3.94   Donor insemination is a simple non-medical procedure involving the placing of semen in the woman's vagina. Donor insemination should be distinguished from fertility treatment such as in vitro fertilisation (IVF) which involves complex medical treatment and which would normally only be undertaken if there is some medical reason preventing conception. In vitro fertilisation can be an extremely expensive procedure and it is unlikely that it will be available on the NHS to a lesbian other than in very exceptional circumstances.

3.95   Donor insemination can be effected without any medical assistance whatsoever. For a variety of reasons (including that sperm provided by a licensed clinic will be screened for disease) some lesbians choose to attend a clinic for donor insemination. The availability of donor insemination on the NHS will vary from health authority to health authority. Although a relatively inexpensive procedure, the provision of donor insemination to lesbians is unlikely to top the list of most health authorities' expenditure.

3.96 There are a number of licensed clinics in the private sector which will offer donor insemination and fertility treatments to lesbians, subject to the conditions laid down by the Human Fertilisation and Embryology Act 1990.

3.97 There are no statistics to show how many lesbians conceive by way of donor insemination but for many lesbians this is now the procedure of choice. Some lesbians undergo donor insemination at a licensed clinic and others enter into private arrangements with either known or anonymous donors. These private arrangements fall entirely outside the scope of the HFEA 1990.

1 Donor insemination provided at a licensed clinic

3.98 Donor insemination by a clinic involves the use of stored sperm and is governed by HFEA 1990, s 4(1)(b). All clinics providing this service must be licensed by the Human Fertilisation and Embryology Authority and are subject to strict requirements and inspections by the Authority. In accordance with HFEA 1990, s 13(5):

> 'A woman shall not be provided with treatment services unless account has been taken of the welfare of any child who may be born as a result of the treatment (including the need of that child for a father) and of any other child who may be affected by the birth.'

3.99 Section 13(5) presents no legal bar to a clinic providing donor insemination to a lesbian. Provided the need for a father has been considered, there is compliance. It should be noted that the reference is to 'that child' and not 'the child', allowing the doctor fairly wide discretion but a clinic may refuse to provide a service to a lesbian if, in the judgment of the medical practitioner, the child's welfare would be adversely affected by the absence of a social father.

(i) Parentage of a child conceived by donor insemination at a licensed clinic

3.100 The unmarried mother of a child conceived by donor insemination is the child's only legal parent (unless the service is provided to an unmarried woman and her male partner). By virtue of HFEA 1990, s 28 a child conceived in this way has no legal father and has no claim of any nature against the donor or his estate.

(ii) The legal status of the donor

3.101 The donor is not regarded as the child's legal father and therefore has no legal obligations or responsibilities in respect of the child. The donor is not a parent for the purposes of the Child Support Act 1991.

3.102 The donor is required to consent to information about himself being kept on a central record. A child born by donor insemination may apply under HFEA 1990, s 31 for access to this information for the purposes of finding out if he or she is related to an intended spouse.

2 Donor insemination not through a licensed clinic ('self-insemination')

3.103   There is no law governing self-insemination and a woman is free to enter into a private arrangement with a donor with the intention of becoming pregnant. It is legal for a woman to advertise for a donor and for a newspaper or magazine to publish such an advertisement. There is no law preventing a person helping a woman to conceive in this way eg by acting as an intermediary in obtaining and delivering fresh sperm. (The situation would be different if the sperm was to be frozen as such arrangements would probably be caught by the HFEA 1990, s 4(1)(b), although it would be necessary to show that a 'treatment service' was being provided by the intermediary).

(i)   Parentage of a child conceived by self-insemination

3.104   A child conceived by self-insemination is the legal child of both the mother and donor.

(ii)   Legal status of the donor

3.105   Whether known or anonymous the donor is the child's legal father and has all the rights and responsibilities of an unmarried father by virtue of the CA 1989. A donor may:
(*a*)   apply for a parental responsibility order (CA 1989, s 4(1)(a));
(*b*)   enter into a parental responsibility agreement with the child's mother (CA 1989, s 4(1)(b));
(*c*)   apply without leave for an order (CA 1989, s 8);
(*d*)   apply for a declaration of parentage (Family Law Act 1986, s 56);
(*e*)   apply to the court on the mother's death to be appointed the child's guardian (CA 1989, s 5).

3.106   There are, as yet, no reported cases concerning applications by donors for residence or contact orders. It is difficult to predict how a court would deal with such an application. As in all such cases, the court would have to apply the welfare checklist and to consider, inter alia, the nature of the relationship between child and donor.

(iii)   Financial responsibility

3.107   As the child's father, the donor has a responsibility to maintain the child and is an absent parent for the purpose of the CSA 1991 and like any absent parent can be required to provide financial support for the child. A mother in receipt of state benefit who has conceived by donor insemination is required by CSA 1991, s 6 to authorise the Secretary of State to take action under the Act to recover child support from the absent parent (ie, the donor). The mother cannot be required to give this authorisation if she can show that by so doing 'there would be a risk of her, or any child living with her, suffering harm or undue distress as a result'[1].

1   CSA 1991, s 6(2).

3.108   Failure to comply with the requirements of s 6 can result in a reduced benefit direction (CSA 1991, s 46). In practice it seems that some child support officers accept that pursuing a donor would cause the mother and/or child harm whilst others do not.

3.109   For the purpose of an application under the Inheritance (Provision for Family and Dependants) Act 1975 a child conceived by donor insemination would be entitled to claim against the donor's estate if he failed to make reasonable financial provision for the child.

(iv)   Donor agreements

3.110   There is nothing at law to prevent a woman entering into an agreement, written or otherwise, with a donor setting out the terms on which the insemination is to proceed. An agreement may, for example, deal with arrangements (or not) for the donor's contact with the child.

3.111   An agreement may purport to restrict each party's right to apply to the court for an order under CA 1989, s 8 or to seek financial support for the child. Just as all private agreements which seek to oust the jurisdiction of the court are unenforceable so donor agreements are unenforceable. In all probability they are also void on the grounds of public policy.

3.112   Notwithstanding the questionable legal status of donor agreements, in drafting an agreement care should be taken to ensure that both parties have independent legal advice before signing the agreement. In the event of a dispute between the mother and donor such an agreement may be of evidential value when considering the intentions of the parties. The parties are purporting to enter into a legal agreement and there is always the possibility of future conflict.

3.113   In practice, donor agreements can be very useful. They can, for example, establish a framework for dealing with disputes between the mother and donor by including a provision to seek mediation before any court proceedings are issued. These can also be useful in concentrating the parties' minds as to the nature and extent of the donor's involvement.

3   Fertility treatments and ova donation

3.114   In vitro fertilisation is defined by HFEA 1990, s 1(2)(a) as 'where fertilisation began outside the human body whether or not it was completed there'.

3.115   This treatment involves the extraction of a human egg which is then mixed with semen (producing an embryo) and transferred back to the mother once it has been fertilised. 'In vitro' means literally 'in glass'. Such treatment is governed by the HFEA 1990 and the requirements for clinics to be licensed, inspected and to have regard to the needs of the child for a father all apply (HFEA 1990, s 13(5), see para **3.99**).

(i)   Parentage of a child conceived by IVF

3.116   At law any child conceived by IVF is the child of the mother. If the sperm is provided by a known donor he is the father. If the egg is fertilised using the sperm of a man who has anonymously donated it to a licensed clinic then the donor is not the child's father.

(ii)   Ova donation

3.117   This is legally a much more problematic area than donor insemination or IVF. There is now no medical reason why one woman cannot donate an egg or eggs to another and for the recipient to then become pregnant by way of donor insemination. This arrangement seems to fall outside HFEA 1990, s 27(i) which defines a mother as 'the woman who is carrying or has carried a child as a result of the placing in her of an embryo or of sperm and eggs...'. No mention is made of where an egg or eggs only are donated.

3.118   It is unlikely that such a treatment would be offered in this country to a lesbian couple who wished to 'mix' their eggs in order to produce a baby to whom they were both genetically linked. There are however clinics in the United States offering this service. Which of the women would be the child's legal mother? Could the egg donor seek a declaration of maternity? There is no statutory provision dealing with this point and therefore it is entirely a matter of speculation as to how a court would deal with an application by the egg donor to also be recognised as the child's mother.

(iii)   Surrogacy

3.119   There has been some recent media interest in gay men who attempt to enter into surrogacy arrangements in order to become fathers. The number of such arrangements is unknown but is likely to be tiny. Subject to the restriction on the payment of money, there is nothing legally to prevent gay men or lesbians entering into an arrangement with another woman to carry a child for them. In response to a number of headline cases, the Surrogacy Arrangements Act 1985 was introduced. It was largely based on the recommendations of the Warnock Report [1] and deals primarily with commercial surrogacy arrangements. We await the outcome of the further report into surrogacy commissioned by the government in 1997.

1   (1984) Cmnd 9314.

(iv)   What is a surrogacy arrangement?

3.120   A 'surrogate mother' is defined by the SAA 1985, s 1(2) as:

> 'a woman who carried a child in pursuance of an arrangement—
> (*a*)   made before she began to carry the child, and
> (*b*)   made with a view to any child carried in pursuance of it being handed over to, and [parental responsibility being met] (so far as practicable) by another person or other persons.'

3.121 A surrogacy arrangement should be distinguished from an arrangement whereby a man donates sperm outside a sexual relationship in order to parent a child with the child's mother. There are more and more examples of lesbians and gay men conceiving children together. Some have shared care arrangements whereas others agree that the child's main home will be with the mother whilst having contact with the father. This is not a surrogacy arrangement.

(v)   Donor as commissioning party

3.122 A gay man or gay couple may enter into a surrogacy arrangement with a woman with one of the men donating his sperm. This is known as a partial surrogacy. A total surrogacy is where the surrogate mother receives an egg into her womb which is either already fertilised or is to be fertilised. It would seem that the legal position of the commissioning and donating father is the same as any other unmarried father. He can acquire parental responsibility by virtue of a parental responsibility agreement or order under CA 1989, s 4 but the surrogate mother cannot transfer or delegate her parental responsibility to him in any other way (other than on adoption) as this would contravene CA 1985, s 2(9). Careful consideration should be given as to whether the commissioning father should make any application at all to the court. As he could acquire parental responsibility by virtue of a parental responsibility agreement (which should resolve practical problems such as the giving of consents, etc) an application to the court may be best avoided. It is unlikely that most judges would look favourably on an arrangement involving a gay man or gay couple although short of appointing the official solicitor to investigate it is difficult to see how, in the absence of grounds for a care order, the court could interfere with the arrangements for the child.

(vi)   Commissioning party not donor

3.123 This is likely to be an extremely rare occurrence. A woman could commission another woman to have a child for her and a man could do the same (not donating sperm). The case of *Re H (a minor) (s 37 direction)* [1] is a case where during her pregnancy (rather than before) a woman decided she would not be able to care for the child and placed it immediately at birth with a lesbian couple. This was deemed to have been a private fostering arrangement which was eventually regularised by the making of a joint residence order in favour of the lesbian couple. Scott Baker J referred to the situation as being very similar in result to surrogacy arrangements where a couple bear a child specifically for the purpose of handing it over to somebody else.

1   [1993] 2 FLR 541.

(vii) Commercial surrogacy arrangements

3.124 It is an offence contrary to SAA 1985, s 2 for any person (other than the surrogate mother and commissioning parents) on a commercial basis to:

'(*a*) initiate or take part in any negotiations with a view to the making of a surrogacy arrangement;

    (*b*) offer or agree to negotiate the making of a surrogacy arrangement; or

    (*c*) compile any information with a view to its use in making or negotiating the making of, surrogacy arrangements.'

An offence under s 2 is punishable by a fine or a term of imprisonment not exceeding three months.

3.125   It is illegal for a newspaper (as a commercial enterprise) to carry an advertisement containing an indication that any person may be willing to enter into a surrogacy arrangement (SAA 1985, s 3). An offence under this section is punishable by fine only.

3.126   It is not illegal for a third party to introduce a woman to another person with a view to a surrogacy arrangement provided this is not for gain. It is not illegal to provide legal advice for payment to the surrogate mother or commissioning party.

(viii)   Disputes arising from a surrogacy arrangement

3.127   In the event of a dispute between a surrogate mother and the commissioning party who has donated sperm, his remedy would seem to be to apply to the court as an unmarried father for an order under CA 1989, s 3. In *A v C* [1] the court refused to make a contact order in favour of a commissioning father where the surrogate mother refused to hand over the child or agree to contact.

1   [1985] FLR 445.

3.128   In the event of a dispute concerning a surrogate mother and a commissioning party who had not donated sperm, then the commissioning party could apply for an order under CA 1989, s 8 (leave would be required unless the commissioning party was entitled to apply as of right under CA 1989). He or she could also issue wardship proceedings. In the absence of some very compelling evidence it is difficult to think that a court would make an order in favour of a lesbian or gay applicant against the wishes of the surrogate mother.

F   ADOPTION

3.129   A growing number of lesbians and gay men consider adoption as a way of parenting children. It is impossible to know how many adoption orders have been made in favour of lesbian and gay applicants. This issue is still the subject of considerable public debate and the recent cases of *Re W (adoption: homosexual adopter)* [1] and *AMT (known as AC) (petitioners for authority to adopt SR)* [2] are very useful to the lesbian or gay applications.

1   [1997] 2 FLR 406 .
2   [1997] Fam Law 8.

3.130   Adoption by lesbians and gay men was touched on by the *Review of Adoption Law: Report to Ministers of Inter-departmental Working Group* [1]:

    'We do not propose any changes to the law relating to single applicants, including lesbians and gay men. There are examples of extremely successful adoptions, particularly of older children with disabilities, by single adopters...'.

1   (October 1992).

3.131   A review of the reported and unreported decisions confirms that on the whole it is still very difficult to place children with lesbians or gay men with a view to adoption.

1   Applying to an adoption agency

3.132   An application to adopt must be made to an adoption agency. An adoption agency is a local authority or an approved adoption society. Most prospective adopters apply to their local authority fostering and adoption unit to be considered for an adoption placement. It is not necessary to live in the area of the local authority to which the application is made and there may be considerable advantages to the prospective applicant of applying to a local authority with a known record of placing children with lesbians and gay men. A number of local authorities have publicly stated that they will consider applications from all sections of the community and therefore should not discriminate against lesbian or gay applicants or refuse to consider to assess them as potential adopters. To do so could possibly open the local authority to an application for judicial review.

3.133   An application to adopt can also be made to an approved adoption society. Some adoption societies have publicly stated that they will not accept applications from lesbians and gay men whilst others do not discriminate in this way.

3.134   The adoption assessment process can be lengthy and can often take up to a year to complete. It will include police and medical record checks. If the applicant is living on his or her own the question of disclosing his or her sexual orientation during the assessment period often arises. In many cases the applicant will disclose his or her sexual orientation at the outset. In other cases however it may not have been discussed. This would seem particularly true in the case of single female applicants. If this information is not disclosed by the applicant, but later comes to the attention of the adoption agency, the applicant may be regarded as unreliable and the application prejudiced.

(i)   The adoption panel

3.135   If the initial assessment is favourable the application is referred to the local authority or adoption society's adoption panel. The panel must consist of no more than ten people and from 1 November 1997 must include at least three lay people. The panel does not make the decision to approve the adoption application but makes recommendations to the adoption agency. Having considered the panel's recommendation the adoption agency is responsible for making the decision itself.

3.136   Whilst there are no reported cases of a panel's recommendation to place a child with a lesbian or gay applicant not being followed, there have nevertheless been a number of instances where there has been considerable reluctance on the adoption agency's part to follow the panel's recommendation. It is possible that a refusal to ratify a panel's decision simply on the basis of the applicant's sexual orientation could be judicially reviewed if it could be shown that no reasonable agency would have come to that decision. The applicant has the right to be given reasons if he or she is not considered suitable and to make representations to the panel for the application to be reconsidered [1].

1   Adoption Agencies Regulations 1983, SI 1983/1964, reg 11A.

(ii)   The placement

3.137   The majority of children placed with lesbian or gay men concern what the agencies define as 'hard to place' children. This can have a very broad meaning and can include children with physical or mental disabilities, children who have been sexually and/or emotionally abused and children with learning difficulties. They can also include siblings who need to be placed together. When advising a prospective applicant it should be borne in mind that they may be unaware of all the child's past difficulties and indeed may only become fully aware of the background once they have seen the papers in any previous proceedings concerning the child. Great care should be taken in relaying this information to the client as it can be of a highly sensitive nature and it should not be assumed that the prospective applicant is privy to such information.

(iii)   Illegal placements

3.138   The Adoption Act 1976, s 11(1) provides that:

> 'A person other than an adoption society shall not make arrangements for the adoption of a child, or place a child for adoption, unless—
> (*a*)   the proposed adopter is a relative of the child, or
> (*b*)   he is acting in pursuance of an order of the High Court.'

Section 11(3) of the Adoption Act 1976 makes it a criminal offence to take part in the making of arrangements for adoption or to receive a child in contravention of s 11(1) of that same Act.

3.139   Depending on the circumstances of the case an adoption order may still be made (see *Re G (adoption: illegal placement)*)[1] but any application arising from an illegal placement must be made in the High Court. Where the child was not placed with the applicant by an adoption agency the applicant must, at least three months before the date of the order, give notice of the application to the local authority in whose area he has his home.

1   [1995] 1 FLR 403.

(iv)   Who can adopt a child?

3.140   A child can be adopted by a single person but cannot be adopted by more than one person unless the applicants are married. The applicant must be domiciled in the UK and must have attained the age of 21 [1].

1   AA 1976, s 15.

3.141   An adoption order may therefore not be made in favour of a cohabiting couple whether heterosexual, lesbian or gay but the case of *Re W* [1] (see para **3.157**) confirms that there is no legal impediment to an adoption by a single lesbian or gay applicant who intends to bring the child up alone or as part of a stable relationship.

1   [1997] 2 FLR 406.

(v)   Disclosure of the applicant's sexual orientation in adoption proceedings

3.142   The question of what information should be given to the birth family about the applicant's sexual orientation needs to be carefully considered. In many cases this information will already have been given to the birth family by the adoption agency's social worker. There are some cases however where this information has not been disclosed before the adoption application is issued. It is important to establish the position at the outset as there may be some exceptional cases where disclosure would not be in the child's best interests. A parent's right to oppose an adoption application does not entitle him as of right to information about the prospective adopter but there is a general expectation that the parents are entitled to know if for example their child has been placed with a lesbian or gay applicant. It can be argued that without this knowledge a parent cannot make an informed decision as to whether to consent to an order being made. In an unreported case *Re P (a minor)* [1] Singer J ordered disclosure to the mother of the applicant's sexual orientation on the basis that whilst a parent was not entitled to information which could identify the applicant (eg, name, address and in some cases occupation) he or she was entitled to as much information about the applicant as did not undermine the placement, including information that the applicant was a lesbian. This decision is very much in line with the later House of Lords' decision of *Re K (adoption: disclosure of information)* where the court reviewed the whole question of disclosure of information in adoption cases.

1   (1995) unreported.
2   [1997] 2 FLR 74.

3.143   If there are concerns that disclosure will jeopardise the placement then consideration should be given to an application to the court for leave not to disclose. In a proper case as soon as the adoption application is issued an agreement should be sought from the reporting officer or the guardian ad litem that he or she will not disclose information concerning the applicant's sexual orientation to the parent without first seeking directions from the court. Such an application should be on notice. The application may be heard by a district judge. Although there is no provision in the Adoption Rules 1984 for the filing of evidence it can be helpful to file a statement setting out the reasons why the applicant does not wish his or her sexual orientation disclosed.

(vi)   Which court?

3.144   Section 62 of the Adoption Act 1976 provides that proceedings may be issued in:
(*a*)   the High Court;
(*b*)   the divorce county court within whose district the child is, or any divorce county court within whose district a parent or guardian of the child is;
(*c*)   a magistrates' court within whose area the child is.

3.145 If the child is not in Great Britain when the application is made, the application can only be brought in the High Court. Similarly if the applicant is seeking ratification of an illegal private placement (see para **3.137**) proceedings must be commenced in the High Court. In practice the majority of adoption applications are issued in the county court although consideration should be given in lesbian or gay cases as to whether the High Court is a better forum. There are disadvantages in issuing potentially complex cases in the Family Proceedings Court. In *Re PB (a minor) (application to free for adoption)* [1] it was held that the Family Proceedings Court might not be a suitable forum for a hearing likely to last for several days.

1   [1985] FLR 394.

3.146 Moreover, it may be considered that the justices are not best placed to consider what are still regarded as unusual applications.

(vii)   Procedure

3.147 Proceedings are commenced by way of originating application and will include either a statement that the application is made with parental consent or a statement of facts setting out the basis on which the applicant seeks an order dispensing with parental agreement.

(viii)   Dispensing with parental agreement

3.148 The grounds for dispensing with parental agreement are set out at AA 1976, s 16(2). Most contested adoption applications rely on the ground that the parent is withholding his agreement unreasonably.

(ix)   Appointment of reporting officer/guardian ad litem

3.149 If the child is free for adoption or it appears that the parent is willing to agree to the adoption, a reporting officer will be appointed by the court (if the parent lives outside England and Wales a guardian will usually be appointed). If it appears that a parent is unwilling to agree to an adoption order the court will appoint a guardian ad litem to act for the child. Sometimes this is a panel guardian and sometimes the official solicitor. In the High Court the guardian ad litem must be the official solicitor unless the applicant applies for some other person to be guardian (for example if a guardian was involved in care proceedings and continuity is felt desirable).

2   Reports

(i)   Schedule 2 report [1]

3.150 In every application for an adoption order a Sch 2 report must be filed by the adoption agency. The report must contain detailed information about the applicant, the child and the child's parents. It must also give an opinion as to whether the adoption order should be made. The Sch 2 report is an extremely important document and should usually address the issue of the applicant's sexual orientation. For some social workers often working without legal advice, this can be a difficult area. In most cases it is in the applicant's best interests for the issue to be covered in full. Sexual orientation is still a factor to be taken into account albeit one to which less weight is now being given but it is important that the Sch 2 report deals with the effect on the child of being parented by a lesbian or gay man.

1   Adoption Rules 1984, SI 1984/265, Sch 2.

(ii)   *Reporting officer's report*

3.151   This will normally be prepared after the Sch 2 report has been filed. The reporting officer's duties are set out in the Adoption Rules 1984 [1]. It is the reporting officer's duty not only to ensure that a parent's consent is freely given but also to report to the court about any matters which in his opinion may be of assistance to the court. The reporting officer should therefore deal with the applicant's sexual orientation and may draw the court's attention to the existence of the available expert evidence (see research of Golombok et al at para **3.32**). It can often be very helpful for the applicant's solicitor to discuss matters with the reporting officer and if appropriate provide copies of any relevant research.

1   SI 1984/265.

(iii)   *Guardian ad litem*

3.152   The guardian ad litem must investigate matters raised in the statement of facts and Sch 2 report. Like the reporting officer he must draw the court's attention to any matters which he feels will assist the court. In a case where leave has been granted not to disclose the applicant's sexual orientation to a parent, the guardian ad litem may consider it prudent to prepare a main report, making no reference to sexual orientation, and a supplemental report dealing with the issue in full.

(iv)   *Disclosure of reports*

3.153   The Sch 2 report, the reporting officer's report and the guardian ad litem's report are all confidential. The applicant is allowed access to those parts of the reports dealing with him/her, subject to any directions given by the court. In *Re D (minors) (adoption reports: confidentiality)* [1] it was held 'non-disclosure should be the exception not the rule'.

1   [1996] AC 593, HL.

(v)   *Expert evidence*

3.154   Until *Re W* (see para **3.157**) in cases where the official solicitor was appointed to act as guardian ad litem he would routinely require a lesbian or gay applicant to undergo a psychiatric assessment. It would seem that this is no longer the case at least for lesbian applicants.

3.155 On behalf of a lesbian applicant, it can be argued that not only is there overwhelming evidence to show that a child's development is not harmed by being brought up by a lesbian but also that the decision in *Re W* makes it quite clear that there is no bar to an adoption order being made even in favour of a cohabiting lesbian.

3.156 The position of male gay applicants is less clear and there is a paucity of research on gay men as parents. It is interesting to note that even in the 1996 case of *AMT (known as AC)* (see para **3.160**) the court considered the 1977 House of Lords' case of *Re D* (see para **3.44**) and found that although in *Re D* some members of the House of Lords had expressed concern about whether, if a child were adopted by a homosexual applicant the child might be cut off from 'normal' society, this was not a generalisation about all homosexual applicants.

3   Recent case law

3.157 In *Re W* [1], a local authority had placed a girl with a lesbian couple with a view to adoption. The child was subject to a care order and justices had found that she had been neglected by her parents and exposed by them to moral danger. She had had several unsuccessful placements but in 1995 was placed with a prospective adopter who was living with her lesbian partner of ten years who was herself a mother and grandmother. The local authority sought an order freeing the child for adoption and the mother objected on the grounds that it was contrary to public policy to make an adoption order in favour of a party living in a same-sex relationship. A freeing order was made and it was held that:

'(*a*)   the court should not construe the provision of AA 1976, s 15 narrowly;

(*b*)   the provisions were drawn widely and did not exclude as a matter of public policy a homosexual cohabiting couple or a single person with homosexual tendencies from applying to adopt a child;

(*c*)   the court had a duty to give first consideration to the need to safeguard and promote the welfare of the child.'

1   [1997] 2 FLR 406.

3.158 On making a freeing order Singer J held that the Adoption Act 1976:

'Permits adoption application to be made by a single applicant, whether he or she at that time lives alone, or cohabits in a heterosexual relationship with another person who is proposed should fulfil a quasi-parental role towards the child. Any other conclusion would be both illogical, arbitrary and inappropriately discriminatory in a context where the court's duty is to give first consideration to the need to safeguard and promote the welfare of the child throughout his childhood … I am prepared to accept the likelihood that the framers of this legislation did not contemplate that a single homosexual applicant might apply for and obtain an adoption order. Indeed were such an applicant's sexual orientation to be known, they might well have thought it implausible that he or she would be successful whether living alone or in cohabitation… The likely attitude of adoption agencies (for the most part, local authorities) would again,

I am prepared to accept, 20 years ago have been to withhold approval from would be applicants whose homosexual orientation was clear. But since then times, and the attitude of adoption agencies have clearly changed, and whereas it has not been commonplace for children to be placed in the care of homosexual carers whether for fostering or prospective adoption purposes, it is by no means unknown.'

(i)   Re E (adoption: freeing order) [1]

3.159   *Re E* is another freeing case concerning a seven year old girl placed with a lesbian who wished to adopt her at some future point. The local authority sought a freeing order. The judge at first instance made the order and dispensed with the mother's consent. The mother appealed. The Court of Appeal considered whether the judge had applied the correct principles to the evidence before him which included expert evidence as to the possible effects upon a child of being brought up in a lesbian household. The judge at first instance had reservations about the placement and said 'prima facie, it is undesirable that [the child] should have gone to a lesbian... but this case is a special one.' The Court of Appeal was satisfied that the judge at first instance had exercised his discretion properly and the mother's appeal failed.

1   [1995] 1 FLR 382.

(ii)   AMT (known as AC) (petitioner for authority to adopt SR) [1]

3.160   Although a number of adoption orders have been made to gay men there are no reported English cases concerning gay male applicants. *AMT* is a Scottish case where the Inner House of the Court of Session considered an application by a gay man to adopt a five year old boy. The application had been refused at first instance by the Lord Ordinary on two grounds:
(a)   that the mother had not agreed to the adoption and that her agreement was not being unreasonably withheld (Adoption (Scotland) Act 1978, s 16(2)(a)); and
(b)   the proposed adoption of the child by a single male applicant, living with his partner in a homosexual relationship, raised a fundamental question of principle about adoption.

1   [1997] Fam Law 8.

3.161   The child suffered from a genetic disorder. He had abnormal forearms, a cleft soft palate and an abnormality in one eye. He was also profoundly deaf, without speech and was unable to walk unaided. The mother was unable to care for the child. The local authority found it extremely difficult to place the child because of his special needs. The applicant was a nurse with experience in nursing children and adults with physical and mental disabilities. He was involved in a stable relationship with his partner of ten years. His application was supported by the child's guardian ad litem.

3.162   The judge at first instance held that as the mother had failed to reply to the reporting officer about her willingness to agree to an adoption she had not given her consent and he did not find grounds to dispense with her consent. On appeal, it was held that any objective reasonable parent in these circumstances would have consented to the adoption and the mother's consent should have been dispensed with. It was also held that the decision in the House of Lords case of *Re D* (see para **3.44**) was no bar to a gay man being granted an adoption order.

3.163 The Lord President, Lord Hope, held:

> 'There can be no more fundamental principle in adoption cases than that it is a duty of the court to safeguard and promote the welfare of the child and issues relating to sexual orientation, lifestyle, race, religion or other characteristics of the parties must of course be taken into account as part of the circumstances. But they cannot be allowed to prevail over what is in the best interests of the child. The suggestion that it is a fundamental objection to an adoption that the proposed adopter is living with another in a homosexual relationship finds no expression in the language of the statute.'

(iii)   Joint residence orders

3.164 Although a same-sex couple cannot jointly adopt, an application can be made by the non-adopter for a joint residence order. Proceedings under AA 1976 are classified as 'family proceedings' under CA 1989. In such proceedings the court may make a s 8 order with respect to a child. In *Re AB (adoption: joint residence)* [1] an adoption order was made in favour of a single heterosexual applicant coupled with a joint residence order in favour of the adopter and partner. In *Re M (minors)* [2] Wall J made such an order in favour of a lesbian couple. A joint residence order may be made without formally issuing an application but it is good practice for the non-adopter to issue an application returnable on the date of the adoption hearing. The application may be issued at any time after the adoption application and if such an order is to be sought the reporting officer or guardian ad litem should be advised so the issue may be addressed in their reports. There is no requirement to serve the residence application on any party, other than the adopter, as such an order will be made after the adoption order but it is sensible to give notice to the reporting officer or guardian ad litem. On the making of a joint residence order the non-adoptive parent will acquire parental responsibility (see para **3.71**).

1   [1996] 1 FLR 27.
2   (3 July 1998, unreported), HC.

(iv)   Publicity

3.165 There is still considerable media interest in cases where a child is placed with a lesbian or gay adopter. It may be contempt of court to publish information knowing that it relates to adoption proceedings heard in chambers. It appears however that little can be done to prevent media coverage which does not identify the child in the proceedings (see for example *Re W (wardship: publication of information))*. [1]

1   [1992] 1 FLR 99.

(v)   Costs

3.166   As a general rule legal aid is not available to an applicant for an adoption order if the application is unopposed. Given the controversy which still surrounds placements with lesbians and gay men legal representation would still seem highly desirable whether or not there is parental agreement. If the applicant is not financially eligible for legal aid or if legal aid is refused his or her legal costs may be met by the local authority. If the official solicitor is appointed to act as the child's guardian ad litem the local authority should be requested to indemnify the applicant in respect of the official solicitor's costs.

G   FOSTERING

3.167   A number of local authorities employ lesbian and gay foster parents and it may be considerably easier for a lesbian or gay man to be approved as a foster parent than as a prospective adopter. Indeed some are recruited specifically because of their ability to care for lesbian and gay teenagers.

3.168   A foster arrangement may be:
(*a*)   a private placement;
(*b*)   a local authority placement;
(*c*)   a voluntary organisation placement; or
(*d*)   a child subject to a care order placed with his parents.

1   Private foster placements

3.169   The Children Act 1989, s 66 provides that a child is privately fostered if he is:
(*a*)   under 16 years old (age is attained at the commencement of the relevant anniversary of his date of birth); or
(*b*)   disabled, under 18 years old;
and he is cared for and provided with accommodation by someone other than:
(*a*)   a parent of his;
(*b*)   a person other than a parent who has parental responsibility for him, or a relative of his;
and he has been thus cared for and accommodated (fostered) by that person either:
(*a*)   for 28 days or more, or
(*b*)   where the period of actual fostering is for less than 28 days, the foster parent intends to foster him for a period of 28 days or more.

3.170   If the child does not spend more than 28 days with the foster parents and there is no intention of the arrangement continuing it is not a private fostering arrangement. Private foster placements are subject to the Children (Private Arrangements for Fostering) Regulations 1991 [1] and notice must be given to the local authority.

1   SI 1991/2050.

3.171 The local authority has the power to disqualify or prohibit a person from being a private foster carer (CA 1989, ss 68, 69). There are no reported cases of a lesbian or gay man being disqualified or prohibited from fostering solely on the basis of sexual orientation.

3.172 The case of *Re H* (see para **3.123**) concerned an application by a lesbian couple for a joint residence order in respect of a child placed with them by its mother in what was unbeknown to them a private fostering arrangement. The local authority had disqualified one of them from fostering by virtue of a conviction for assault and prohibited the other on the ground that she suffered severe depression. Notwithstanding the local authority's decision a joint residence order was eventually made in the High Court.

3.173 It is a criminal offence for a person to foster a child if he is disqualified or prohibited. An appeal against a local authority's decision is to the magistrates' court and there is no power under the Children Act 1989 for the justices to remit the appeal to be heard at the same time as any pending application in another court (eg, for a residence order).

2 Local authority placements

3.174 The vast majority of fostering arrangements are made by a local authority. Department of Health guidance has stated [1]:

> 'It would be wrong arbitrarily to exclude any particular group of people from consideration. But the chosen way of life of some adults may mean that they would not be able to provide a suitable environment for the care and nurture of a child. No one has a right to be a foster parent. Fostering decisions must centre exclusively on the interests of the child.'

1   Department of Health circular 3/1991 *Family placements.*

3.175 In order to be approved as a local authority foster parent the applicant has to undergo a detailed assessment in accordance with the requirements of Foster Placement (Children) Regulations 1991 [1]. The local authority must obtain information relating to the applicant's religion, race, culture and any previous criminal convictions. The local authority will consider any previous conviction when making its decision. Certain convictions and cautions operate as an automatic ban on acting as a foster parent. For example, a conviction for gross indecency (such as cottaging) would automatically disqualify an applicant unless he was under the age of 20 at the time of the offence [2].

1   SI 1991/910.
2   See Children (Protection from Offenders) (Miscellaneous Amendments) Regulations 1997, SI 1997/2308, reg 2.

3.176 Before effecting a foster placement or making any decision with respect to a child whom a local authority is looking after it must, as far as reasonably practicable, ascertain the wishes and feelings of the child, the parents, any other persons with parental responsibility, and other person whose wishes and feelings the local authority considers to be relevant (CA 1989, s 22(4))

3.177 The local authority has a duty to consider and promote the welfare of the child and 'in making the placement, the local authority must be satisfied that the child's needs arising from his cultural background and racial origin will be met so far as practicable'. Where possible the child should be placed with foster parents who are of the same religious persuasion as he is, or who undertake to bring him up in that persuasion [1].

1   Foster Placement (Children) Regulations 1991, SI 1991/910, reg 5(2).

3.178 The local authority is under a duty to consult about the details of the placement and a proposed placement with a same-sex couple could be opposed by the child's family and there has been at least one example of a local authority not placing a child with a lesbian couple because of opposition from the child's family. However, in an unreported case in 1997 the London Borough of Southwark did not withdraw a child from a placement with two gay male foster carers despite the mother's opposition and despite much media interest.

3   Placing the lesbian or gay child

3.179 Many lesbians and gay men feel they were born gay. As society's attitudes have become more accepting of lesbian and gay sexuality more teenagers are 'coming out' but still in some cases this has led to the young person being rejected by his or her family. Some lesbian and gay men leave home at a very early age and can find themselves being accommodated by a local authority or subject to a care order. Some lesbian and gay teenagers specifically state a preference to be fostered by lesbian or gay foster parents and some local authorities specifically seek such foster parents. Organisations such as the Albert Kennedy Trust specialise in placing lesbian or gay teenagers. Whilst the local authority may have a duty to consider a child's race and cultural origin there is no duty to consider his or her sexual orientation. In an unreported case in 1998 a gay teenager in the care of the London Borough of Wandsworth won the right to be placed with gay foster parents.

H   CARE PROCEEDINGS IN RESPECT OF YOUNG LESBIANS AND GAY MEN

3.180 Life for some young lesbians and gay men can be extremely hard. Homophobic bullying at school is still commonplace and some young lesbians and gay men are rejected by their families if they come out at home. Gay teenagers leave home at a very early age and some enter the care system. A local authority will accommodate a child in accordance with CA 1989, s 20 if:
(*a*)   there is no person who has parental responsibility;
(*b*)   he has been lost or abandoned;
(*c*)   a person who has been caring for him has been prevented (for whatever reason) from providing him with suitable accommodation or care.

3.181 There are no grounds for a young person to be made subject to a care order simply because of his or her sexual orientation. If however, he or she is found to be beyond parental control an order may be made. If an order is sought on this basis then the child must be in a state of being so beyond parental control that it must have caused him significant harm or created the risk of such harm. There is no need to show culpability on the part of the parents. So for example, if a lesbian or gay young person engages in under age sex with an older person (which is detrimental to his or her welfare) he or she may be regarded as beyond parental control and a care order made. The imminent equalisation of the age of consent to 16 should go some very considerable way to improving the position.

Chapter 4

The family home

A   INTRODUCTION

4.01   In any cohabitation relationship, the family home, whether rented or purchased, is usually the focal point of that relationship. Sharing a home is, after all, what sets cohabiting couples apart from others who are 'romantically' involved with one another and at the same time imbues their relationship with some of the same features and problems which occur in marriage. The family home is often a cohabiting couple's most valuable asset and the place where one or both of them wish to continue to live when the relationship ends due to breakdown or the death of one partner. However, whereas the law has come to recognise the special nature of the matrimonial home, accepting, for example, that the structure of married relationships makes the application of strict rules of property law inappropriate in determining each party's occupation rights or their respective shares in the home on divorce, it has yet to concede this in any consistent way in respect of other family homes. Thus, despite the obvious parallels which can be drawn between the nature and needs of married and cohabitation relationships (whether same-sex or heterosexual), there is not yet a holistic family law approach to the legal rights and remedies affecting the family home within these less conventional family structures. The Court of Appeal decisions in the cases of *Burns v Burns* [1] and *Fitzpatrick v Sterling Housing Association* [2] are clear examples of the harsh injustice which this can cause. The Law Commission is currently looking at the options for reform of the law relating to the property rights of unmarried couples and other 'homesharers', a term which undoubtedly includes same-sex cohabitants. Yet, although it is acknowledged that the current law is 'unfair, uncertain and illogical', the political and pragmatic difficulties that such reform will entail are evidenced by the fact that we still await the Law Commission's consultation paper.

1   [1984] Ch 317, discussed further at para **4.100**.
2   [1998] 1 FLR 43, discussed further at para **4.76**.

4.02   For the present at least, family law still has a tiered approach to regulating family life and the family home—an approach which privileges heterosexual marriage. Thus, it will nearly always provide a family law remedy when issues arise concerning the home of married couples [1]. Increasingly, though, the growing numbers of heterosexual cohabiting couples [2] are also being recognised as a family structure in law, although not for all purposes [3]. Same-sex cohabitants, on the other hand, are only just beginning to be acknowledged as a family structure of which the law should take account [4]. There is certainly no divorce law equivalent which enables the court to settle disputes between same-sex partners on relationship breakdown taking account of financial and homemaking roles, even though same-sex cohabitants may have pooled their income and divided the wage-earning and homemaking roles in a way traditionally associated with married relationships [5]. Neither have the UK courts developed a doctrine of unjust enrichment as an alternative mechanism for taking account of such qualitatively different contributions to a relationship as has occurred in Australia and Canada [6]. Rather, disputes relating to the family home on breakdown of a cohabitation relationship are still decided in this jurisdiction according to strict property law rather than family law. Here, little or no account is or can be taken of the familial nature of the relationship or of any indirect contributions which may have been made to the home.

1   Thus, as illustrated in the House of Lords decision in *Gissing v Gissing* [1971] AC 886, a wife who had no beneficial interest in the matrimonial home because she had made neither any agreement nor any direct contribution to the acquisition of the home sufficient to give rise to a resulting or constructive trust, was awarded nothing on divorce after a 20-year marriage with one child. The Matrimonial Causes Act 1973, Pt II now affords the courts greater discretion when adjusting property rights on divorce and can take contributions made to the welfare of the family into account (see MCA 1973, s 25). Where a spouse dies, in addition to the right to inherit on intestacy (Administration of Estates Act 1925, s 46), the surviving spouse also has the right to apply for reasonable financial provision under the Inheritance (Provision for Family and Dependants) Act 1975 (IHA 1975), s 1(1)(a), where any contributions to the welfare of the family will similarly be taken into account (s 3(2)). This is not the case however during the marriage—see, for example, *Lloyds Bank v Rosset* [1991] 1 AC 107, discussed further at para **4.100**. Spouses do have automatic occupation rights in respect of the matrimonial home—see the Family Law Act 1996 (FLA 1996), s 30.
2   Statistics show a clear increase in the trend towards heterosexual cohabitation. The number of women between the ages of 18–49 cohabiting with a man in Great Britain has risen from 11% in 1979 to 25% in 1995 (*Social Trends, 27*, the Stationery Office, 1997).
3   Thus, in contrast to spouses, there is no automatic right of occupation of the family home, no general ability to make financial provision for dependent cohabitants on relationship breakdown and no right to automatically inherit on intestacy. Often the law offers a similar but diminished remedy to cohabitants. This is the case with financial provision on death under IHA 1975, s 1(1A) where the award is limited to such as would be reasonable to receive *for their maintenance*. Family Law Act 1996, Pt IV also provides a more limited occupation order remedy for unentitled cohabitants as opposed to unentitled former spouses—contrast s 35 with s 36. It also, for the first time, permits in FLA 1996, Sch 7 the transfer of the family home between cohabitants on relationship breakdown, on similar but modified criteria to those which apply to married couples.
4   Note that as of 13 October 1997 same-sex cohabitants may apply for immigration rights under the Home Office 'concession outside immigration rules for unmarried partners', although the criteria are stricter than for heterosexual partners who are able to marry. Under FLA 1996, Pt IV same-sex cohabitants can now apply for non-molestation orders as by virtue of living in the same household they fall within the definition of 'associated persons' under FLA 1996, s 62(3)(c). However, they are specifically excluded from the definition of cohabitants under s 62(1) and, as discussed further at paras **4.55ff** may only obtain occupation orders if they are they are entitled to an interest in the family home under FLA 1996, s 33.
5   This is in contrast to several other jurisdictions including Sweden, Norway and Denmark. See for example the Danish Registered Partnership Act 1989.
6   Indeed, Lord Browne-Wilkinson V-C has expressed himself to be against the use of unjust enrichment as a device for settling home ownership disputes: 'there are great dangers in seeking to turn equity into one comprehensive law of unjust enrichment based on some sweeping fundamental concept [of unconscionability]' Browne-Wilkinson 'Constructive Trusts and Unjust Enrichment' (1996) 10 *Trust Law International* 98 at 101. However in Canada and Australia, it is accepted that the court may impose retrospectively what is referred to as a 'remedial constructive trust'. Here the court does not need to search for

any common intention to share ownership, but imposes a constructive trust to prevent unjust enrichment. Alternatively it may order payment of monetary compensation. See the Canadian cases of *Pettkus v Becker* (1980) 117 DLR (3d) 257; *Sorochan v Sorochan* (1986) 29 DLR (4th) 1 and *Peter v Beblow* [1993] 1 SCR 980 and the Australian case of *Baumgartner v Baumgartner* (1987) 62 ALJR 29.

4.03   This state of affairs means that all cohabitants and same-sex partners in particular are in much greater need of good legal advice on the consequences of joint enterprises undertaken or proposed by them than their married counterparts. Prevention is always better than cure and if disputes after death, relationship breakdown or even home repossession proceedings are to be minimised or avoided, people need to be made aware of their legal position at the outset.

4.04   This chapter therefore aims to look first at the possibility of prevention. It will consider the feasibility of cohabitation agreements within lesbian and gay relationships as well as the need for a declaration of trust where the family home is owner-occupied [1]. It will then go on to consider the remedies available where disputes arise—where a 'cure' is sought. Family homes and domestic violence legislation [2], which extends in part to same-sex cohabitants, will be examined, followed by consideration of the position of same-sex cohabitants on the death of one partner in the context of the rented family home. Finally, the complex nature of the law will be discussed together with the remedies available when family home disputes arise due to relationship breakdown.

1   For a draft declaration of trust agreement see Appendix II, p 206.
2   This is contained in the Family Law Act 1996, Pt IV.

B   PREVENTION

1   Cohabitation agreements and the family home

4.05   In some jurisdictions, such as that of California, heterosexual and same-sex cohabitation relationships can be regulated by enforceable cohabitation contracts, which must nonetheless be carefully drafted [1]. This enables the parties to agree in advance how their property is owned during the relationship and set out how it will be divided should the relationship break down, in the same way that a will provides for the eventuality of death. However, the position in England and Wales is not so clear cut. Whilst there is no problem in declaring the respective interests of each of the parties in any property they own during the relationship in a way that is legally enforceable [2], there is no recent authority on the validity of comprehensive cohabitation agreements which deal with every aspect of the relationship in our jurisdiction. In fact, such authority as there is [3] points to agreements of this nature being void on public policy grounds as they constitute contracts for immoral purposes and/or contracts prejudicial to the institution of marriage. However, given the changing moral climate, the consensus of opinion [4] is that this is not a real obstacle to creating an enforceable cohabitation agreement. Nonetheless, care must be taken to draft the agreement in such a way that will avoid it being declared void under the normal rules of contract law [5]. Let us first consider the advantages and disadvantages of cohabitation agreements in same-sex relationships.

1   Compare the Californian cases of *Jones v Daley* 122 Cal App 3d 500 (1981) and *Whorton v Dillingham* 248 Cal Rptr 405 (1988).

2   See Appendix II for an example of a declaration of trust in respect of the family home.
3   See *Fender v St John-Mildmay* [1938] AC 1 at p 42
4   See, for example, Bailey Harris *The Family Lawyer's Handbook* Law Society, Hodson *The unmarried family: property rights*, p 153.
5   For a full discussion see Barlow *Cohabitants and the Law* (1997) Butterworths, pp 12–23.

(i)   *Why enter into a cohabitation agreement?*

4.06   Although viewed by many as unromantic, the clear advantage of a cohabitation agreement is that it enables the couple to take legal advice and then thoroughly discuss and agree upon all aspects of their relationship, including the possibility of breakdown, before any dispute arises between them. This clarifies the parties' respective positions during the relationship and should minimise dispute in the event of separation. Although it may involve extra legal costs at the outset, it is far less costly in both financial and emotional terms than expensive litigation at the end of the relationship or on the death of one partner. At the very least, it will provide to any court charged with resolving a dispute, strong evidence of the parties' intentions at the time of the contract. If executed as a deed it may, for example, be used to make clear the agreed joint beneficial ownership of the family home legally vested in the name of only one partner. However, the parties need to be made aware that the agreement will regulate matters as between themselves but can only bind the parties to the agreement. It cannot, for example, affect each party's liability to any third party such as a mortgagee. Thus if there is a joint mortgage which one partner undertakes in the cohabitation agreement to pay in total, they will still, of course, each be jointly and severally liable to the mortgagee for the mortgage debt.

4.07   A cohabitation agreement cannot avoid the need to make wills and take out, where possible, life assurance to provide for their partner's needs in the event of their death. An agreement can, however, make clear the beneficial interests and mortgage liability of each of them in respect of the family home during the relationship, thus avoiding disputes or confusion between the parties as to what has been agreed. It can also provide a mechanism for compensating any failure to keep to the financial commitments made in the agreement.

4.08   However, it must be recognised that the contents of the agreement are unlikely to be capable of being settled once and for all. There is therefore a clear need to keep the agreement under review so that it can be revised (if appropriate) to reflect changing circumstances. Clear legal advice to couples on this issue is critical.

(ii)   *Contents of the agreement*

4.09   The exact contents of each agreement are clearly a matter for the individuals concerned. A framework agreement has been provided in Appendix I and provides guidance on the issues which it is thought could be included in an enforceable agreement. The most essential features to reach agreement on and incorporate into any cohabitation agreement would be:
(*a*)   beneficial ownership of the home during the relationship;
(*b*)   contributions to the mortgage and other outgoings in respect of the home;

(c)   ownership of personal property and other assets acquired before and during the relationship;
(d)   joint debts and bank or building society accounts;
(e)   procedure for review and termination of the agreement;
(f)   financial provision on relationship breakdown; and
(g)   a commitment to mediation and/or arbitration in case of dispute over the interpretation of the agreement.

4.10   The role of the legal adviser is to draft the agreement in a way which maximises its chances of enforceability (discussed further at para **4.11**) and consideration should be given as to whether it may be best to do this by creating a series of separate agreements. Whereas a comprehensive cohabitation agreement aims to deal with all aspects of the relationship, each one of the series would instead deal individually with them. Thus, for example, one would cover personal aspects of the relationship, a second would deal with property and maintenance during the relationship and a third would cover property and maintenance on breakdown. In any event, the goal of enforceability dictates that the personal aspects should be kept separate, even if the other issues are dealt with together in a single document. Couples may well want the personal aspects of such an agreement to be set out and there is no reason why details such as: the amount of time the couple agree to spend together; whether or not they are permitted to have other sexual relationships; right down to the minutiae of the cooking and washing-up rota, should not be formally committed to writing. However, the law would not, in common with all contracts for personal services, enforce such commitments by requiring specific performance. Neither are the courts likely to award damages for breach as they would not regard the parties as having intended to be legally bound by these rules other than to provide evidence of relationship breakdown. To include these in a cohabitation contract may therefore detract from the enforceability of the property and maintenance issues and thus in all cases it is best to separate them from the main body of the agreement.

(iii)   Enforceability of cohabitation agreements

4.11   To ensure as far as possible that a cohabitation agreement will be enforced by the courts, legal advisers need to have in mind the demands of the law of contract. Providing the hurdles laid down by the common law are successfully cleared, contract terms detailing how property which is brought into the relationship or purchased subsequently is to be dealt with both during the relationship and on breakdown should be enforceable. Let us now consider the main hurdles.

Illegality on grounds of public policy

4.12   Contracts for immoral purposes, including sexual immorality, are illegal and consequently unenforceable. Contracts prejudicial to the marital state are also contrary to public policy and void. Despite the changing tide towards both heterosexual and to a lesser extent same-sex cohabitation in some statutes, these common law principles of the law of contract remain unchanged. Current thinking is that no cohabitation agreement would actually be struck down on this ground, but this has yet to be definitively tried and tested in the courts. Advisers need to take steps to avoid this potential pitfall if they can. It seems most unlikely that an agreement between a same-sex couple would in any event be considered prejudicial to the institution of marriage, as it could be argued that the parties would be unlikely to enter into heterosexual marriage—the only form of marriage recognised in our jurisdiction [1]. Arguably, a contract between gay or lesbian cohabitants might be more susceptible to a finding by the courts that it is void as it promotes sexual immorality than that of a similar agreement between a heterosexual couple. However, given the wider recognition of the reality of same-sex couples as families by both Parliament and the courts [2], it is hoped that this too is a fairly remote possibility. The courts have certainly never raised this as an issue in property disputes concerning agreements between heterosexual or same-sex cohabitants in recent times [3]. Nonetheless, to enable a cohabitation contract to clear this first hurdle, it is clearly important to ensure that the agreement does not indicate that provision of sexual services is the consideration for the agreement. A contract which did would certainly be a contract for immoral purposes and declared void. To avoid the need to expressly state any form of consideration for the contract, advisers should ensure that any cohabitation agreement is drafted and executed in the form of a deed. No consideration at all is then required yet the agreement is enforceable. This is the format which has been adopted in the framework cohabitation agreement in Appendix I.

1   Marriages between persons of the same sex are void. See MCA 1973, s 11(c). This is in contrast to the position in some other jurisdictions eg Sweden, Norway, Hawaii.
2   See note 4 to para **4.02** and *Wayling v Jones* [1995] 2 FLR 1029 and *Tinsley v Milligan* [1994] 1 AC 340, both involving same-sex couples.
3   See for example *Wayling v Jones* [1995] 2 FLR 1029 and *Tinsley v Milligan* [1994] 1 AC 340.

(iv)   Absence of intention to create legal relations

4.13   Another aspect of contract law which needs to be heeded is the rebuttable presumption that parties to agreements concerning domestic arrangements have no intention to be legally bound [1]. However, the inclusion of clear words indicating the intention to be bound in the agreement will be sufficient to rebut the presumption and where legal advice has been taken and a formal document drawn up, this potential pitfall is easily avoided. As was stated by Scott J in *Layton v Martin* [2]:

> 'In family or quasi-family situations there is always the question whether the parties intended to create a legally binding contract between them. The more general and less precise the language of the so-called contract, the more difficult it will be to infer that intention.'

1   See *Balfour v Balfour* [1919] 2 KB 571.
2   [1986] 2 FLR 227 p 239.

(v)   Contract void for uncertainty

4.14   The provisions of the cohabitation agreement need to be certain. If they are too vague, either the offending terms will be ignored or, if they are fundamental to the operation of the contract, the whole agreement could be held void for uncertainty. For example, a term agreeing to make financial provision on relationship breakdown, without any indication of the amount to be paid or the rules according to which it could be ascertained would be void. Advisers need to make sure that if the parties' respective interests in property or the sum of maintenance agreed to be paid on breakdown is not precisely fixed at the time of the contract, the agreement makes clear how they can be calculated.

(vi)   Contract voidable for undue influence

4.15   A finding of undue influence exercised by one party over the other inducing that person to enter into the contract will vitiate the contract in its entirety. Thus if the terms of the agreement are heavily weighted in favour of one of the parties, it may be susceptible to such a finding. In contracts between spouses, there is no presumption of undue influence; to defeat the contract it has to be proven. Yet such a presumption can arise between engaged couples. Here, the advantaged party must prove that no undue influence was exercised over the other party to induce them to enter into the agreement [1]. There does not appear to be any such presumption operating in relation to agreements between cohabitants, yet the nature of the relationship undoubtedly means that undue influence could be exercised and should be guarded against if the contract is to be enforceable. As legal advisers may only advise one party to an agreement (to avoid potential conflict of interest), it is desirable to ensure where there is any hint of inequality of bargaining power that the less favoured party is urged to seek independent legal advice and that this is signalled in a recital to the agreement.

1   See, for example, *Zamet v Hyman* [1961] 1 WLR 1442.

4.16   Finally, agreements should always include a severance clause (see clause 22 of framework cohabitation agreement in Appendix I) so that if any part of the agreement is found to be illegal or unenforceable, providing this is subsidiary to the main agreement [1], this may be severed, leaving the remainder of the agreement enforceable.

1   See *Bennett v Bennett* [1952] 1 KB 249.

2   Acquiring the family home—what about a declaration of trust?

4.17   A comprehensive cohabitation agreement may well take the form of a declaration of trust. Indeed for it to effectively govern the interests in the owner-occupied family home it must take this form if it is to be valid, as noted at para **4.06**. However, where it is decided either to enter into separate agreements governing different aspects of the relationship, or where no cohabitation agreement as such is envisaged but the parties need to clarify their shares in the home, a declaration of trust dealing solely with ownership of the home is appropriate. A declaration of trust limited to declaring the parties' respective interests in the family home will not encounter any of the difficulties of enforceability outlined in respect of comprehensive cohabitation agreements. Clear legal advice on the agreed interests does need to be taken by each party. Yet the opportunity for giving such advice may be limited.

(i)   Deciding to share the home of one partner

4.18   When cohabitation commences, a decision is usually made to live initially in the home of one partner which may be a rented or owner-occupied property.

The other partner may well give up a tenancy or sell a property and 'invest' any capital realised or income saved in their new family home. Yet cohabitants rarely seek legal advice in these initial stages and if no formal agreement is made, cohabitants have to rely on the vagaries of the case law governing implied, resulting and constructive trusts arising under the Law of Property Act 1925, s 53(2) to determine their interests as discussed below. Those who do seek advice, should be strongly encouraged to discuss the basis upon which such 'investments' are being made and to enter into a cohabitation agreement to make clear the legal implications, if any, of these new living arrangements undertaken for the parties' mutual emotional benefit. If a full-scale cohabitation agreement is not wanted, it is possible to make a declaration of trust in respect of the home already vested in the name of one cohabitant, to make clear that a beneficial interest has been acquired by their partner, if this is what has been agreed. This will then be decisive in determining each party's share on relationship breakdown or the death of one partner. The declaration may simply set out the shares as percentages of the net or gross equity of the home. Or may be more complex if the respective shares are 'floating' but will crystallise later, say on the sale or transfer of the home, in accordance with the provisions of the declaration [1]. However, providing it is in writing and has been executed as a deed to comply with the requirements of LPA 1925, s 53(1) and has not been superseded by a subsequent declaration of trust, it will be effective to determine their respective beneficial interests.

1   See for example clause 1(a) of the framework cohabitation agreement in Appendix I and clause 5 of the draft declaration of trust set out in Appendix II.

(ii)   Purchasing a joint home

4.19   The most likely time for same-sex cohabitants to seek legal advice is if the couple decide to purchase a property together. This is probably the best opportunity for legal advisers to ensure that couples take stock of their legal position and either enter into a comprehensive cohabitation agreement or, at the very least, make a declaration of trust in respect of their shares in the family home so that the beneficial ownership of the home is put beyond dispute. Indeed, for advisers not to do so is likely to result in a finding of negligence [1].

1   See *Walker v Hall* [1984] FLR 126 and criticisms made in *Springette v Defoe* [1992] 2 FLR 388 of solicitors who had transferred the property into joint names without declaring the beneficial interests.

4.20   If a family home is to be purchased by same-sex cohabitants for their joint use, a decision needs to be made first whether the legal title of the property is to vest in their joint names or just the sole name of one of them. In either case, they need to agree, following clear and careful legal advice to each of them, what their respective beneficial interests in the home are to be. It is perfectly possible for a property to be purchased in the name of one partner, but for the beneficial interest in the home to be owned jointly. Whatever the decision about legal ownership, wherever there is joint beneficial ownership, a couple needs to decide whether this is to take the form of a beneficial joint tenancy or tenancy in common. A declaration of trust in proper form will expressly declare the beneficial interests each partner has in the family home regardless of how the legal title is held. Once again, providing it is in writing, it will normally be conclusive should dispute arise. The legal consequences of each option will now be considered.

(iii)   Purchase in sole name

4.21   As noted above, if for tax or other bona fide reasons, cohabitants who are both contributing to the purchase of a property wish it to be purchased in the sole name of one party, it is still possible to have a declaration of trust as to how the equity is held. Although this will only give an equitable, rather than a legal, interest in the property to the non-purchaser cohabitant, it would still be clear evidence of the parties' respective interests in any subsequent dispute between them. A non-owner partner who has contributed in money or money's worth is likely in any event to prove a beneficial interest in the proceeds of the sale by virtue of a resulting or constructive trust and can make an application under the Trusts of Land and Appointment of Trustees Act 1996 (TLATA 1996), s 14 as discussed at para **4.81**. Accordingly, where a beneficial interest is acknowledged or apparent from the outset, a declaration of trust should be drawn up, setting out the respective interests under the resulting trust and reciting the contributions made by each party.

4.22   Where an adviser is acting for a mortgagee as well as a sole purchaser, enquiries must be made in respect of others who will be occupying the property. If the existence of a cohabitant is thereby revealed, then the cohabitant will be required to sign a declaration that any interest in the property that they may have does not have priority over that of the mortgagee. Enquiries as to whether the cohabitant is contributing to the purchase price should be made of both parties, and if a contribution is confirmed, further questions as to the basis upon which this is being done would seem to be entirely appropriate. Such a revelation would in any event provide an opportunity, if not always a duty, to discuss the possible consequences of cohabitation in a home purchased by one cohabitant, and to advise on the merits of drawing up full documentation to record the parties' intentions with regard to the property which is to be the family home. Independent advice will, following decisions on undue influence in the married context such as *Barclays Bank plc v O'Brien* [1] and *Midland Bank plc v Cooke* [2], always be appropriate for the non-purchasing cohabitant to make clear the position concerning any interest they may claim to have in the home and, indeed, its relationship with any mortgagee's interest [3]. Such advice at an early stage may prevent the need for litigation later and to that extent must be of benefit to all concerned in the proposed transaction. Enquiries may reveal that the proposed contribution takes the form of a loan or a gift and not a contribution to the purchase price, in which case the loan agreement or deed of gift should be drawn up as appropriate and the desirability of independent advice clearly explained.

1   [1994] 1 AC 180.
2   [1995] 4 All ER 562.
3   See now *Royal Bank of Scotland v Etridge (No 2)* [1998] 2 FLR 843, CA.

4.23   As noted at para **4.18**, the need for a declaration of trust may arise where parties agree to cohabit in a property already owned by one of them and the incoming partner pays for improvements to be done to the property or contributes to the mortgage repayments. It is open for them to transfer the legal and equitable title of the property into joint names but this may involve obtaining a mortgagee's consent and possibly paying stamp duty, land registration fees, legal costs and disbursements as on a new purchase. Some cohabitants may prefer just to make a declaration of trust, although from the non-owner cohabitant's point of view, this would confer only an equitable rather than a legal interest and would be enforceable against their partner only.

4.24   Wherever a property is purchased, the need for wills to be drawn up should be considered. In the case of beneficial co-owners, if they hold the property as tenants in common, their shares will devolve as part of their respective estates. This is in contrast to the position of equitable joint tenants, where their interests pass by operation of law to their co-owner on their death.

4.25   As developed at para **4.18**, where the legal title of the home is vested in the name of one partner, the other may fear on relationship breakdown that the home could be sold without their consent. A later purchaser for value of the property would normally raise enquiries about the interests of any other adult occupier of the property, and where the cohabitant is in actual occupation of the property, the owner cohabitant will not be able to give vacant possession without their partner's co-operation. Thus a purchaser is likely to be put on notice. A cohabitant would, in any event, have an overriding interest where the title is registered [1] and they remain in actual occupation of the home and a declaration of trust gives the non-owner cohabitant documentary evidence of his or her interest in the property which can be protected by registration as a minor interest (see para **4.84**) and will be enforceable as against their partner in case of dispute through an action under TLATA 1996, s 14 [2].

1   Land Registration Act 1925, s 70(1)(g).
2   This is discussed at para **4.84** in the context of relationship breakdown.

Undue influence and purchase in sole name

4.26   Another issue that needs to be addressed, where just one partner is purchasing a family home which is for joint use, is that of undue influence. There have been a plethora of recent cases considering the issues of misrepresentation and of undue influence where a spouse or cohabitant is asked by their partner to consent to a mortgagee's charge against the family home to secure the business debts of that partner, usually the man in the heterosexual context. This will occur during the currency of the relationship and may apply whether or not the home is vested in their joint names. Effectively, the House of Lords in *Barclays Bank v O'Brien* (see para **4.22**) recognised that where one partner (normally the wife) could show that she generally trusted and had confidence in her partner in financial matters a presumption of undue influence arises, placing a heavier burden on the mortgagee. If in rare cases, the husband acts as the mortgagee's agent, then they will be unable to enforce the charge against the wife's equity. Otherwise, the ability to enforce would depend on whether or not the mortgagee was fixed with actual or constructive notice of the undue influence. The House of Lords made it clear that these principles would apply as much to cohabiting couples, whether heterosexual or homosexual:

> '[T]he same principles are applicable to all other cases where there is an emotional relationship between cohabitees. The "tenderness" shown by the law to married women is not based on the marriage ceremony but reflects the underlying risk of one cohabitee exploiting the emotional involvement and trust of the other. Now that unmarried cohabitation, whether heterosexual or homosexual, is widespread in our society, the law should recognise this. Legal wives are not the only group which are now exposed to the emotional pressure of cohabitation.' [1]

1   Per Lord Browne Wilkinson in *Barclays Bank plc v O'Brien* [1993] 4 All ER 417 at 431.

4.27   The case of *CIBC Mortgages v Pitt* [1] (where unlike in *O'Brien*, the matrimonial home was in joint names and as far as the mortgagees were aware the loan was purportedly for a joint holiday home) emphasised that in the *O'Brien* situation, where the home was in the man's sole name and the loan was for his business, the risk of undue influence was greater. In *Massey v Midland Bank* [2] it was confirmed that *O'Brien* applied to the cohabitation context, although the bank here were entitled to rely on the fact that they had required Ms Massey to seek independent advice. Furthermore, in *Barclays Bank plc v Boulter* [3] it was confirmed that it was for the mortgagee to prove they did not have constructive notice of the undue influence, and that whether the land was registered or unregistered was irrelevant in cases of this nature. The question was whether the creditor had actual or constructive notice of the facts on which the equity to set aside the transaction was founded. Thus advisers need to be aware both of the potential conflict of interests between cohabitants and of their own professional position when advising in these situations.

1   [1994] 1 AC 200.
2   [1995] 1 All ER 929.
3   [1997] 2 All ER 1002.

(iv)   Purchase in joint names

4.28   If a property is purchased and the legal and equitable title is vested in the joint names of same-sex cohabitants each has the right to occupy it. Neither can lawfully exclude the other without having first obtained a court order to do so. In addition, as both names are on the title deeds, one joint owner cannot sell, mortgage or charge the property without the consent of the other, whose signature will be required to effect the sale or create the legal charge. This also means that if one co-owner wishes to sell and the other refuses, an application has to be made to the court for an order to resolve the issue. The court will either order the sale or agree to a postponement of the sale in certain circumstances. This situation usually arises on breakdown of the relationship between cohabitants and is explored in more detail at paras **4.81**ff.

4.29   All joint purchasers hold the legal estate of their property as joint tenants in law. By virtue of the Trusts of Land and Appointment of Trustees Act 1996, s 5 and Sch 2, where there is joint ownership, a statutory trust of the land is implied. Co-owners are therefore trustees and hold on trust for themselves as either joint tenants or tenants in common in equity. As the law allows joint owners to hold their beneficial interest in the property either as joint tenants or as tenants in common, all co-owners should be advised at the time of purchase of the broad implications of both options, so they can make an informed decision which properly reflects their intentions. This decision is of tremendous importance to all co-owners and particularly to cohabitants. Failure to keep a record of the legal advice given at the time of the purchase is likely to amount to negligence on the part of a solicitor and members of the profession are often criticised for failing to explain clearly to joint purchasers at the time of purchase the options open to co-owners and their implications. The courts, with justification, have become increasingly critical of inadequate advice given to joint purchasers which has in turn led to costly and unnecessary litigation between cohabitants on relationship breakdown. In *Walker v Hall* [1] the Court of Appeal found that a solicitor who failed to find out the beneficial interests of joint purchasers for whom he was acting and had declared a tenancy in common without declaring any shares was guilty of negligence. Such practice was further lamented in *Springette v Defoe* [2] where property had been transferred to the parties as joint tenants in law without any declaration as to their beneficial interests in the property having been made in the transfer. In the more recent decision of *Huntingford v Hobbs* [3] a majority of the Court of Appeal rejected the contention that the standard declaration on the transfer of registered land form, that the survivor of the two cohabitant joint proprietors could give a valid receipt for capital money arising on the disposition of the land, constituted a declaration of trust that they held the property as beneficial joint tenants.

1   [1984] FLR 126, CA.
2   [1992] 2 FLR 388, CA.
3   [1993] 1 FLR 736, CA.

4.30   Joint purchasers have often decided between themselves how they are going to contribute to the purchase of the property and then to the outgoings in respect of the home. They may decide to apply one partner's income towards the mortgage repayments and the other's towards all other outgoings or they may decide to make unequal contributions towards these to reflect the differences in their salaries at the time of the purchase. Unless close enquiries have been made at the time of purchase, these arrangements may not have been communicated to their solicitor and will not then be contained in any legal document. Many cohabitants will be completely unaware that these different arrangements may well affect their beneficial interests in the property and that these arrangements may prove critical if there is ever a dispute. Some joint purchasers may not even expressly discuss with each other their understanding of the implications of the agreed arrangements they have made to contribute to the purchase price and mortgage repayments as was the case in *Springette v Defoe*.

4.31   In order to avoid negligence claims and disputes between cohabitants at a later stage, it is important when taking instructions on a purchase to ask crucial questions about the source of the purchase money, the proposed contributions to the mortgage and intentions as to beneficial ownership. All the options and implications need to be carefully explained, including the implications of relationship breakdown and death. It is important for advisers to discover whether there are any other potential beneficiaries who would be adversely affected by the right of survivorship in the case of a beneficial joint tenancy and if appropriate to suggest the need for the drawing of new wills and explain the ramifications of the Inheritance (Provision for Family and Dependants) Act 1975 if one or both cohabitants have former spouses or minor children by other relationships.

4.32   Another issue that needs to be addressed is whether the life assurance usually offered to cohabitant joint purchasers on standard terms is appropriate to their individual circumstances. So-called 'joint life, first death' endowment policies can give unexpected results where death of both cohabitants takes place within a short space of time, particularly if, as has been common practice, the mortgagee does not take an assignment or notice of deposit of the policy, as the right of survivorship applies to the proceeds, potentially not protecting the estate of the longest surviving cohabitant. Consideration needs to be given to whether a mortgage protection policy or policies taken out by each purchaser on their own life might be more appropriate, although obtaining any form of life assurance may currently prove difficult in practice for gay men. Alternatively, where there is a joint life policy, a declaration of trust needs to be drawn up in relation to the proceeds of the joint life policy to avoid such an anomaly, not intended by the parties.

4.33 The relative merits of the main considerations to which both advisers and joint purchasers should apply their minds will now be considered.

(v) Joint tenancy or tenancy in common

4.34 Regardless of their actual contributions to the purchase price, joint proprietors, who must hold as joint tenants in law under a statutory trust of land, have the option of declaring that they hold their beneficial interests either as joint tenants or as tenants in common. One of the most important effects of this decision is seen on the death of one of the joint tenants. If the couple are beneficial joint tenants and neither has severed the joint tenancy thereby creating a beneficial tenancy in common, the survivor of them will succeed to the deceased joint tenant's legal and equitable interests by operation of law, notwithstanding the terms of deceased joint tenant's will. However, where there is a beneficial tenancy in common, then the deceased co-owner's share will form part of that person's estate on death and devolve according to will, or in the absence of a will, the rules on intestacy. Where there is no will, this means that the deceased partner's share will be inherited by his or her next of kin, and not by their surviving partner. This makes it critical for advisers to ensure that couples are aware of the need to make wills if there is to be a beneficial tenancy in common and they wish their partner to inherit their share of the home. Otherwise, a surviving same-sex partner has to rely on the proceeds of any life policy to purchase the deceased partner's share from the beneficiary or if they were dependent on the deceased, on a precarious application under the Inheritance (Provision for Family and Dependants) Act 1975, which would not necessarily enable the applicant to remain in the home [1].

1   See Ch 5.

4.35 What, therefore, should determine whether cohabitants should be joint tenants or tenants in common and how should this best be reflected in the purchase documentation? Where the capital contribution made by each of the cohabitants is broadly equal, it is also intended that they should contribute to the mortgage in roughly equal shares and they expressly agree that their shares in the home are and should remain equal even if circumstances change, the crucial issue is whether they wish the right of survivorship to apply. If they decide that they wish the other to inherit their share of the property without having to make a will to that effect, then a beneficial joint tenancy should be created.

4.36 However, it can be argued that given the inability of the courts to intervene and adjust the shares of same-sex cohabitants on relationship breakdown, it might never be appropriate to recommend a beneficial joint tenancy to them, in case on relationship breakdown the original desire to have equal shares in the home becomes unacceptable from the perspective of one of the parties. From an adviser's point of view, the safest course of action is to declare a beneficial tenancy in common together with clear written advice to make mutual wills. Yet there is often a formidable, if not altogether logical, reluctance to will-making on the part of cohabitants, who prefer the advantage of a beneficial joint tenancy to deal with succession of the home, without having to make difficult decisions about the destination of their other assets. Another potential difficulty is that a beneficial tenancy in common expressly declaring the proportionate beneficial interests based on actual and intended contributions to capital and mortgage at the time of the purchase, may not provide a flexible enough assessment of the parties' true intentions as to their interests in the property. Where one is providing mainly capital and the other mainly mortgage repayments, these issues may be magnified in the effects they produce. Often parties feel that the fairest method of assessing respective interests in the home is a retrospective one at the date the property is to be sold, taking account of the actual contributions made and not just the promise made at the date of purchase of, for example, mortgage repayments. There is judicial approval [1] for such deferred ascertainment of the beneficial interests, where it can be inferred that this was clearly intended by the parties and this approach was approved in *Springette v Defoe* [2]. It seems that a possible solution to the practitioner's dilemma is a declaration which creates a beneficial joint tenancy until severance by either party, whereupon a beneficial tenancy in common is created, to be held in shares specified with reference to the parties' contributions. This idea has been reflected in the framework cohabitation agreement and draft declaration of trust in Appendices I and II and is discussed further at para **4.44**.

1   See for example *Passee v Passee* [1988] 1 FLR 263, particularly at pp 270–272.
2   [1992] 2 FLR 388.

4.37   It falls to the practitioner acting for the purchaser to record the intentions about how the beneficial interests are to be held. In unregistered land, the conveyance should, as a matter of course, always contain an express declaration as to whether the purchasers hold beneficially as joint tenants or tenants in common. This, in the absence of any later evidence of a different joint intention or of fraud or mistake, will be conclusive. Where the purchase involves registered land, an express declaration can and should, be included in the transfer document, although traditionally the majority of solicitors have done no more than complete the declaration on the standard form of transfer stating that the survivor can give a valid receipt for capital monies arising on disposition of the land. For many years it was not clear whether this declaration would be sufficient to create an express beneficial joint tenancy. In *Bernard v Josephs* [1] the Court of Appeal held that where property had been transferred to two cohabitants jointly, without any express declaration as to the nature of the beneficial ownership, there was no presumption that the parties held the property in equal shares. Instead, a court should look at all the evidence, such as respective contributions, and see whether it indicates any intention to hold the property other than in equal shares. In that case, it was decided that the parties did have equal interests in the property, but much time and expense would have been saved if the transfer had indicated the parties' intentions at the time of purchase. In the more recent decision of *Huntingford v Hobbs* [2] a majority of the Court of Appeal rejected the contention that the standard declaration on the transfer of registered land form (that the survivor of the two cohabitant joint proprietors could give a valid receipt for capital money arising on the disposition of the land) constituted a declaration of trust that they held the property as beneficial joint tenants. They found that because such wording could equally have been employed to indicate that they were holding the beneficial interest as trustees on behalf of a third party, it did not constitute a declaration of their beneficial interests in the property. Furthermore, extrinsic evidence was not admissible in this context and thus the interests fell to be decided in accordance with the principles of resulting, implied or constructive trusts.

1   [1982] 3 All ER 162, CA.
2   [1993] 1 FLR 736, CA.

4.38   To create a beneficial joint tenancy, an express declaration of trust unambiguously to this effect must be entered into by the joint purchasers. Where the conveyance or transfer does not include a declaration of the beneficial interests, a separate declaration of trust document, executed by both parties, should be drawn and placed with the title deeds. Once there is an express beneficial joint tenancy, then each party will be deemed to have an equal interest in the proceeds of the sale, even if the joint tenancy is subsequently severed [1], unless as suggested in para **4.36**, each party's beneficial interest on severance has been specified in the original declaration. Where there is an initial joint tenancy, it can later be severed by either of the joint tenants, by service of a notice of severance on the other party or by course of dealing. As soon as a joint tenancy is severed, a tenancy in common arises and the right of survivorship no longer applies. Each co-owner's share will then devolve separately with his or her estate. If an adviser is instructed to sever a joint tenancy, the client should be advised to make a new will.

1   See *Goodman v Gallant* [1986] 1 All ER 311.

4.39   Even if the parties have contributed in unequal shares to the purchase price of the property, they may still, if they wish, purchase as beneficial joint tenants. However, even after the tenancy has been severed, they will normally still hold the property in equal shares [1], although where separation takes place some adjustment may be made to reflect varying contributions made after the separation.

1   See *Goodman v Gallant* [1986] 1 All ER 311.

4.40   Where there are unequal contributions to the purchase price and the parties wish this to be reflected in their respective interests in the property on purchase, then a beneficial tenancy in common is needed. To create a beneficial tenancy in common an express declaration should be made in the conveyance or transfer, or in a separate declaration of trust document, clearly stating the proportions in which the property is held by the co-owners in proper form [1].

1   As noted at para **4.18** it must be in writing and follow the requirements of Law of Property Act 1925, s 53(1). An example has been provided in Appendix II.

4.41   Where advisers are acting for joint purchasers, it should be standard practice to ask whether they wish to hold the property as joint tenants or tenants in common. Whatever the answer, an express declaration should be made at the time as it can avoid future disputes. Where there is to be a beneficial tenancy in common with floating shares, it will be appropriate to record not only the capital contributions to the deposit, but also any credit to be given for a 'right to buy' discount; the parties' proposed present and future contributions to the mortgage and other outgoings; and the planned use of the property as a family home. In effect, a small-scale cohabitation agreement dealing specifically with the parties' intentions in relation to the home could and should be drawn up.

4.42   To summarise, any adviser instructed to create a tenancy in common should immediately advise on the position of each cohabitant on death. Without a will leaving their interest in the property to the other, a partner's share will devolve according to the intestacy rules on their next of kin, which may not reflect his or her true wishes. In the case of registered land, an adviser must also indicate on the transfer and on the land registry application form, whether or not the survivor can give a valid receipt on the subsequent sale of the property. As discussed at para **4.37**, this on its own is not sufficient to determine the interests in the property and a declaration of the beneficial joint tenancy or tenancy in common and the relative shares of tenants in common, must in any event be recorded on transfer or in a separate declaration of trust.

4.43   Parties purchasing as tenants in common, specifying fixed shares, should also be advised that the declaration of trust can be varied in the future but only by agreement. If joint purchasers' true common intention is reflected by declaring neither a beneficial joint tenancy nor a beneficial tenancy in common in specific shares, there are two further possibilities to consider. First, it may be possible to create a beneficial tenancy in common which builds in flexibility in the way in which the shares are calculated, declaring so-called 'floating shares'. A deferred ascertainment clause recording the common intention of the method by which the beneficial interests are to be calculated would be a way of achieving this. The advantage is that important issues like the value of contributions in kind, such as home improvements or perhaps childcare, could be built into the method of assessment. A method of dealing with negative equity if this was considered in need of different treatment to the proposed division of positive equity could also be addressed. The potential difficulty with this approach is that it is open-ended, requires the couple to keep careful records of expenditure during the relationship and leaves them with too much to argue over should the relationship break down. However, it does at least leave the couple with a clear common intention, which with careful drafting could provide a couple with the flexibility to take future events into account, yet provide them with a fixed framework for determining their interests on relationship breakdown. See Appendices I and II.

4.44   Second, there seems to be no reason why cohabitants who are purchasing a property jointly and who wish during the currency of the relationship to be beneficial joint tenants taking advantage of the right of survivorship—yet who, should the relationship break down, do not necessarily want to hold the property in equal shares on severance of the joint tenancy—should not be able to enter into an effective 'hybrid' declaration of trust. The declaration should make clear either the proportions in which the beneficial interest is to be held on severance, or the method of calculating them if deferred ascertainment is preferred. For a draft declaration of trust see Appendix II.

4.45   Neither of these possibilities should be used unless they clearly coincide with the joint purchasers' intentions at the time of purchase. Thought needs to be given to these options where the parties are not satisfied that either of the two more straightforward options meets with their true intentions. Both alternative options suggested have the advantage of flexibility but the disadvantage of lack of immediate certainty. It could be argued that, framed in the right way, they can effectively achieve for same-sex cohabitants a fairer method of dividing property on relationship breakdown in accordance with principles decided by the couple when they were together and which they may accordingly be happy to agree to abide by with the minimum of dissension on breakdown.

3 Good practice checklist for advisers of same-sex cohabitants purchasing property

4.46 (*a*) Take very full instructions as to the relationship, the contributions to the deposit, details as to whom any right to buy discount is attributable, anticipated contributions to the mortgage repayments and implications of any proposed improvements to the property.

(*b*) Take instructions on the basis upon which the parties intend to hold the property in law and in equity, fully explaining the implications of the right of survivorship, the need to draw wills, the possibility of or difficulties in obtaining life assurance, the effect on any potential beneficiary. Consider and discuss the ramifications of whether beneficial interests should be expressed as a proportion of the gross or net proceeds of sale in the light of capital and mortgage contributions and consider whether a negative equity situation will affect the proposed beneficial interests. Wherever possible confirm instructions in a letter to each of the purchasers to ensure that there have been no misunderstandings.

(*c*) Ensure that a firm conclusion is reached in relation to the holding of the beneficial interests, whilst bearing in mind that certainty does not rule out flexibility. Include a declaration in the transfer or conveyance, making reference to a separate declaration of trust where a more complicated calculation of the beneficial interest is preferred. This may be particularly appropriate where one party is contributing mainly capital and the other intends to take prime responsibility for the mortgage repayments. Be aware that the communicated common intention of the purchasers at the time of purchase is critical, although deferred ascertainment of the beneficial interests is a permissible common intention.

(*d*) Consider the appropriateness of the life assurance arrangements in the light of anticipated contributions to the mortgage repayments and any dependency by one partner upon the other as well as the effect on other potential beneficiaries.

(*e*) Advise on the need to draw wills, where appropriate and the possibility of a cohabitation agreement.

C CURE

4.47 When relationships break down, same-sex cohabitants have no cohesive family law based remedies to guide the settlement of any disputes that arise in relation to the family home. This is why cohabitation agreements and declarations of trust concerning the family home are regarded as particularly beneficial in such relationships. For at the very least, they provide evidence of what the parties intended when they entered into the agreement and will usually provide an enforceable remedy for the partner seeking to rely on the agreement following separation. Where there has been no agreement or declaration of trust, same-sex cohabitants are, of course, dependent on the application of strict property law. In this situation, where one partner claims an interest in the home which is purportedly owned by their partner, their only likely remedy is to prove the existence of an implied, resulting or constructive trust. However, unlike in Australia and Canada, no doctrine of unjust enrichment has been developed in the UK to soften the operation of strict rules of property law in the family law context. An alternative remedy is to ask the court to apply the doctrine of proprietary estoppel. Yet the case law relating to both implied trusts and proprietary estoppel is acknowledged to be extremely complex and uncertain in its application. From the adviser's perspective, it is difficult to predict a certain outcome. From the cohabitants' point of view, litigation is expensive and time consuming. Hence the recommendation that prevention in the form of a cohabitation agreement or declaration of trust is better than cure.

4.48   Whilst cohabitation agreements are effective to determine property rights and financial provision during and after the relationship, they cannot oust the application of legislation designed to protect family members. Thus whilst an agreement can set out the parties' intentions with regard to children of the family, it cannot oust the jurisdiction of the court to decide these issues under the Children Act 1989 (CA 1989). Similarly, the domestic violence legislation cannot be ousted and any court order made under FLA 1996, Pt IV affecting occupation rights in the family home would be capable of delaying the enforcement of the cohabitation agreement for the duration of the occupation order.

4.49   Where the family home is rented, whilst there is a remedy for heterosexual cohabitants under Sch 7 to the FLA 1996 permitting an application for transfer of the family home from one partner to another on relationship breakdown, same-sex cohabitants have been left without any remedy at all. Where they have a rented joint tenancy, this means that there is complete stalemate unless an occupation order can be obtained, as discussed at para **4.56**. Yet on death of a sole tenant of a rented family home, as the law stands at the moment, their partner has no right whatsoever to remain in the home whatever security of tenure their partner had, as the cases of *Harrogate Borough Council v Simpson* [1] and more recently *Fitzpatrick v Sterling Housing Association* [2] graphically illustrate.

1   [1986] 2 FLR 91.
2   [1998] 1 FLR 43.

4.50   There will inevitably be situations where litigation or at least the threat of litigation cannot be avoided and whilst mediation is to be considered and encouraged wherever appropriate, advisers need to be aware of the disparate areas of law governing such disputes which arise most frequently on relationship breakdown or death.

1   Domestic violence remedies affecting the family home [1]

4.51   Domestic violence can and does occur in same-sex relationships but this has traditionally been ignored by the law. For the first time, same-sex cohabitants are now eligible to apply for some domestic violence remedies under Pt IV of FLA 1996 which also governs occupation rights within the family home. It therefore seems appropriate to summarise here the main features of the legislation as it relates to same-sex cohabitants. The new legislation may be particularly helpful to those advising lesbian and gay cohabitants on disputes concerning a family home rented in joint names. A new-style occupation order may be the only remedy available to assist.

1   For a fuller account of the law and procedure relating to domestic violence in the cohabitation context, see Barlow *Cohabitants and the Law*, (1997) Butterworths, Ch 7.

4.52   Although they have been specifically excluded from the definition of cohabitants in FLA 1996, s 62(1) which is clearly heterosexual [1], same-sex cohabitants do fall within the definition of 'associated persons' in s 62(2)(c)—those living or having lived in the same household otherwise than merely by reason of one of them being the other's employee, tenant, lodger or boarder [2]. This means they can apply for non-molestation orders under s 42 which aims to protect a person's personal safety and well-being by prohibiting 'molestation'. Providing they are 'entitled'—that is they have a legal or beneficial interest in the home or contractual or statutory rights of occupation—they can also apply for an 'occupation order' under s 33 which may adjust the occupation rights of each partner in respect of the family home.

1   Section 62(1)(a) defines 'cohabitants' as a man and a woman living as husband and wife.
2   The Law Commission foresaw that the test for determining whether people are 'living together in the same household' would be that developed in the matrimonial law context to establish the degree of community of life between them (see for example *Fuller v Fuller* [1973] 2 All ER 650 and *Mouncer v Mouncer* [1972] 1 WLR 321). Lesbian and gay cohabitants, it is thought, should have no difficulty in showing that they are or have been living in the same household. Thus although all the authorities relate to married or heterosexual cohabiting couples, the existence of an intimate relationship together with shared meals and domestic arrangements should bring them within the definition. Indeed the Law Commission Report *Family Homes and Domestic Violence* (Law Com no 207) specifically refers to homosexual couples as falling within this 'family relationship' in the broader sense (see para 3.19).

(i)   Non-molestation orders

4.53   The aim of such an order is to restrain a party from molesting the applicant or any relevant child. The term 'non-molestation order' has been retained and is designed to convey, as it did under the old law [1], that violence per se is not a prerequisite for obtaining an order. There is no definition of 'molestation' contained in the Act; a deliberate omission, designed to ensure that the pre-existing level of protection was not reduced. Thus authorities such as *Vaughan v Vaughan* [2] where 'pestering', by a man who called upon his estranged wife morning and evening, at home and at work, making a thorough nuisance of himself and *Spencer v Camacho* [3] where, following a series of other incidents, a man rifling through his partner's handbag were both held to amount to molestation, remain good law. In essence, where any conduct harassing the victim, violent or non-violent, which warrants intervention by the court could and can still be the subject of an injunction and both physical and mental harassment fall within the scope of the new law as they did with the 1976 legislation. However, in *Johnson v Walton* [4] the court took the view under the 1976 Act that, in addition to the actual harassment not amounting to violence, there must also be an intent to cause distress or alarm for it to amount to molestation. In most cases, such an intention will be apparent, yet it is questionable as to whether the difference in approach between actual violence and harassment should be sustained. If where there has been actual violence, the harm caused rather than the actual intention is the test, as decided in *Wooton v Wooton* [5] where violence during epileptic seizures amounted to molestation, why should a similar harm-based approach not be taken to other forms of harassment? It is also hoped that non-molestation orders will be thought appropriate even where the parties intend to continue living together in contrast to the approach taken in *F v F (protection from violence: continuing cohabitation)* [6] where a non-molestation order was refused on these grounds. There is nothing in the wording of the new legislation to indicate that such restriction was intended, although this was equally true of the old law. Such restrictive interpretation appears unnecessary as there may be situations where parties genuinely feel that a non-molestation order may be an effective means of saving a relationship from further violence and they should be given the opportunity to test this with the protection of an order.

1   This, as far as heterosexual cohabitants were concerned, was the Domestic Violence and Matrimonial Proceedings Act 1976.
2   [1973] 1 WLR 1159.
3   (1983) 4 FLR 662.
4   [1990] 1 FLR 350.
5   [1984] FLR 871.
6   [1989] 2 FLR 451.

4.54   In terms of the criteria for granting a non-molestation order, s 42(5) provides that in deciding whether to exercise its powers under this section and, if so, in what manner, the court shall have regard to all the circumstances including 'the need to secure the health, safety and well-being' of the applicant and any relevant child. The term 'well-being', it is hoped, is sufficiently wide to ensure that courts do not feel restricted to making orders only in cases where violence or threat of violence can be proven. The term 'relevant' child, as defined in s 62(2), is wide [1] and might encompass a situation where, for example, a child came to stay with an applicant on contact visits, or was cared for during the day by an applicant, although did not reside with them.

1   It includes any child who lives or might reasonably be expected to live with either party to the proceedings, any child in respect of whom an order under the Adoption Act 1976 or the Children Act 1989 is in question in the proceedings and any other child whose interests the court considers relevant.

4.55   There is no minimum period of living in the same household required before an applicant within this category of associated person may apply.

(ii)   Section 33 occupation orders

4.56   Unlike heterosexual cohabitants or married couples, same-sex cohabitants may only apply for an occupation order under FLA 1996, s 33 and thus must show not only that they are 'associated' under s 62(3)(c) but also that they are entitled in their own right to occupy the family home [1]. To be eligible to apply for a s 33 occupation order in respect of the family home, a same-sex cohabitant must be able to show two things. First, that they have an entitlement to occupy the accommodation and second, that the accommodation either was or was intended to be their home jointly with a person with whom they are associated. Section 33(1) defines entitlement to occupy, either through having a legal or beneficial estate or interest, or by virtue of contractual or statutory rights including 'matrimonial home rights' defined by s 30 but which do not extend to either heterosexual or same-sex cohabitants. Therefore lesbian and gay cohabitants who are sole or joint beneficial owners, or sole or joint tenants (whether contractual or statutory) in the rented sector may apply for an order against their partner or former partner regardless of their partner's legal status in relation to occupation of the home. A non-entitled lesbian or gay cohabitant without an interest or contractual or statutory right to occupy, is not eligible to apply for an occupation order and, in contrast to heterosexual cohabitants [2], their remedy is limited to a non-molestation order. Furthermore, where there is a dispute as to one same-sex cohabitant's entitlement to occupy, this dispute must be resolved before that cohabitant can make a s 33 application, in contrast to heterosexual cohabitants who again have an alternative remedy under s 36 in such a situation.

1 The home must comprise a dwelling house for the order to be made, as defined in s 63(1) as:
'(*a*) any building or part of a building which is occupied as a dwelling,
(*b*) any caravan, house-boat or structure which is occupied as a dwelling,
and any yard, garden, garage or outhouse belonging to it and occupied with it'.
2 See FLA 1996, s 36.

Nature of the s 33 occupation order

4.57 An occupation order may be either declaratory or regulatory under s 33, and can do any of the following:
(*a*) enforce the applicant's entitlement to remain in occupation as against the respondent;
(*b*) require the respondent to permit the applicant to enter and remain in the dwelling house or part of it;
(*c*) regulate the occupation of the dwelling house by either or both parties;
(*d*) where the respondent has entitlement to occupy the home other than by virtue of matrimonial home rights, prohibit, suspend or restrict the exercise by him/her of his/her rights to occupy the dwelling house;
(*e*) where the respondent has matrimonial home rights in respect of the dwelling house, restrict or terminate those rights;
(*f*) require the respondent to leave the dwelling house or part of it;
(*g*) exclude the respondent from a defined area in which the dwelling house is included.

4.58 The court therefore has great flexibility in terms of the type of declaratory and regulatory orders that can be made and their usefulness to same-sex joint tenants of the rented family home is obvious. This is particularly true given that additional provisions in respect of matters such as maintenance of the property, taking care of furniture and payment of rent, mortgage or other outgoings can be included in a s 33 occupation order (see s 40). These provisions only apply for the duration of the order. On making an occupation order under s 33 or at any time thereafter, the court may:
(*a*) impose on either party obligations as to repair and maintenance of the dwelling house or the discharge of relevant rent or mortgage payments or other outgoings;
(*b*) order a party occupying the dwelling house or part of it (regardless of whether or not they are entitled to occupy the accommodation in their own right) to make periodical payments in respect of the accommodation to the other party, who, but for the order would themselves be legally entitled to occupy the accommodation;
(*c*) grant either party possession or use of furniture or other contents of the dwelling house;
(*d*) order either party to take reasonable care of any furniture or other contents of the dwelling house; and
(*e*) order either party to take reasonable steps to keep the dwelling house, furniture or other contents secure.

4.59 In deciding how the court should exercise its powers under this section, s 40(2) provides that the court should have regard to all the circumstances of the case including:

(a)   the financial needs and financial resources of the parties; and
(b)   the financial obligations which they have or are likely to have in the foreseeable future, including financial obligations to each other and any relevant child.

4.60   Advisers must think through exactly what their client will need to effectively occupy the accommodation or to be compensated for their loss of it. Enquiries must be made of clients to ascertain details of rent and mortgage payments and other outgoings. A priority must be to ensure that these payments continue to be paid either by the occupant or by the excluded partner. The court can however now also make an order for periodical payments of what may be termed an 'occupation rent' to the excluded party.

4.61   As noted above, this order is of great potential use where there is a joint tenancy of a rented family home as it is the only remedy available to curtail the occupation rights of one partner in a same-sex cohabitation relationship. Whether or not the court would be prepared to act in this way depends on the application of the criteria for making an order.

(iii)   Criteria for making a s 33 occupation order

4.62   As with the non-molestation order a violent situation is not a necessary prerequisite to the making of an order. Section 33 (6) sets out the matters to which the court must have regard in considering whether to make an occupation order but these are subject to a 'balance of harm' test introduced in s 33(7). The court is directed to have regard to all the circumstances including:
(a)   the respective housing needs and housing resources of the parties and relevant child;
(b)   the respective financial resources of the parties;
(c)   the likely effect of any order, or of any decision by the court not to exercise its powers to make an order on the health, safety or well-being of the parties and of any relevant child; and
(d)   the conduct of the parties in relation to each other and otherwise.

4.63   However, the application of these standard criteria is subject to s 33(7) which states that if it appears to the court that the applicant or any relevant child is likely to suffer significant harm if an order is not made, then the court shall make the order unless:
(a)   the respondent or any relevant child is likely to suffer significant harm if the order is made; and
(b)   the harm likely to be suffered by the respondent or child in that event is as great or greater than the harm likely to be suffered by the applicant or child if the order is not made.

4.64   This is known as 'the balance of harm test' and it creates a presumption in favour of an order where a child or the applicant is likely to suffer significant harm without one. This can only be avoided where it can be shown that as great or greater harm is likely to be suffered by the respondent or child if an order is not made. Presumably, where the balance of harm is exactly equal, the court is free to choose whether or not the order should be made. The term 'significant harm' is borrowed from CA 1989. 'Harm' is defined in FLA 1996, s 63(1) as meaning ill-treatment or impairment of health and, in the case of a child, development. What is significant may be judged in the context of its effect on the victim and is clearly not confined to physical health. However, once this threshold of significant harm has been reached by an applicant, then the occupation order must be made unless equal or worse significant harm would be suffered by the respondent or relevant child. Depending on where the threshold is placed, this is potentially a welcome shift towards a harm centred approach to the application of this remedy.

4.65   It is still likely to be the case that the court is more likely to grant an occupation order excluding the respondent if the applicant can show that the respondent can easily find other accommodation with a member of his or her family, or has the means to rent other accommodation [1].

1   See *Baggott v Baggott* [1986] 1 FLR 377.

Duration of s 33 orders, ex parte applications and powers of arrest

4.66 Occupation orders under this section may be made for a specified period, or until a specified event or further order (s 33(10)). Although provisionally, both non-molestation and occupation orders are available in all courts, s 59 denies magistrates' courts jurisdiction to hear cases involving determination of a dispute as to beneficial interests or occupation rights in respect of a property. Where there is no dispute, or where it is not necessary to determine the dispute, the magistrates' court does have jurisdiction.

4.67   Section 45 of FLA 1996 now states that both non-molestation and occupation orders may be made ex parte when the court considers it is 'just and convenient to do so'. To determine appropriate cases for exercising this power, the court shall have regard to all the circumstances including:

(*a*)   any risk of significant harm to the applicant or a relevant child if the order is not made immediately (s 45(2)(a));

(*b*)   whether it is likely the applicant will be deterred or prevented from pursuing the application if an order is not made immediately (s 45(2)(b)); and

(*c*)   whether there is reason to believe that the respondent is deliberately evading service and that the applicant or a relevant child will be seriously prejudiced by the delay involved in effecting service of the proceedings in the magistrates' court or effecting substituted service in any other court (s 45(2)(c)).

4.68   Where ex parte orders are made, s 45(3) provides that the respondent must be given an opportunity to make representations relating to the order as soon as just and convenient at a hearing on notice.

4.69   Section 47(2) of FLA 1996 now provides that on making a non-molestation or occupation order, the court shall attach a power of arrest 'where it appears…that the respondent has used or threatened violence against the applicant or a relevant child' unless the court is satisfied in all the circumstances that they will be adequately protected without such a power of arrest. A power of arrest is by far the quickest and most effective method of enforcement of a non-molestation order, enabling a police officer to arrest the respondent without a warrant where there is reasonable cause to suspect that the terms of the order to which the power of arrest has been attached, have been breached (s 47(6)). This presumption in favour of a power of arrest does not however apply to orders made ex parte. In this situation the court has a discretion to attach a power of arrest where the respondent has used or threatened violence to the applicant or relevant child and there is a risk of significant harm to either of them if the power of arrest is not attached immediately (s 18(3)).

4.70   Where no power of arrest has been attached to the order or to that part of it which has been breached, a warrant of arrest supported by evidence on oath may now be applied for at the court which made the relevant order.

4.71   Despite the Law Commission's recognition of the unsatisfactory nature of the previous law as concerned heterosexual cohabitants, former cohabitants and former spouses [1] it has been prepared to leave gay cohabitants, who have no estate or interest in the family home vested in their partner—arguably a very vulnerable group—without an occupation order remedy in relation to their home, even in a violent situation. In addition, an extension through case law of the remedies under the general law of tort to assist non-entitled cohabitants has been effectively quashed by the House of Lords decision in *Hunter v Canary Wharf Ltd; Hunter v London Docklands Development Corp* [2]. This overruled the decision in *Khorosandijan v Bush* [3] insofar as it held that a mere licensee could sue in private nuisance. Despite Lord Cooke delivering a dissenting judgment on the point, saying that for him occupation of the property as a home was an acceptable criterion for entitlement to sue in private nuisance and one which was consistent with international standards, it seems that the usefulness of this remedy in the family context has been greatly reduced for those unable to use the domestic violence legislation, including lesbian and gay non-entitled cohabitants.

1   *Family Homes and Domestic Violence* (Law Com no 207) and see note 2 to para **4.52**.
2   [1997] 2 All ER 426.
3   [1993] 3 All ER 669, CA.

2   The rented family home, relationship breakdown and succession

4.72   As noted above, the position of same-sex cohabitants on both relationship breakdown and death is often very unsatisfactory. In some situations, there is no legal remedy available as same-sex cohabitants are not consistently recognised as a family unit and are denied the remedies which have been extended to heterosexual cohabitants.

(i)   Relationship breakdown and rented tenancies

4.73   On relationship breakdown, only heterosexual cohabitants are able to apply for transfer of the tenancy of the family home under Sch 7 to FLA 1996. Same-sex cohabitants are left in the unenviable position of having to reach agreement, subject to the restrictions of landlord and tenant law. Alternatively, particularly where there is a joint tenancy, they may have to deal with the consequences of complete stalemate where no legal remedy is available unless a court can be persuaded in the circumstances to grant a s 33 occupation order. There is also the risk in the cases of joint secure or assured periodic tenancies that the partner who wishes to leave and be relieved of the joint and several obligation to pay rent will give the landlord notice to quit. This will be effective to bring the whole tenancy to an end regardless of the other partner's wish to remain in the home [1]. Again, the only possibility here is for the remaining partner to apply for a s 33 occupation order which can adjust the occupation rights and declare the rent liability as between the parties. Even where agreement is reached, given that most tenancies now are not capable of assignment, the landlord's consent may well be needed and may not be forthcoming, particularly in the case of a sole tenancy, whether in the private or social rented sector. Thus the nature of the tenure under which the tenancy is held may mean it is not possible to put the agreement into effect by assigning the tenancy, without jeapordising the tenancy itself [2].

1   *Hammersmith and Fulham London Borough Council v Monk* [1992] 1 AC 478.
2   For a full discussion of these issues see Barlow *Cohabitants and the Law* pp 239–247.

(ii)   Succession to tenancies on death

4.74   Where cohabitants are joint tenants, the survivor will automatically succeed to the tenancy on the death of his or her partner. From this perspective, it is best for same-sex cohabitants to take out or if possible have their tenancy put into joint names. However, this will be subject to the consent of the landlord, which may well not be forthcoming. Where only one cohabitant is the tenant of the family home, it is now clear that whatever the nature of the tenancy, their non-tenant partner will not be able to succeed to the tenancy on the tenant's death, no matter how long they have lived together in the family home. The position concerning secure public sector tenancies has been clear for some time. In *Harrogate Borough Council v Simpson* [1] the Court of Appeal found that a surviving partner of lesbian cohabitants of long-standing, whose family home was vested in the name of the deceased partner, could not be said to have lived together in their home 'as her husband or wife', as the essential ingredients of this involved a man and a woman living in the same household. Consequently, although a heterosexual cohabitant who had lived together with their partner for 12 months prior to the tenant's death could have done, she, as a same-sex cohabitant, could not succeed to the council tenancy under the Housing Act 1985, s 87. A subsequent complaint to the European Commission on Human Rights on the facts of this case alleging breach of art 8 of the Convention, was also rejected [2].

1   [1986] 2 FLR 91.
2   See Application no 11716/85: *S v United Kingdom* (unreported).

4.75   In the case of assured periodic tenancies, statutory succession to the tenancy is limited to spouses and no other members of a family are entitled to succeed. Spouses in this context are however defined to include those 'living with the tenant as his or her wife or husband' [1]. Yet this wording effectively ensures in the light of the *Harrogate* decision that same-sex cohabitants are excluded from the ambit of this provision.

1   See Housing Act 1988, s 17(4).

4.76   The position with regard to Rent Act tenancies was not, however, so clear cut. Since the decision in *Fitzpatrick v Sterling Housing Association* [1] it is though now clear that same-sex cohabitants are also denied succession rights in this context. This case involved two gay men who had lived together for 18 years before the death in 1994 of Mr Thompson who was the tenant of their home and who for the last eight year of his life was a tetraplegic requiring constant nursing care. His partner, Mr Fitzpatrick, had for these eight years nursed him at home and in the words of Waite LJ 'dedicated himself to providing, with love and devotion, the constant care which he [Mr Thompson] required.[2]' The family home was owned by a charitable landlord but the tenancy was governed by the Rent Acts. On Mr Thompson's death, Mr Fitzpatrick claimed the right to succeed to the tenancy. The first issue the court had to consider was whether Mr Fitzpatrick was entitled to succeed to the tenancy under the Rent Act 1977, Sch 1, para 2(2) because he was 'living with the tenant as his/her husband or wife'. The majority of the court here felt bound to follow the *Harrogate* decision given the proximity of the wording in the two statutes and accordingly rejected this claim on the ground that the phrase applied to heterosexual couples only. The court then went on to consider the alternative claim that there was a right to succeed to the tenancy on the ground that Mr Fitzpatrick was a member of the tenant's family within the meaning of the Rent Act 1977, Sch 1, para 3(1) who had lived with him for at least two years. The majority again rejected this contention, distinguishing between those who live together as a family who are not entitled to succeed to a tenancy unless they are heterosexual cohabitants who have been specifically provided for in the statute, from those who are members of a family through kinship or marriage who are so entitled.

1   [1998] 1 FLR 43.
2   [1998] 1 FLR at p 7G.

4.77   Interestingly, however, there was a powerful dissenting judgment by Ward LJ in which he indicated that he would have reached the opposite conclusion to each of the questions posed. Given the changing political climate and the awaited direct incorporation of the European Convention on Human Rights into our law which is likely to enable the courts to look again at this issue, careful consideration of the dissenting judgment is merited. Ward LJ's approach to the statutory interpretation of the Rent Act reflected the fact that it is an Act which is 'always speaking' and so should be given a construction that continuously updates its wording to allow for changes to family structures since the Act was initially framed [1]:

> 'Since families are dynamic, the statutory interpretation must equally reflect the motive forces, physical or moral, affecting behaviour and change in domestic organisation.'[2]

1   [1998] 1 FLR 6 at p 26C
2   [1998] 1 FLR 6 at p 38B.

4.78   Reviewing the case law under the Act, which had in the past extended the boundaries of the types of family to which the Act could apply [1], he found that there was essentially no difference between a homosexual and a heterosexual couple which both bore some of the same hallmarks of a married relationship in terms of their function of providing love, nurturing, fidelity, durability, emotional and economic interdependence [2]. Accordingly he found that Mr Fitzpatrick had lived with the deceased as his husband or wife. In considering if he could in any event fall within the definition of a member of the deceased's family, he preferred to look at function of the familial nexus rather than its structure and components. On this test there was clearly a recognisable family, a view which he felt was strengthened by the fact that this was how the couple had considered themselves and would have been considered by others. He went on to state:

'I am satisfied that the ordinary man is liberated enough to accept in 1997 or even in 1994 looking broadly at the appellant's life and comparing it with other rich patterns of family life he knows, that the bond between the appellant and the deceased was de facto familial.'[3]

In concluding his judgment, he clearly endorses the need for change in the law:

'As the Master of the Rolls, Sir Thomas Bingham said in *R v Ministry of Defence, ex p Smith*[4]: "A belief which represented unquestioned orthodoxy in year X may have become questionable by year Y and unsustainable by year Z." I have come to the conclusion that *Harrogate Borough Council v Simpson* was decided in year X; my Lords, for reasons with which I could well have agreed, believe us to be in year Y; whereas I have been persuaded that the discrimination would be thought by the broad mass of the people to be so unsustainable that this must by now be year Z. To conclude otherwise would be to stand like King Canute, ordering the tide to recede when the tide in favour of equality rolls relentlessly forward and shows no sign of ebbing.'[5]

1   See for example *Dyson Holdings v Fox* [1976] QB 503 which, before the expansion of the definition of 'spouse' by the Housing Act 1988 to include cohabitants, accepted that a heterosexual cohabitation relationship constituted a family for the purposes of Rent Act succession. This was followed (reluctantly) in *Helby v Rafferty* [1979] 1 WLR 13.
2   [1998] 1 FLR 6 at p 39H.
3   [1998] 1 FLR 6 at p 41D–E.
4   [1996] QB 517 at p 554C.
5   [1998] 1 FLR 6 at p 42B–C.

4.79   The current legal position regarding the inability of same-sex cohabitants to succeed to the tenancy of a rented family home is highly unsatisfactory and results in grave injustice to lesbian and gay couples. Since the decision in *Fitzpatrick*, the government has issued guidance to local authorities advising them to treat same-sex cohabitants in the same way as heterosexual cohabitants in relation to tenancy succession. However, this is in no way binding and in any event has no effect on private or housing association tenancies, unless they themselves have chosen to adopt a similar policy. Both the Law Commission in their review of the rights of 'homesharers' and the Department of Environment, Transport and the Regions are reportedly considering the possibility of legislation [1]. It is to be hoped, therefore, that reform of the law to at least bring the rights of same-sex cohabitants in line with the position of heterosexual cohabitants both in the context of succession and on relationship breakdown will be enacted sooner rather than later.

1   Communicated to the solicitor of Mr Fitzpatrick, the appellant, in correspondence between October 1997 and April 1998, referred to in Current Developments [1998] JSWFL vol 20 no 3 pp 320–22.

3   The owner-occupied family home on relationship breakdown

4.80   The legal position on relationship breakdown of gay and lesbian cohabitants whose family home has been purchased by one or both of them is, together with the rights of other 'homesharers', currently under scrutiny by the Law Commission. Their long awaited report on the reform of the law relating to shared ownership of property is not now likely to be published until at least the spring of 1999. Until it is and any recommendations it makes following the consultation process are acted upon by Parliament, resolution of disputes between same-sex cohabitant co-owners on relationship breakdown remains very much a matter of property law rather than family law.

4.81 There have, however, been significant recent reforms to the law of property as well as developments in the case law which affect how the courts deal with disputes relating to the owner-occupied family home arising between cohabitants on relationship breakdown. In particular the Trusts of Land and Appointment of Trustees Act 1996 [1] has abolished settled land for the future and effectively existing and future, express and implied trusts for sale as well. Both categories have been replaced by the new 'trust of land', itself modelled on the old-style trust for sale. The fiction of the doctrine of conversion has also been abolished (s 3) and co-owners have been given new powers as trustees (ss 6, 7) and rights of occupation (s 12). The remedy previously used by co-owners to resolve ownership disputes relating to the family home was Law of Property Act 1925, s 30 which gave the courts jurisdiction to order the immediate or postponed sale of beneficially jointly owned land held under a trust for sale. This has been repealed and replaced by TLATA 1996, s 14 which gives the court wider powers than to order or not order sale. Any trustee or beneficiary under a trust of land or any secured creditor of a beneficiary may apply to the court under s 14 for any such order as the court thinks fit relating to the exercise by the trustees of any of their functions or for a declaration as to the nature or extent of a person's interest in the property subject to the trust. This obviously gives the court a broader range of options for resolving disputes. Section 15 directs the court to statutory criteria relevant to determining applications. It has also made clear that where a beneficial interest under a trust, including a resulting or constructive trust can be shown, then TLATA 1996, s 12 now gives a right of occupation, as opposed to a mere interest in the proceeds of sale as was the case under the old law. Although TLATA 1996, s 13 gives trustees the new right to restrict occupation by a beneficiary, these powers may not be exercised to oust any beneficiary already in occupation by virtue of s 12 or otherwise. Where an informal trust has arisen between same-sex cohabitants in relation to the family home occupied by them both therefore, the non-owning cohabitant will have both a right of occupation and protection from being excluded by use of the s 13 power. In practice, where there is a beneficial interest of a party who is not a legal owner and who is no longer in occupation and the land is unregistered, it is usually advisable to issue proceedings under Trustee Act 1925, s 41 for the appointment of another trustee if the legal owner refuses to do so. Proceedings under TLATA 1996, s14 can then follow if appropriate as this is now the mechanism for resolving disputes about the extent of a cohabitant's beneficial interest, either because they are not a legal owner or because no express trust was declared at the point of acquisition. The court has far wider powers on such applications than was the case under LPA 1925, s 30. It is still possible to apply for an order for sale, where this cannot be agreed and the new powers are also wide enough to include an order preventing sale or exercise of other powers by trustees. In addition orders that a beneficiary occupying the property pay an occupation rent to a beneficiary out of occupation are within the court's powers, in contrast to the position under the old law.

1   The Act came into force on 1 January 1997 and has acted upon the reforms put forward by the Law Commission in their report *Transfer of Land: Trusts of Land* (Law Com no 181 (1989)).

4.82   In making orders under s 14 (other than where the application is made by a trustee in bankruptcy, which is governed by the Insolvency Act 1986, s 335A), the court must have regard to the matters set out in s15, which may be summarised as:

(*a*)   the intentions of the person(s) who created the trust;

(*b*)   the purposes for which the property subject to the trust is held;

(*c*)   the welfare of any minor who occupies or might reasonably be expected to occupy the property as their home; and

(*d*)   the interests of any secured creditor of any beneficiary.

4.83   It is, however, clear from the wording of the section that this list is not exhaustive and other relevant factors may be taken into account, where appropriate. The introduction of these criteria, although broadly reflecting the case law developed under LPA 1925, s 30 to discover the 'collateral purpose' of the trust, can be seen to be particularly helpful in the family law context. Furthermore, the specified criteria which include the intentions of those creating the trust and the original purpose of the trust, which may often be to provide a family home, as well as an express direction to consider the welfare of any minor child who resides or may in the future reside in the property, arguably provide greater opportunity for a family law based approach to prevail. Nevertheless, there is no guidance on the relative priority that the court is to give to these factors.

4.84   Wherever s 14 proceedings are issued, a caution or landcharge on the basis of a pending land action should immediately be lodged; this will give any purchaser of the home actual notice of the non-owner's beneficial interest. This is particularly important in the case of unregistered land. Where the land is registered a beneficial interest can be protected as a minor interest by way of caution, restriction or notice and this should be done without delay where the non-legal owner is no longer in actual occupation of the home. Where they are, they will have an overriding interest which will bind a purchaser but which cannot of itself be protected by caution, restriction or notice [1].

1   See *Williams & Glyn's Bank v Boland* [1981] AC 487.

4.85   Although the statutory basis for resolving disputes has changed, the determination of beneficial ownership of property is still governed by the law of trusts. Thus, although the court may have greater discretion as to what remedy to offer and can, for example, postpone sale but order that an excluded co-owner be paid an occupation rent by an occupying co-owner. However, determination of their respective beneficial interests is still governed by the doctrines of express, implied, constructive and resulting trusts.

4.86   The starting point for any adviser is to see whether the legal title of the home is vested in the joint names of the cohabitants or just the sole name of one of them. Once this is established, it is necessary to see whether there is any express declaration of trust or cohabitation agreement setting out the beneficial interests of each cohabitant in the home. If so, this would normally be conclusive. If there is a beneficial joint tenancy, consideration should be given to severing the joint tenancy and the need to revise any will that has been made. If there is no documentation relating to beneficial ownership and there is a dispute as to the parties' respective interests in the home, the adviser then needs to consider whether an implied, resulting or constructive trust has come into existence.

(i)   Express trusts

4.87   Where there is an express declaration of trust setting out the interests of each of the parties and declared in proper form in accordance with the requirements of LPA 1925, s 53(1)(b), this will be conclusive in the absence of fraud or mistake. If it was induced by fraud, it will be set aside. If it is as a result of a mistake which means it does not reflect the parties' true intentions, then rectification can be sought, although this will not be granted if it would prejudice a bona fide purchaser for value [1].

1   See *City of London Building Society v Flegg* [1988] AC 54.

4.88   Where a cohabitation agreement or declaration in the form of a trust has been made by same-sex cohabitants, then their shares will be determined in accordance with this document. Where there are fixed shares, these will be determined as a proportion of the current market value of the property, subject to the mortgage liability of each party as set out in the documentation. Where the declaration reveals 'floating' shares, advisers need to ensure that either there is clear agreement as to what the crystallised shares are, or that all relevant receipts are carefully scrutinised to determine the shares at the date of sale or transfer, see Appendix II.

4.89   Even if the agreement does not comply with the formal requirements of a declaration of trust, any written agreement will be evidence of the parties' intentions at the date of acquisition and may be useful were a party to attempt to show a common intention as to the beneficial ownership of the property by virtue of an implied, resulting or constructive trust.

4.90   If there is no express declaration, a resulting or constructive trust [1] may yet be discovered to have come into existence with respect to the family home. In neither case is there a need for written evidence of the intention to share beneficial ownership. But in each there must be some evidence that the non-legal owner has acquired a beneficial interest in the property.

1   Although the statute refers to an implied trust there do not appear to be any specific rules that segregate an implied trust from either a resulting or a constructive trust. Both of the latter seem to be instances of the former. See Barlow *Cohabitants and the Law* p 263.

(ii)   Resulting trusts

4.91   The resulting trust is the simpler of the two. It comes into effect when two parties have contributed directly to the acquisition of property [1]. The fact of their contribution gives rise to a presumption of an intention to share beneficial ownership of the property [2] and in the absence of any agreement to the contrary the proportion in which they share is determined by their contributions to its acquisition.

1   *Midland Bank v Cooke* [1995] 4 All ER 562, CA.
2   This is a presumption that may be rebutted by proof that the contribution was intended as a loan, a gift or rent. See *Sekhon v Alissa* [1989] 2 FLR 94, ChD and *Richards v Dove* [1974] 1 All ER 888, ChD.

4.92   The non-legal owner's contribution must be in money or money's worth and should relate directly to the purchase of the property [1]. The legal owner then holds the property in trust in shares relative to the respective contributions.

Equity presumes that, where two parties contribute to the purchase, they intend to share the property beneficially in proportion to their contributions. Where these are made in money the valuation of the respective shares is simple. Thus, in *Tinsley v Milligan* [2] resulting trust principles were applied to the shares of a house jointly paid for by a lesbian couple but placed in the sole name of only one of them. The House of Lords held that each was entitled to a share of the equity proportionate to her direct contribution to the purchase price by virtue of the presumed resulting trust [3].

1   See, for example, *Springette v Defoe* [1992] 2 FLR 388.
2   [1994] 1 AC 340.
3   Indeed, the 'non-owner' was not even disqualified from this equitable remedy by the illegality of the couple's motive for disguising her ownership. They intended to enable Ms Milligan to claim means-tested welfare benefit to which she would not have been entitled as the owner of property.

4.93   The fact that the contributions combine money and money's worth need not make the division of beneficial ownership any more difficult. In *Springette v Defoe* [1] the courts held that a woman's share in a council house, which she had bought with her partner, was based on her contribution to its acquisition which included her right to buy discount, as well as her capital contribution and her share in the mortgage liability. The couple were allocated their respective shares in the property on the basis of their respective broad financial contributions to its purchase [2].

1   [1992] 2 FLR 388, CA.
2   See too *Evans v Hayward* [1995] 2 FCR 313, where the court held that the council house discount was to be applied as a direct contribution by the person in whose favour it operated.

4.94   However, the approach of the courts has sometimes been ambivalent in the context of contributions made in money's worth (either alone, or combined with small monetary contributions) which has led to a blurring of the distinction between resulting and constructive trusts as developed below [1].

1   See *Cooke v Head* [1972] 1 WLR 518, CA at 520F and more recently, *Drake v Whipp* [1996] 1 FLR 826, CA; *Midland Bank v Cooke* [1995] 2 FLR 915, CA. The confusion stems from statements made in *Gissing v Gissing* [1971] AC 886, see Lord Diplock pp 904–5. In *Lloyds Bank v Rosset* [1991] 1 AC 107, HL at 133A Lord Bridge purported to remove the possibility of creating a constructive trust by virtue of indirect contributions. See para **4.100**.

(iii)   Constructive trusts

4.95   The common intention constructive trust [1] is regarded as more problematic than the resulting trust. In the law of England and Wales it comes into effect when two parties have reached a common intention to share the beneficial ownership of property. Here there is no necessary contribution which gives rise to a presumption of intention (as there is in the case of resulting trusts). However, establishing a common intention [2] will only be the first stage in identifying a constructive trust. Further elements are then required. Only once the non-legal owner, relying on the common intention, acts in a way which is to her detriment, can a beneficial interest be established. The court must then go on to quantify the non-legal owner's share of the equity.

1   Invented in *Gissing v Gissing* [1971] AC 886.
2   Express agreement is evidence of constructive trust: *Eves v Eves* [1975] 3 All ER 768.

4.96   In *Grant v Edwards* [1] Mustill LJ clearly sets out the four possible situations in which a common intention to establish a constructive trust will be discovered by a court:

> '(*a*)   An express bargain whereby the proprietor promises the claimant an interest in the property in return for an explicit undertaking of the claimant to act in a certain way.
>
> (*b*)   An express but incomplete bargain whereby the proprietor promises the claimant an interest in the property, on the basis that the claimant will do something in return. The parties do not themselves make explicit what the claimant is to do. The court therefore has to complete the bargain for them by means of implication, when it comes to decide whether the proprietor's promise has been matched by conduct falling within whatever undertaking the claimant must be taken to have given sub silento.
>
> (*c*)   An explicit promise by the proprietor that the claimant will have an interest in the property unaccompanied by any express or tacit agreement as to a quid pro quo.
>
> (*d*)   A common intention not made explicit to the effect that the claimant will have an interest in the property, if she subsequently acts in a particular way.'

1   [1986] Ch 638 at p 652.

Express common intention

4.97   Where property was registered in the name of one cohabitant because of a deception perpetrated on the other, the court found in *Grant v Edwards* that, despite the lack of mutuality, a common intention could be inferred (under para **4.96**(*c*)) due to her reliance on his representation. In this case the property was registered in the name of a cohabitant. Here the cohabitant had told his partner that the reason the property was not bought in their joint names was to avoid complications in relation to her ongoing matrimonial proceedings. The court held that this ostensible reason raised the clear inference of a common intention that the woman should have an interest in the house.

4.98   *Lloyds Bank plc v Rosset* [1] seemed to compress all of Mustill LJ's categories which referred to an express promise or bargain (ie (*a*), (*b*) and (*c*)). In that case Lord Bridge, finding that there was no common intention to share beneficial ownership, said of an express common intention based on express discussions between the parties, that:

> 'it will only be necessary for the partner asserting a claim to a beneficial interest against the partner entitled to the legal estate to show that he or she acted to his or her detriment or significantly altered his or her position in reliance on the *agreement* in order to give rise to a constructive trust or proprietary estoppel' [emphasis added] [2].

1   [1991] 1 AC 107, HL.
2   [1991] 1 AC 107 at p 132.

4.99   More recently the courts have had to transmute the requirement of 'agreement' in this judgment to do equity between the parties. Waite J in

H v M (property: beneficial interest) [1], returning to Mustill LJ's more flexible approach, expanded the requirement of 'agreement' to include evidence of 'discussions leading to any agreement, arrangement *or understanding* that the property [was] to be shared beneficially' (emphasis added) [2]. Thus, where a cohabitant had used a dishonest excuse to justify his refusal to register his partner as the joint owner of property—tax problems in this case—an inference of common intention could be drawn, despite the fact that there was clearly never a *common* intention to share.

1   [1992] 1 FLR 229.
2   [1992] 1 FLR 229 at p 239B.

Inferred common intention

4.100   Where there is no express indication of a common intention to share beneficial ownership the court must 'divine' one from the facts of the case. The court will look to the circumstances of the home sharers and may infer a common intention to share beneficial ownership [1]. However, the courts will no longer infer a common intention lightly. In *Burns v Burns* [2] the court refused to acknowledge that raising children and caring for the home, in a 19-year heterosexual cohabitation relationship, could have given rise to an inferred common intention to share beneficial ownership of the home [3]. *Lloyds Bank v Rosset* [4] made the restrictions on inferring a common intention explicit. Where the matrimonial home was purchased in the husband's sole name because of the terms of the trust from which he funded the purchase but his wife (who was an interior designer) worked extremely hard to renovate it, no common intention that she should have a beneficial interest in the property was found [5]. In limiting the facts from which a common intention could be inferred, Lord Bridge said that:

> 'direct contributions to the purchase price by the partner who is not the legal owner, whether initially or by payment of mortgage instalments, will readily justify the inference necessary to the creation of a constructive trust. But as I read the authorities, it is at least extremely doubtful whether anything less will do.' [6]

1   See Mustill LJ in *Grant v Edwards* [1986] Ch 638 at p 652 and see para **4.96**.
2   [1984] Ch 317.
3   The contribution to the welfare of the family was not considered to be a contribution to the 'home' even in 'money's worth'.
4   [1991] 1 AC 107.
5   Cf *Cooke v Head* [1972] 2 All ER 38.
6   [1991] 1 AC 107 at p 133A.

4.101   This strict approach to inferring common intention is still good law [1]. Thus, until *McHardy v Warren* [2] and *Midland Bank plc v Cooke* [3] it seemed that the only way to infer a common intention constructive trust was to find—if necessary creatively—an express agreement [4]. In *McHardy v Warren*, instead of treating a direct contribution to the purchase price as giving rise to a resulting trust, the court inferred a common intention constructive trust, allowing the parties to hold the beneficial interest in shares other than those indicated by their direct contributions. Here the parents' wedding gift to their son and daughter-in-law was the deposit on their matrimonial home which was registered in his sole name. There was no express agreement as to beneficial ownership. Principles of resulting trust could, therefore, have prevailed, which would, in the circumstances of this case, have given the wife a small beneficial interest in the home. However, Dillon LJ, in the Court of Appeal, said:

> 'To my mind it is the irresistible conclusion that where a parent pays the deposit ... on the purchase of their first matrimonial home, it is the intention of all three of them that the bride and groom should have equal interests in the matrimonial home, not interests measured by reference to the percentage half the deposit [bears] to the full price, certainly not an intention that the wife should have no interest at all because the property was put into the sole name of the husband.'[5]

1   See, for example, *Ivin v Blake* [1995] 1 FLR 70 where a daughter failed to establish a direct contribution to the home she shared with her mother, despite having worked in her mother's pub for nothing in order to save the business and to enable the purchase of the home.
2   [1994] 2 FLR 338.
3   [1995] 2 FLR 915.
4   See *H v M (property: beneficial interest)* [1992] 1 FLR 229; *Savill v Goodall* [1993] 1 FLR 755, CA and *Stokes v Anderson* [1991] 1 FLR 391.
5   At p 340F.

4.102   This case confuses the source of the common intention to share beneficial ownership. Even though there was nothing to rebut the presumption that a resulting trust should arise, the court applied constructive trust principles of quantification of the beneficial interests rather than resulting trust principles.

4.103   After *Rosset* it seemed that only two alternatives sources were available to found a constructive trust. One was the direct contribution to the purchase price and the other was an express agreement to share beneficial ownership. Only in the latter instance was quantification of the respective shares determined by reference to 'all payments made and *acts done by the claimant*' [emphasis added][1] which were treated as:

> 'illuminating the common intention as to the extent of the beneficial interest. Once you get to that stage, as Lord Diplock [2] recognised, there is no practicable alternative to the determination of a fair share. The court must supply the common intention by reference to that which *all the material circumstances* have shown to be fair' [emphasis added][3].

1   *Stokes v Anderson* [1991] 1 FLR 391 at p 400B, per Nourse LJ.
2   *Gissing v Gissing* [1971] AC 886 at p 909D.
3   *Stokes v Anderson* [1991] 1 FLR 391 at p 400B, per Nourse LJ.

4.104   Where there was a direct contribution to the purchase price and no express agreement, only the parties' respective contributions—under principles of resulting trust—seemed capable of affecting the shares in which beneficial ownership was held. In *Springette v Defoe* Dillon LJ made it clear that alternative sharing could be based on nothing less than clear agreement between the parties:

> 'the common intention of the parties must, in my judgment, mean a shared intention communicated between them. It cannot mean an intention which each happened to have in his or her own mind but had never communicated to the other. '[1]

1   [1992] 2 FLR 388 at p 393E.

4.105   What *McHardy v Warren* [1] achieved was the ability of the courts to find a common intention to share by virtue of a direct contribution but to avoid the restrictive effects of a resulting trust on the quantification of shares.

1   [1994] 2 FLR 338.

4.106   *Midland Bank plc v Cooke* [1] endorses this approach. It also, however, undermines any attempt to retain a clear distinction between resulting and constructive trusts. In that case, Mrs Cooke's only contribution to the purchase of the property was her half share of a wedding gift, which was used as part of the deposit on the property (amounting to less than a 7% share of the purchase price). She had, however, made significant contributions to household expenditure and carried out minor decorative improvements. The court held that it could infer an intention to share beneficial ownership from her direct contribution to the purchase of property. But the extent of her share was not necessarily to be determined by the traditional resulting trust principles. Rather, as Waite LJ indicated, the courts would

'undertake a survey of the whole course of dealing between the parties relevant to their ownership and occupation of the property and their sharing of its burdens and advantages. That scrutiny will not confine itself to the limited range of acts of direct contribution of the sort that are needed to found a beneficial interest in the first place. It will take into consideration all conduct which throws light on the question what shares are intended.' [2]

1   [1995] 2 FLR 915.
2   [1995] 2 FLR 915 at p 926G.

4.107   The court went on to find that despite express evidence from Mr and Mrs Cooke that at the time of the purchase there had been no discussion as to how the property was to be owned beneficially, there was an inferred agreement that the beneficial interests should be shared equally. Effectively, the court was prepared to impute an agreement as to quantification of the parties' shares, where there was none, by taking account of the parties' dealings with each other as a whole. It distinguished the approach to quantification in *Springette v Defoe* on the facts. That case involved a middle-aged cohabiting couple whose dealings were, in their view, more akin to commercial partnership. In the absence of any communicated intention to share in a way other than in proportion to their shares of the purchase price, the court was not prepared to look behind the parties' direct contributions. Simple resulting trust principles applied.

4.108   *Midland Bank v Cooke* was followed in *Drake v Whipp* [1]. In that case cohabitants purchased a barn in the sole name of the man with a view to converting it into a shared residence. No declaration of trust was made, but Ms Drake contributed almost 20% of the original purchase price and conversion costs. Mr Whip contributed the balance. They each also contributed their labour in the proportions 70% to Mr Whip and 30% to Ms Drake. She provided all food and household expenditure out of her salary. Four years later, when the relationship ended, Ms Drake sought a declaration as to their respective beneficial interests. At first instance, resulting trust principles applied and she was found to be entitled to a share of almost 20%. On appeal, however, this was increased to one third. The court held that the trust had been incorrectly characterised as a resulting trust and was, rather, a constructive trust. Once the existence of a constructive trust was established, the broad-brush approach to quantum of the shares with reference to the parties' whole course of conduct could be adopted. In this case, their intention to set up a joint home, their labour contributions, the existence and financing of a joint bank account and Ms Drake's contributions to household expenses and housekeeping were taken into account and her share was assessed at one third.

1   [1996] 1 FLR 826.

4.109   These two cases have extended the principles relating to the quantification of beneficial shares in property. The discretion the courts had adopted in cases where express agreement to share the property had been found (but not in which proportions the sharing would take place) was extended to cases where the common intention to share was found in the direct contributions of the parties to the acquisition of property. Outcomes like the one in *Springette v Defoe* are no longer necessary. Courts can look to much wider circumstances than just the contributions of the parties to the purchase price.

4.110   There is, therefore, a two-stage approach adopted in the case of constructive trusts. The courts find the common intention to share beneficial ownership (either in express agreement or in direct contributions to the purchase of property) and then go on to establish what shares each is entitled to. This is determined on the basis of further evidence as to their common intention concerning the extent of their sharing. Here their contributions more generally to the relationships are relevant considerations.

4.111   Although the ability to gain some credit for what can broadly be termed contributions to the welfare of the family through domestic labour is to welcomed on one level, the new approach to quantification throws up some practical difficulties. Why, for instance, was Mrs Cooke awarded a half-share, whereas Ms Drake's share was limited to one-third? Ms Drake's direct financial contribution was far greater than that of Mrs Cooke and her labour contribution to the barn conversion was not negligible. This coupled with her payment of household bills and undertaking of domestic work could arguably have resulted in her being awarded a larger share. Unfortunately, the method of calculation is not clear. Reform of the law in this area is keenly awaited and a comprehensive checklist of factors to be weighed in the equation in such cases would hopefully provide greater clarity and consistency in approach. Pending legislative reform, we are left with an unsatisfactory two-stage and two-tier approach to the establishment and determination of beneficial interests under a constructive trust.

4.112   In the first stage, in the absence of express discussions, the court will only impute a common intention to share beneficial ownership from direct or indirect financial contributions followed by acts of detriment referable to the common intention in accordance with *Rosset* [1]. The degree of detriment seems to be greater for those relying upon indirect financial contributions than for those relying upon express discussions or direct financial contributions, so that contributions to the welfare of the family will not suffice as detriment in the former category but will in the latter categories, providing two tiers within the first stage. Such contributions to welfare of the family alone are certainly not in the first stage regarded as evidence of a common intention to share the property beneficially and are not even universally accepted as evidence of detriment. Thus recent developments in the case law have not helped the cohabitant in the *Burns v Burns* [2] situation.

1   [1991] 1 AC 107, HL.
2   [1984] Ch 317.

4.113   Yet in the second stage, once through the narrow gateway, having established common intention, providing there is no express agreement as to the proportion of the beneficial interests, the court looks at the whole course of dealings between the parties and may impute an agreement from this as to their respective beneficial interests. Here, contributions to the welfare of the family assume far greater significance and can greatly enhance a cohabitant's share beyond that which would be presumed on resulting trust principles, as seen in *Cooke*. Yet why should such contributions be valid evidence of an imputed common intention as to the size of a couple's shares in the second stage but not of their intention to share beneficially in the first? The distinction seems artificial, certainly in terms of its effect. For it widens the gulf between those who are arguably deserving, such as Mrs Burns, yet fail to get through the gateway to the second stage, receiving nothing; and those, such as Mrs Cooke, who by virtue of an imputed, small but direct financial contribution pass through the gateway and are then deemed to have evidenced by conduct very similar to that exhibited by Mrs Burns, an agreement that she owned a half-share in the family home.

4.114   From an adviser's perspective, therefore, this area of law is a minefield. The courts, whilst having rejected an unjust enrichment approach adopted elsewhere [1], have still been prepared to intervene on a more ad hoc basis to remedy the difficulties which the application of strict property law to family situations often engenders.

1   As in Australia and Canada. See note 6 to para **4.02**.

4.115   Another area of law which has been used in this way is the doctrine of proprietary estoppel which offers another mechanism under which a beneficial interest in property can be established by a non-legal owner. However, this too gives the court a wide discretion and does not provide outcomes that are any more certain.

(iv)   Proprietary estoppel

4.116   The conventional distinction between this doctrine and that of the constructive trust revolves around the concurrence of view of the parties to the property relationship [1]. The common intention constructive trust requires a bilateral understanding or agreement that if the non-owner acts in a particular and detrimental way, they will obtain an agreed or, failing that, a fair share in the family home. Proprietary estoppel, on the other hand, requires only unilateral conduct by the legal owner which leads the partner to believe that they have an equitable interest in the home. If the partner then acts to their detriment in reliance upon that conduct it becomes unconscionable for the legal owner to insist upon his legal rights in the property. For that reason the court will intervene to prevent the unconscionable conduct from affecting the non-owner detrimentally.

1   There is a considerable degree of overlap and confusion between the doctrines of proprietary estoppel and constructive trusts. In *Grant v Edwards* [1986] Ch 638

Browne Wilkinson V-C remarked that, in constructive trust cases, useful guidance might be obtained from the principles underlying the law of proprietary estoppel which are closely akin to the constructive trust approach laid down in *Gissing v Gissing* [1971] AC 886. David Hayton 'Equitable Rights of Cohabitees' (1990) 54 The Conveyancer 370. But see Browne Wilkinson 'Constructive Trusts and Unjust Enrichment' [1996] 10 *Trust Law International* 98 (who argues that 'common intention' constructive trusts were invented in *Gissing v Gissing* and were a confusion of the principles underlying traditional resulting and constructive trusts).

4.117   From a practical perspective, the problem with relying on proprietary estoppel is that outcomes remain substantially unpredictable. In *Pascoe v Turner* [1] a claim for proprietary estoppel succeeded where a woman, relying on an ex-partner's assurance that 'the house and everything in it is yours', spent a large portion of her capital on the property. The court decided that awarding her a licence to retain possession of the home would be insufficient to satisfy the equities and, therefore, perfected the gift by transferring the home to her. However, in *Greasley v Cooke* [2] although a proprietary estoppel was established, it was held to be sufficient to give rise only to a right to occupy the property rent free for life.

1   [1979] 1 WLR 431, CA.
2   [1980] 1 WLR 1306.

4.118   In the company of these decisions, *Coombes v Smith* [1] becomes entirely surprising. Here a woman who found herself pregnant by her lover, left her husband and job to move into a home owned by the lover, but in which he did not live. He assured her, however, that he would always look after her. When he decided to evict her from the property her claim to proprietary estoppel failed. The court was not satisfied that the assurance had led her to believe she would acquire an interest in the property. Nor had she, it found, acted to her detriment by leaving her husband and job and having the child.

1   [1987] 1 FLR 352.

4.119   Yet a more generous approach was adopted in *Wayling v Jones* [1]. Same-sex cohabitants had lived together for some sixteen years when Mr Jones died. Wayling assisted Jones by helping him in his hotel and other business ventures. He received no salary but was promised he would inherit the hotel. By the time of his death the hotel specified in the will was not the hotel currently run by the couple. Wayling's proprietary estoppel claim succeeded and he was awarded the proceeds of the sale of the hotel. The court held that the promises relied on did not have to be the sole inducement for Wayling's conduct. Once it had been established that promises had been made and there was detrimental conduct from which inducement could be inferred, the burden shifted to the defendant to prove that the plaintiff had not relied on the promises. Despite conflicting evidence the court was not prepared to find that the defendant had satisfied the burden of proof.

1   [1995] 2 FLR 1029 following *Re Basham* [1987] 2 FLR 264.

4.120   From this survey of the cases it is evident that proprietary estoppel is also an unreliable and uncertain remedy for homesharers in dispute, but one which advisers need still to have in mind.

Quantification of shares and equitable accounting

4.121   Once the size of the couple's respective beneficial interests in the home has been established, it is still necessary to precisely quantify the shares. It should first be noted that the date for quantifying the shares is the date of sale (or transfer, where one co-owner agrees to buy out the other's share) and not the date of separation [1]. It is also usually necessary to make any appropriate adjustments in respect of mortgage repayments or other outgoings made or not made after separation. These may or may not be offset by the paying party having had sole occupation of the home and in respect of which an order to pay occupation rent may have been made under either TLATA 1996, s 13 or FLA 1996, s 33. The process of weighing payment of outgoings against sole occupation of the home following separation is known as equitable accounting. The issue of whether or not an occupation rent should enter the equation is a difficult one where no order has been made. Such authorities that exist are in conflict, particularly where one partner has left voluntarily [2]. If an occupation rent has been ordered by the court, this must of course be taken into account. Unfortunately, the opportunity to fully consider the conflicting existing authorities in other situations was missed in the most recent decision of *Re Pavlou (a bankrupt)* [3]. This case did make it clear that co-owners must account to each other for any increase in value of the property brought about by expenditure of just one of them after separation and thus payment for improvements or capital payments on mortgage instalments, which reduce the mortgage debt and increase the equity must be credited to the party who made the payments. The position relating to payment of mortgage interest and its relationship to whether this equates with the payment of an occupational rent is less clear. The starting point is that a co-owner is entitled to occupy the property and if he or she chooses not to do so this should not affect their rights and liabilities. Thus ostensibly, they remain liable for half the interest and capital payments on a joint mortgage, but conversely could return to the home at any point. If on the other hand they were excluded by the other co-owner, it would normally be equitable that they should be entitled to an occupation rent, often assessed in practice as half the mortgage interest payments. This placed great importance on the issue of whether or not a party was excluded. In contrast to *Suttil v Graham*, the court in *Re Pavlou* seemed to favour a broad examination of the parties' conduct premised upon the starting point that no occupation rent will normally be payable. However, it was also stated that the ultimate test is what is fair and equitable and thus arguably a co-owner who has voluntarily left and would be welcomed back to the family home would be unlikely to be awarded an occupation rent.

1   *Turton v Turton* [1988] Ch 542.
2   Compare and contrast *Cracknell v Cracknell* [1971] 3 All ER 552, *Eves v Eves* [1975] 3 All ER 768 and *Dennis v McDonald* [1981] 2 All ER 632, *Jones v Jones* [1977] 2 All ER 231 and *Suttill v Graham* [1977] 3 All ER 1117.
3   [1993] 2 FLR 751.

Negative equity and mortgage arrears

4.122   Cohabitants facing relationship breakdown today may all too often face the added problem of dealing with negative equity and/or mortgage arrears. Given that co-owners are jointly and severally liable for a mortgage debt, it may often be difficult to get a mortgagee's consent to a transfer of property order in a negative equity situation. The attitude of mortgagees to this problem varies. However, where the repayment record is good and there is sufficient income or income support available to meet repayment of the interest element, it should be possible to negotiate the desired outcome. Borrowers who have taken out a mortgage on or after 2 October 1995 are now subject to a 39 week delay before income support will be paid to meet mortgage interest repayments and insurance may not be available. Particularly where the property market remains depressed, however, there is little for a lender to gain in forcing a sale in adverse conditions if the interest payments are being made.

4.123 Where a sale is the only option in a negative equity situation on relationship breakdown, it is generally financially advisable for the borrowers to take urgent action to sell the home themselves as they are likely to obtain a higher purchase price than the mortgagee selling in possession and where no other option is possible both parties should agree to limit the damage to each of them. However, consent of the mortgagee to the sale is needed in a negative equity situation or the sellers will not be able to redeem the mortgage and secure the release of the charge on completion of the sale. If the mortgagee refuses, then the borrowers can apply to the court pursuant to LPA 1925, s 91 to enable the court to direct sale on terms that the court considers appropriate [1]. Such proceedings must be issued in the High Court where the total mortgage debt exceeds £30,000.

1   See *Palk v Mortgage Services Funding plc* [1993] Ch 330, CA.

4.124 Another matter to consider in a negative equity situation where there is an endowment mortgage of at least ten years' standing, is for the couple to switch to an ordinary repayment mortgage and for the life policy to be sold to a specialist broker for a price much higher than the surrender value. The proceeds can then be applied to discharge or reduce the negative equity.

4.125 Where there are arrears and possession proceedings, suspension of any possession order should be made where it can be shown that the mortgagor will pay off the arrears and be able to pay the repayments after a 'reasonable period'[1]. In *Cheltenham and Gloucester Building Society v Norgan* [2] in assessing a reasonable period the whole of the remaining period should be taken into account. Where, as is often the case with second mortgages, the loan is under £15,000 and governed by the Consumer Credit Act 1974, time orders under s 129 are available 'if it appears to the court just' to make one in respect of any sum owed to the lender at a rate which is reasonable taking into account the debtor's financial position. This is an easier hurdle to overcome than the AJA 1970 and 1973 test and the provision enables both further time to pay and the rescheduling of payments beyond the original term of the loan. It is also possible for the debtor under the 1974 Act to apply for the order without awaiting proceedings being issued by the lender.

1   See Administration of Justice Act 1970 and Administration of Justice Act 1993, s 8.
2   [1996] 1 All ER 449, CA.

4.126 Finally, the possibility of a mortgage rescue scheme can be explored. These are operated by many mortgagees and some local authorities and involve a housing association buying the property and enabling the current occupier to remain either as a tenant or under a shared ownership scheme. This may be particularly useful where one cohabitant and the children wish to remain in the home, but cannot afford to take on the mortgage debts. The availability of schemes is patchy and initiative needs to be taken to see whether the mortgagee concerned or local authority for that area do operate such a scheme.

4.127 Following sale, legal co-owners will remain jointly and severally liable for the balance of the mortgage debt not met out of the sale proceeds and if there have been possession proceedings, then a money judgment may also have been obtained. Although the mortgagee can in theory seek to enforce the whole of the debt against either of the co-owners, an agreement as between the former cohabitants as to how this should be borne should be considered on relationship breakdown. Where there has been an agreement as to the proportions in which the mortgage repayments were made, then the debt would be shared between them in these same proportions.

Legal aid

4.128 As in the matrimonial context, any advice given to same-sex cohabitants concerning a dispute relating to the family home, must include information about both costs and where appropriate, the availability of legal aid, the consequences of the requirement to pay a contribution and the legal aid statutory charge under Legal Aid Act 1988, s 16(6).

4.129 In relation to proceedings under TLATA 1996, s 14 brought to establish the beneficial interests in the family home, there is now power for the Legal Aid Board (LAB) to postpone enforcement of the charge where property recovered or preserved is to be used as a home for the assisted person or their dependants [1]. Similarly, where a sum of money is recovered under such proceedings for the purpose of purchasing a home in accordance with the order or agreement, the charge may also be deferred providing the property is bought within a year of the order or agreement and in both cases, the Board has power to agree to the purchase of a substitute property to which the charge will be transferred [2]. Postponement is always at the discretion of the LAB and is dependent upon the property concerned offering sufficient security for the sum charged. The court order must also make it clear that the property or sum awarded is to provide a home for the assisted person or their dependants and it is critical that advisers ensure that this wording is included in the wording of the order or agreement [3]. Simple interest on the charge accrues at the rate prescribed (currently 8%) on the charge as of the date of registration and an assisted person may at any time make repayments in respect of the charge which will be applied first to the outstanding interest [4]. The exemption of the first £2,500 of the charge does not apply in the context of proceedings under TLATA 1996, s 14 [5].

1   Civil Legal Aid (General) Regulations 1989, SI 1989/339, as amended, regs 96(1) and 97(1).
2   SI 1989/339, reg 98.
3   See *Practice Direction (Statutory Charge: Form of Order of the Court)* [1991] 3 All ER 896 and Annex D at para **4.133**).
4   Civil Legal Aid (General) Regulations 1989, SI 1989/339, as amended, reg 99.
5   SI 1989/339, reg 94.

4.130 The Court of Appeal decision in *Parkes v Legal Aid Board* [1] also makes it clear that where as in this case an order for sale is successfully resisted, under LPA 1925, s 30 (or now under TLATA 1996, s 14) even though the extent of the beneficial interests were not in dispute, there had been a recovery of the exclusive right to possession which had previously been a shared right. This brought the property within the Legal Aid Act 1988, s 16(6) and the property would be subject to the statutory charge to the extent of the costs incurred under the legal aid certificate.

1   [1996] 4 All ER 271.

4.131 It may even be necessary to consider the implications of the statutory charge wherever a legally aided co-owner acquires through proceedings an exclusive right of occupation for a substantial period. For the statutory charge could in theory at least apply to long term occupation orders granted in respect of an owner-occupied property under FLA 1996, Pt IV where the successful applicant has a beneficial interest in the family home.

(v)   Conclusion

4.132   From the above, it seems clear that prevention is better than cure wherever possible and cohabitation agreements and declarations of trust are to be encouraged at every opportunity. As things stand at the moment and it is hoped that reform is now on the horizon at least, the law relating to property disputes between same-sex cohabitants is highly unsatisfactory, primarily because its uncertainty makes it very difficult for advisers to give advice which avoids the need to litigate. Where possible and appropriate, conciliatory negotiation or mediation may well provide a more acceptable solution than long drawn out and expensive litigation, which can only increase the hostility between the parties. Otherwise it is all too easy for the equity in the home to disappear in legal costs, which is not in the interests of either party.

4   Practitioners' checklist on cohabitant co-ownership disputes

4.133   Establish legal ownership of the family home and the rights of any third parties, including the mortgagee.
(a)   Gather detailed evidence as to equitable ownership and in particular look to what the intention was at the date of purchase and subsequently, including:
  (i)   documentary evidence (eg title documents, written agreements, correspondence, declarations of trust);
  (ii)   evidence as to express discussions between the parties;
  (iii)   detrimental acts by the non-legal owner;
  (iv)   the history of the relationship and the whole course of dealing between the parties during the period of ownership;
  (v)   direct and indirect contributions made to the purchase price;
  (vi)   direct and necessary indirect contributions to the mortgage repayments; and
  (vii)   details of who carried out improvements to the property and on what basis.
(b)   Consider whether there is an express trust or whether resulting or common intention constructive trust case law is appropriate to establish the parties' respective interests, remembering the different approaches to stages 1 and 2.
(c)   Consider issues relating to proprietary estoppel.
(d)   Quantify the share claimed and consider the date of valuation and whether equitable accounting will be appropriate.
(e)   Notify and liaise with the mortgagee where appropriate.
(f)   Consider whether conciliation or mediation would be appropriate.
(g)   Consider whether an occupation order should be applied for.
(h)   Consider the statutory provisions available and case law applicable in relation to determining the shares in and disposition of the family home.
(i)   Consider the impact of costs, legal aid and the statutory charge.

D ANNEX

Statutory charge: form of order of the court

4.134   As set out in the practice direction, the following wording completed with the details relevant to the particular case should be included in the court order where postponement of the statutory charge is sought in respect of a family home.

> 'And it is certified for the purpose of the Civil Legal Aid (General) Regulations 1989 [that the lump sum of £x has been ordered to be paid to enable the applicant/respondent to purchase a home for himself/herself (or his/her dependants)] [that the property (address) has been recovered/preserved for the applicant/respondent (or his/her dependants)].'

Chapter 5

Inheritance and succession

5.01 This chapter will consider the devolution of a deceased person's estate in the absence of a will and thereafter consider some possible wills that might be appropriate for lesbians and gay men. Going one step further, tax planning exercises will be looked at, in order to reduce the Inland Revenue's share of the client's estate and hence increase the share to be taken by the surviving partner. These subjects will be dealt with in chronological order, considering first action that needs to be taken during the client's lifetime to reduce Inheritance Tax (IHT) that is chargeable on death.

A   LIFETIME INHERITANCE TAX PLANNING

1   Introduction

5.02 Inheritance Tax affects the moderately well off and those with even greater wealth. Generally speaking, an individual may make outright gifts of capital of any value without being subject to IHT providing he or she survives for seven years after making the gift. This is called a Potentially Exempt Transfer (PET). There is a cumulative charge on transfers made within the period of seven years prior to death and on death. The rate of tax is 40% on the excess of the estate over the nil rate band. There is however, tapering relief if a gift is made over three years prior to death but such relief only applies to larger gifts. If the lifetime gift does not exceed the nil rate band at the date of death there is no advantage in the gift having been made over three years before death. If no lifetime gifts have been made or if they were made over seven years before death an individual can leave an estate of up to the nil rate band before IHT is charged.

5.03 There are a number of exemptions and reliefs from the incidence of the tax, some of the most useful being as follows:
(*a*)   annual exemption of £3,000 per annum (which can be carried forward one year);
(*b*)   gifts of up to, but not exceeding, £250 per annum per donee;
(*c*)   transfers between spouses;
(*d*)   gifts to charity;
(*e*)   normal expenditure out of income;

(*f*)   transfers of certain agricultural property;
(*g*)   transfers of certain business property.

It follows that persons of modest means, by which we mean those individuals whose estates are worth less than the nil rate band, should not unduly concern themselves with Inheritance Tax planning.

5.04   Those persons whose estates exceed the value of the nil rate band might consider lifetime tax planning to minimise the incidence of the tax on their demise. Presumably the larger the estate the greater the attention that should be given to this exercise.

5.05   Gay people are at a disadvantage to married couples as property passing between married couples does not trigger IHT. Gays are placed in the same position as unmarried couples. However, unmarried couples may be able to marry, if only for this reason, but this ability is denied to gay couples.

5.06   Tax planning for married couples is inherently different from that relating to gay couples. First, property passing between married couples is free from IHT. Their tax planning invariably involves retaining capital for the benefit of their children and grandchildren. Their nearest is already provided for by the tax system. Second, they are able to continue planning after death by using the surviving spouse as a conduit to pass assets to the next generation during the survivor's lifetime.

5.07   Tax planning for gay persons generally involves planning for the benefit of the surviving partner which generally means planning as long as possible before death. This is because the maximum amount that can pass tax-free on death will be the nil rate band—provided that this has not been used during the previous seven years. The fiscal advantage given to married couples and denied to unmarried couples of the same or different sex often causes hardship.

Example

5.08   Ruth and Judith live in a property that is worth, say, £400,000. The property is in Ruth's name and they have little else of value. If Ruth were to die leaving her estate to Judith the present amount of tax payable at 40% is £70,800. As there are no other assets out of which to pay the tax Judith might be forced to sell the property to meet the tax.

5.09   We shall take as our model an individual who has an estate that will exceed the nil rate band on his death. He has a partner whom he would wish to benefit from the majority, if not the whole, of his estate on his death. He would wish to minimise the incidence of IHT payable on his death in order to maximise the assets that pass to his surviving partner. The worst position is that sort envisaged in the preceding example.

5.10   We must distinguish two scenarios as follows:
(*a*)   where the client wishes to transfer assets through to his partner by way of a PET so that the donee has control of those assets during the donor's lifetime; and

(*b*) where the client wishes to make arrangements for assets to pass to the surviving partner on his death, bypassing his estate and so avoiding IHT on his death.

Examples of the former would be an outright gift of cash or a share in the partnership home whilst an example of the latter would be insurance policies or pension benefits placed in trust which would pay out on the donor's death.

5.11 How far the client wishes to go will involve various factors. He may be unwilling to place assets in the hands of his partner prior to his death if he is not absolutely sure that the relationship will last until his death. If the partnership is one of many years' standing there may be more inclination to gift assets with immediate effect. Of course the donor may be fearful that his partner will dissipate what he has been given with the result that he will be no better off.

5.12 What those gifts comprise will depend on several factors not the least of which is the incidence of Capital Gains Tax (CGT). Generally, where a person disposes of an asset other than by way of an arm's length bargain his disposal is deemed to be for a consideration equal to the market value of the asset. The donor of a gift is therefore normally treated as incurring a chargeable gain calculated by reference to the market value at the date of disposal. If this gain is sufficiently large so as to exceed the individual's annual allowance the result is likely to be a CGT bill.

5.13 Capital Gains Tax does not, however, bite on property passing on death. The personal representatives are deemed to acquire a deceased person's assets at market value so that an uplifted value of the assets for CGT purposes is achieved without payment of the tax. One must carefully consider the advantages of making a lifetime gift to save IHT on death if a chargeable event for CGT purposes arises. It might be worth paying IHT on death in the knowledge that the asset in the hands of the personal representatives or beneficiaries can be sold free of capital gains tax.

5.14 Careful consideration must therefore be given as to what assets might comprise a lifetime gift. One's main residence, government securities, chattels up to the value of £6,000, certain insurance policy proceeds and pension benefits and cash do not attract CGT on their disposal and so may be ideal candidates to be gifted to one's partner during one's lifetime in order to reduce the incidence of IHT on death.

5.15 An individual's most valuable assets are likely to be the partnership home, pension and life insurance benefits about which particular mention is now made.

2   Main residence

5.16 It is not uncommon for the partnership home alone to exceed the nil rate band. However by virtue of the home being more than just an investment there may be strong reasons for excluding it from a tax planning exercise. After all, if a partnership fails, insult would be added to injury if the original property owning partner is forced to sell his home because he had previously given a share of it to his partner. If however, the partner who owns the property feels comfortable in transferring part of the home to the other partner, he should consider doing so.

5.17 There are three distinct advantages in utilising this particular asset in tax planning.

(i)   Capital Gains Tax

5.18 The general CGT treatment of a gift has already been referred to. Fortunately the Taxation of Chargeable Gains Act 1992, s 222(1) provides that where a gain accrues to an individual so far as attributable to the disposal of, or of an interest in:
(a)   a dwelling house or part of a dwelling house which is, or has at any time in his period of ownership been, his only or main residence; or
(b)   land which he has for his own occupation and enjoyment with that residence as its garden or grounds up to the 'permitted area';
that gain or a part of the gain, if the property has not been occupied throughout the period of ownership as the main residence, is exempt.

5.19 The 'permitted area' means an area of 0.5 hectares or such larger area as may be required for the reasonable enjoyment of the dwelling house as a residence taking into account the size and character of the dwelling house. If more than one residential property is owned it will be necessary to make an election with the Inland Revenue as to which property is the main residence at any particular time. So generally speaking, a gift of a share in the partnership home to one's partner should not be a chargeable event for capital gains tax purposes.

(ii)   Gifts with reservation

5.20 Section 102(1) of the Finance Act 1986 introduced the concept of gifts with reservation. A gift will be ineffective for IHT purposes if either: (a) possession and enjoyment of the property is not bona fide assumed by the donee; or (b) the property is not enjoyed to the entire or virtually to the entire exclusion of the donor.

5.21 Is the continued occupation of the donor not caught by s 102(1)(b) of the Finance Act 1986? The answer would appear to be no. Each joint owner of property has a right to occupy the whole property with the other remaining owners. The donor therefore occupies by virtue of his remaining share in the property; it is not referable to the share that he has given away and hence it cannot be a gift with reservation. The donor partner must share occupation— which one would expect—and it would appear that the donee must meet his share of the costs of the property. This state of affairs is supported by a House of Commons Statement.

5.22 If however, the donee partner moved out of the partnership home the donor would have to pay full monetary consideration for the use of the share of the property that had been given away if the gift with reservation rules were not then to bite.

(iii)   Discounted value

5.23   It is accepted by the Capital Taxes Office that the value of a joint share in real property should be discounted for IHT purposes with the result that if part of one's home is given away to one's partner the value of the remainder could be discounted by up to 15%.

Example

5.24   Julian transfers to his partner Sandy one half of their home. Julian dies more than seven years later when the value of the property is £400,000. The value of Julian's share in the property for IHT purposes will be £200,000 less a discount of up to 15% (£30,000) ie £170,000. By this exercise the saving of IHT amounts to £92,000 ie 40% of (£400,000 – £170,000)

5.25   This additional assistance is well worth having. By virtue of the IHT provisions regarding connected persons [1] such a discount is not available to married couples—so this is one area where gay couples have a fiscal advantage over their married counterparts.

1   IHTA 1984, s 270.

5.26   In conclusion, the gift of a share in the partnership home has various fiscal advantages over other assets, making it a very suitable candidate for a tax planning exercise. Additionally, by virtue of the value of property generally the performance of this exercise might be all that is needed to reduce the donor partner's estate to below the nil rate band or at least to a level where the incidence of IHT might be manageable. From a practical point of view this exercise is much more likely to be considered in the case of a couple whose relationship is a stable one of many years' standing.

3   Insurance policies

5.27   Insurance policies that will mature on death and have no benefit to the policyholder or alternatively endowment policies maturing before death for which the policyholder does not require or need the proceeds are ideal vehicles to reduce the policyholder's estate.

5.28   By assigning the benefit of the policy to one's partner or alternatively, by declaring trusts of the policy proceeds, the funds payable on maturity will fall outside the estate of the donor when they mature.

5.29   There will be a PET for IHT purposes and the usual survivor rules apply. If the policy is assigned or trusts declared after it has been in existence for some time, the value of the gift will be the surrender value or the cost of the total premiums less any surrenders made [1]. These valuation rules do not apply to term assurance policies of three years or more which will no doubt have no surrender value; or unit linked policies which are valued at the price of the units.

1   IHTA 1984, s 167.

5.30 It often happens that a life policy is set up in trust from the outset in which case the gift element of the premiums should be covered by normal expenditure out of income or, if not, then they are likely to be covered by the £3,000 annual exemption. This means that the PET regulations do not apply so that no part of the nil rate band is utilised if the donor fails to survive for seven years.

5.31 Term assurance, which provides cover only in the event of death, should always be assigned to another or placed in trust. This is because an individual will never benefit personally from the proceeds. To permit the proceeds to fall into one's estate and for IHT to become payable thereon smacks of carelessness.

5.32 There are three options open to the donor.

(*a*) If one's partner alone is to benefit from the policy proceeds an outright assignment of the benefit of the policy would seem to be in order. In this way the policy proceeds will be paid to him as soon as liability is accepted by the insurance company. Unless it is on the maturity of an endowment or similar policy, this will normally be following the inspection of the deceased's death certificate by the insurance company. The donee will therefore have access to the funds at the earliest opportunity. This may assist at a time when other funds are blocked pending probate and of course they may be a source of funds for the payment of IHT before application for probate is made.

(*b*) If one's partner and others are to benefit from the policy proceeds in particular proportions, the most practical way of them benefiting is to assign the benefit of the policy to trustees who are under an obligation to hold the fund, eg for such of A, B and C as shall survive the donor and if more than one, in equal shares absolutely.

(*c*) Alternatively, where the donor requires more flexibility he can assign the policy to trustees for the benefit of one or more primary beneficiaries with an overriding power for the appointment of a wider class of beneficiaries. It is also possible to increase the wider class, eg by inserting a clause in the trust documentation providing for such additional persons as shall be notified by the donor in writing to the trustees during the donor's lifetime or for the class of beneficiaries to include any person who is mentioned in the donor's will. The donor will then no doubt leave with his trustees a letter of his wishes as to the devolution of the policy proceeds in the hope that they will act on those wishes. This letter can be updated as circumstances change.

5.33 The flexibility given by this third option provides a distinct advantage over the first two options. You may be able to add beneficiaries after the trust arrangement has commenced. By prudent choice of trustees a beneficiary, whilst not being removed from the trust, may be excluded from eventual benefit for one reason or another. If a partner were to be the principal beneficiary but he dies in the same accident as the insured, the trustees may direct the policy proceeds elsewhere rather than into the estate of the deceased beneficiary. Insurance companies invariably produce ready-made trust documentation to cover the above situations or alternatively one can draft one's own.

4 Employee pension benefits

5.34 In an approved pension scheme one often finds that if the employee dies before reaching retirement a sum of up to four times their salary becomes payable. Generally the trustees of the pension scheme will have a discretion as to who to pay this sum. This discretion takes the payment outside the IHT regime with the result that what amounts to a large sum passes free of IHT. The trustees may well provide a pro forma for completion by the member of the pension scheme whereby the employee can indicate to the trustees who should benefit on his demise. In the absence of a letter of wishes the trustees will undoubtedly look very favourably on a surviving spouse. That consideration would not necessarily extend to a same-sex partner so that a gay employee needs to be sure that his letter of wishes is in place. Even so, it is not unknown for a letter of wishes not to be adhered to, to the letter, if for example, parents are not slow in coming forward to enquire what they may be entitled to. Prejudices in such circumstances come through and the trustees may well be persuaded to make provision, or greater provision, for members of the deceased employee's family in the face of the deceased's expressed wishes.

Example

The Trustees of ABC Ltd Occupational Pension Scheme

[Date]

When exercising the powers and discretions given to you as trustees of the pension scheme of which I am a member I request you to have regard to my wishes in respect of any death in service or other lump sum benefits as follows:

Names   % of lump sum

This request supersedes all previous requests made by me.

[..........................Signature..............................]

Name

5.35 Additionally the death of an employee before retirement age may trigger a pension becoming payable to his spouse or dependants. Depending on the terms of the pension scheme a same-sex partner may well come within the class of persons who might be entitled to benefit. The more modern the pension scheme the greater is the likelihood that a same-sex partner can be considered for a pension.

5 Personal pension benefits

5.36 Since 1 July 1988 those persons who are self-employed or who are in non-pensionable employment are able to contribute to personal pension plans. If the person dies before retirement there may be a lump sum which will become payable reflecting the pension premiums paid or the value of the pension fund at that time. If the sum payable on death must be paid to the deceased's estate it will be aggregated with the remainder of the estate and IHT will be payable on it. If however, the persons to whom it can be paid are at the discretion of the pension company, the lump sum should be received tax-free. As with employee pension benefits (depending on the scheme) it may be possible to nominate who shall receive the benefit of the sum payable on death.

5.37 The predecessor of the personal pension plan was the retirement annuity policy. These remain in existence and payments can still be made to such policies that were taken out before 1 July 1988.

5.38 As with insurance policies, one may assign the benefit of retirement annuity policies to trustees for the benefit of certain individuals or, alternatively, upon discretionary trusts. Apparently, Inland Revenue practice requires that the whole retirement annuity policy should be placed in trust, with the trustees holding the pension benefit for the absolute benefit of the policyholder and any death benefits for the trust beneficiaries. The preferred course of action would be to assign the benefit to trustees of a discretionary trust whereby the trustees will be able to distribute those funds to a surviving partner or to other persons independently of the deceased's estate. The trust should have flexibility for additional beneficiaries to be added. Whilst pension companies may produce their own documentation, it may be that the client has a multitude of pension policies with different pension providers so that it might be advantageous to prepare a trust deed to provide an umbrella for all the different policies.

B INHERITANCE TAX PLANNING ON DEATH

5.39 Whilst lifetime tax planning is the province of the more well-to-do, everybody should consider the sagacity of making a will. In the absence of a will a person will be subject to the laws of intestacy. These are to be found in the Administration of Estates Act 1925, s 46 . They attempt to make provision for the disposal of assets for Mr and Mrs Average and may work reasonably well for a married person of moderate means. The likelihood is that the spouse will take all the deceased's estate in such circumstances and in the absence of a spouse the children will take equally. We shall not dwell on the trust provisions that affect a surviving spouse and children where the estate is somewhat larger, as they probably fall outside the concerns of the client group for which this book is written. The laws of intestacy take no account of unmarried partners whether of a different or the same sex. In the circumstances that there is no spouse or children the parents alone inherit the deceased's estate and if there are two parents alive they would share it equally. If both parents are dead the deceased's siblings inherit the estate or if there are no siblings, remote relatives become entitled to the deceased's estate in preference to the surviving partner.

5.40 If a gay man or lesbian therefore wishes to benefit his or her partner and possibly friends, it is imperative that he or she makes a will. In the absence of a will the surviving partner's only claim against the deceased's estate will be an application under the Inheritance (Provision for Family and Dependants) Act 1975, about which more will be said later. We now consider various will scenarios.

1 Will A

5.41 The simplest will would be one whereby the deceased leaves everything to his or her partner and appoints him or her sole executor.

2   Will B

5.42   The next scenario may well be a will gifting assets or cash to friends, charities, godchildren etc with the bulk of the estate passing to the surviving partner. In these circumstances it might be appropriate to have a second executor to share the burden of executorship. Of course the testator may prefer the surviving partner not to have to worry about the business of the administration of the estate and may shift that burden to others, possibly professionals.

3   Will C

5.43   A married couple (or possibly an unmarried couple) with children may well have mirror wills leaving their estates to one another with the survivor then leaving their estate to the children. This is the norm and there is every expectation that the survivor would wish to make provision for their joint children. The matter becomes more complicated when there is more than one family when there might be his children, her children and their children. We are then getting close to a gay relationship in that the partners may have different wishes as to who should benefit ultimately on the second death. They may have common long-term friends or charities which they jointly wish to benefit. In these circumstances mirror wills gifting each estate to the survivor, failing which, to X and Y or to a favourite charity will be simple enough.

5.44   Matters become more complicated when each partner has family, possibly brothers and sisters or nieces and nephews whom they would wish to benefit from what remains of their estate after the survivor has died.

5.45   In these circumstances one might suggest a life interest for the survivor of the two partners and after the survivor's death the capital of the estate of the first partner to die passes to their brothers and sisters or favoured nieces and nephews. There could be grafted onto the trusts the ability for the trustees to be able to advance capital to the survivor.

5.46   This suggestion is probably more practical if the estate is larger rather than smaller as there are expenses of running a trust. However a trust could be used in an estate where the main asset was the partnership home owned either solely by one partner or jointly (as tenants in common, of course). The cost of running a trust where the one asset is the partnership home is likely to be small. The terms of the trust can provide for the survivor to meet the outgoings. The trustees will undoubtedly wish to satisfy themselves, for example, that the property is adequately insured. Such an asset will however be less time consuming, and hence less costly, to administer than for example a portfolio of stock exchange securities.

5.47   For IHT purposes the capital value of the funds which the surviving partner has the life interest is aggregated with his own estate on his death. If this has the effect of the combined estates exceeding the nil rate band one might consider creating a discretionary trust for the benefit of the surviving partner and other appropriate beneficiaries the capital value of which would not be aggregated with the surviving partner's estate.

4   Will D

5.48   More lesbians or gay men than one would imagine are married for one reason or another. It may be that they have had a change of orientation somewhat later in the cycle than others. Alternatively it is not unknown for lesbians or gay men to marry to enable their spouse to have residency in this country or for them to obtain residency in another country. A gay man or lesbian who happens to be married at the time of his or her death to someone who is at this time domiciled in this country, is in an advantageous position if their estate is large and they wish to consider more sophisticated tax planning through their will.

5.49   The point to be emphasised here is that a gay man or lesbian who has a spouse must have a will. If theirs is a marriage of convenience the spouse could benefit twice over: first, in obtaining residency and second, in succeeding to the deceased's estate as the surviving spouse on intestacy.

5.50   A will can be drafted to create a life interest for the spouse with power for the trustees to terminate all or part at their discretion. The creation of such a life interest in favour of the spouse does not give rise to IHT on the deceased's demise. The termination of the trust or part of it by way of advancement to the surviving partner is considered a PET by the spouse. Providing that such spouse lives for seven years there would be no IHT payable on the property that has been redirected to the surviving partner.

5.51   If the surviving spouse died within seven years her estate might well become liable to IHT or the liability increased due to the aggregation of the two estates. Certainly her nil rate band or part of it would have been hijacked for the benefit of the surviving partner in whose favour the trust had been broken. This would seem to be a situation in which serious consideration ought to be given to insuring against the death of the spouse. Additionally or alternatively it would seem appropriate to provide some benefit for the spouse who has been used as a conduit for this exercise.

5   Will E

5.52   A gift to charity is exempt from IHT. In the absence of more deserving beneficiaries, a testator may well wish for his partner to benefit from his estate and after his partner's death for his estate to go to a particular charity. If a life interest to the survivor is contemplated, followed by a gift over to a charity, there will be IHT chargeable on the death of the testator although there will be the general exemption from IHT when the surviving partner dies and the estate then passes to charity. I am indebted to Robert Venables QC for a suggested method of possibly avoiding IHT on the first death, as follows.

5.53   The testator bequeaths his estate to Charity A, on condition that Charity A pays to the surviving partner a certain annuity out of its own resources (ie out of assets other than those bequeathed by the testator). Such a bequest should be exempt from IHT. Should Charity A not be willing or able to satisfy this condition there would be a gift over in favour of Charity B and thereafter Charity C and so on. Presumably Charity A would accept the gift if it was satisfied that there was net benefit to it. Mr Venables is of the opinion that the anti-avoidance provisions of IHTA 1984, s 23 are circumvented if the bequest will in any event go to charity. The scope of this particular scheme may be somewhat limited. It probably is only of use in dealing with larger estates and probably where the partners are elderly or alternatively where the life expectancy of the partners is otherwise limited, such as with AIDS sufferers.

Example

5.54   Benjamin and Peter have lived together for forty years. Benjamin's estate consists of the partnership home in his name alone which together with his personal chattels are valued conveniently at the nil rate band. His only other assets consist of investments worth £1,000,000. In his will he bequeaths his home and personal chattels to Peter and the balance of his estate to the National Trust on the condition that it will pay Peter a gross income of £50,000 per annum out of its other assets. There are provisions for other charities to benefit from the estate if the National Trust is unable or unwilling to accept this gift with its attendant condition. At Benjamin's death Peter is aged 70. Let us say that the cost of purchasing an annuity from an insurance company to create an income of £50,000 per annum is £500,000. If the National Trust is willing to purchase such an annuity for Peter the net benefit to it from Benjamin's generosity will be £500,000.

6   Inheritance (Provision for Family and Dependants) Act 1975

5.55   If a gay person makes no will or if his will is hopelessly out of date and no provision is made for his surviving partner, the only avenue open to the surviving partner in order to benefit from the deceased's estate is to make an application to the court under the Inheritance (Provision for Family and Dependants) Act 1975.

5.56   The preamble to this Act states that it is an Act to allow for the court to make orders for the provision for the spouse, former spouse, child, child of the family or dependant out of the estate of a deceased person and for matters connected therewith. For our purposes the surviving partner can only come within s 1(1)(e):

> 'any person (not being a person included in the foregoing paragraphs of this subsection) who immediately before the death of the deceased was being maintained, either wholly or partly, by the deceased'.

5.57   That person may apply to the court for an order under s 2 of the Act on the ground that the disposition of the deceased's estate, effected by his will or the law relating to intestacy, or the combination of his will and that law, is not such as to make reasonable financial provision for the applicant. This is an objective test.

5.58   Reasonable financial provision is defined as:
> '(*a*)   in the case of an application…by a husband or wife…means such financial provision as it would be reasonable in all the circumstances

of the case for a husband or wife to receive, whether or not that
provision is required for his or her maintenance;

(b) in the case of any other application such financial provision as it
would be reasonable in all the circumstances of the case for the
applicant to receive for his maintenance.'[1]

1   Inheritance (Provision for Family and Dependants) Act 1975, s 1(2).

5.59   Section 1(3) indicates that a person is treated as being maintained by the
deceased if, other than for valuable consideration, the deceased was making
a substantial contribution in money or money's worth towards the reasonable
needs of that person. Provision of rent free accommodation can amount to a
substantial contribution.

5.60   An application under the Act must be made within six calendar months
of the issue of a grant of representation in the deceased's estate to the High
Court or county court. The court has wide powers including making orders for
periodic payments, lump sum payments and transfers of property. It can also
make orders in respect of jointly held property that would pass by survivorship
and would otherwise not pass under the deceased's will or into his estate on
his intestacy. Legal aid is available for such applications. Unless a claim is
vexatious, one would expect the costs of all the parties to be met out of
the estate.

5.61   Once again, a gay or lesbian partner is in a much inferior position to that
of a spouse. His or her claim can only be on the grounds of dependency. He
or she is however, probably in no worse a position than an opposite sex
partner. At least that is the theory although in practice an opposite sex partner
might receive superior provision from the court than his/her gay counterpart.

5.62   In the absence of a will making some sort of provision for the surviving
partner, his only recourse is to seek the assistance of the Act. Sadly, its scope
is very limited. It may be applicable to the situation of a 'kept' partner. Here
his dependency upon the deceased can extend beyond death. Where, however,
the relationship is more of an equal one, where each partner works and they
equally provide for their lifestyle together, the benefit of the Act is denied
to the surviving partner. Go one step further and consider the situation
where the surviving partner has possibly provided the greater share of
the costs of their joint lifestyle. He may own the property in which they live,
thus relieving the deceased partner of the cost of accommodation he would
otherwise have to find. The surviving partner is denied assistance from the
Act. His acts of generosity count for nothing. On the other hand, the surviving
partner who has been subsidised by the deceased because he had no
employment or possibly because all his own income went on shopping and
entertainment, will come within the ambit of the Act.

5.63   That old adage used by estate agents springs to mind: the three most
important things in selling a house are location, location and location. As far
as gay people are concerned, the three most important things in getting one's
affairs in order are making a will, making a will and making a will.

C CONCLUSION

5.64   First and foremost, a gay man or lesbian must have a will. One great advantage of a will (or at least until one becomes non-compos mentis) is the ability to change it at any time, to take into account changing circumstances.

5.65   As no fiscal advantages similar to those enjoyed by married couples are given to gay or lesbianpartners, they must make sure that they maximise the tax breaks that are open to them, such as making sure that pension benefits and insurance policy proceeds fall outside their estate for the benefit of those who are close to them and not for the benefit of the Inland Revenue. They may be able to do this in a flexible way so that the benefits for any preferred individual are not set in stone.

5.66   Finally, where there is an overriding wish to benefit a surviving partner in circumstances where one's estate is going to exceed the nil rate band, notwithstanding the precautions taken in para **5.65**, consideration ought to be given to transferring assets during one's lifetime to one's partner if, in all the circumstances, one feels comfortable in doing so.

Chapter 6

Immigration

A   INTRODUCTION

6.01   On 10 October 1997, just five months after the election of Tony Blair's Labour government, the immigration minister, Mike O'Brien, announced a 'concession' whereby at least some categories of gay and lesbian relationships (and unmarried heterosexual relationships) would be recognised for immigration purposes in the United Kingdom.

6.02   Under the terms of this concession, which came into effect on 13 October 1997, the unmarried foreign partner of a British citizen, permanent resident, European Economic Area national living in the UK or certain other categories of individuals based in the UK (including full work permit holders, refugees and other individuals with a status potentially leading to permanent residence) would be granted leave to enter or remain in the UK provided that he or she met five core requirements:
(a)   the parties are legally unable to marry under UK law;
(b)   any previous marriage or similar relationship has permanently broken down;
(c)   the parties have been living together in a relationship akin to marriage which has subsisted for four or more years;
(d)   the parties are able to maintain and accommodate themselves adequately without recourse to public funds;
(e)   the parties intend to live together permanently.

Leave would be granted initially for one year and, provided that such a relationship was continuing at the end of that year, indefinite leave to remain (permanent residence) would then be granted.

6.03   This announcement was heralded at the time as an important breakthrough for gay and lesbian rights in the UK. Indeed, this acclaim was to a certain extent merited. From the international perspective, the UK joined a small handful of other countries—the Netherlands, the Scandinavian countries, Australia, New Zealand and Canada—in recognising same-sex relationships for immigration purposes. From a domestic point of view, this development was—and remains at the time of writing—the only British government action thus far affording some legal recognition to same-sex relationships.

6.04   This achievement was perhaps even more remarkable because its subject matter combined two issues—immigration control and gay and lesbian rights—which traditionally attract little sympathy in the political arena or amongst the public at large. The success in putting the issues so high on the agenda of the incoming government must be attributed to the concerted effort over a period of years by a number of courageous couples who had dared to make honest applications based on their relationships at a time when there was no clear likelihood that these relationships would be recognised for immigration purposes and who were then prepared to dig in their heels and fight long, costly and difficult legal battles.

6.05   They were assisted by lawyers who endeavoured to use every available legal and political method to draw out and pursue their clients' cases and by the strong political and organisational support of the Stonewall Immigration Group. The Stonewall Immigration Group was created by those pioneering couples and their lawyers in 1992 to share important information, lobby for change and educate and advise those contemplating embarking on the process of applying for leave to remain in the UK on the basis of a gay or a lesbian relationship. The strategy which has been followed throughout the campaigning efforts of the couples and those supporting them has been to give the issue a 'human face' by focusing on the simple reality of ordinary couples who wish to remain together because they are in long-term committed and loving relationships.

6.06   This chapter outlines the terms of the concession and offers practical advice for making an application under the concession. It also suggests strategies which may be considered by couples not falling squarely within the terms of the concession or who are pursuing appeals against refusal of leave to remain under the terms of the concession. The chapter also addresses other areas of the UK immigration practice which have a particular relevance in the gay and lesbian context: political asylum and policy with respect to those affected by HIV and AIDS.

6.07   The UK's record in granting of political asylum to individuals claiming to have a well-founded fear of persecution in their home country because of sexuality has, unfortunately, been poor. Unlike the situation in many other countries, there has been considerable reluctance to recognise gay men and lesbians as members of a social group who face a well-founded fear of persecution if returned to their home country.

6.08   The policy of the British government with respect to immigration and HIV and AIDS has, however, been more exemplary. Unlike the situation prevailing in some other countries, the mere fact of being HIV positive has never in itself been an impediment to the granting of leave to enter or remain in the UK. Furthermore, in compassionate cases relating to HIV status, there is often the possibility of an individual obtaining exceptional leave to remain in this country even if the individual does not fall within any category of the immigration rules.

B   CONCESSION RELATING TO UNMARRIED PARTNERS

6.09   The terms of the 'concession outside the immigration rules for unmarried partners' are found in the Immigration Directorate's Instructions [1]. The concession needs to be read alongside the instructions on how the concession should be interpreted and applied. Both the concession and the instructions can be accessed on the Home Office website [2] and the full text of the concession is reproduced in *Butterworths Immigration Law Service* at **D[1031]**.

1   Ch 8, annex Z.
2   http://www.homeoffice.gov.uk/ind/htm.

6.10   Perhaps here it is worth noting that a 'concession', in the context of British immigration law, can best be defined as an established practice, often set down in writing, which is sufficiently detailed, well known and consistently applied as to have a certain predictability. Whereas statutory immigration law needs to be voted upon by Parliament and immigration rules are made by the Home Secretary and must be laid before Parliament (after which they take effect unless either House exercises a negative vote against them), concessions are developed without parliamentary involvement and so are more easily created (and amended or annulled). Since neither the Immigration Act 1971, which establishes the framework for current UK immigration control, nor the most recent set of immigration rules (HC395), refers to entering or remaining in the UK on the basis of a same-sex relationship, the concession fills a major gap.

6.11   The concession applies to both same-sex couples and heterosexual unmarried partners where there is a legal impediment to their marriage (such as the impossibility of obtaining a divorce). The foreign partner may be seeking to join or remain with a British citizen, a European Economic Area national residing in the UK or any other person who has indefinite leave to remain in the UK or falls into one of a number of categories of limited leave to remain which lead to indefinite leave to remain. The concession extends to the foreign partners of persons granted asylum in the UK.

6.12   The central requirement of the concession is that 'the parties have been living together in a relationship akin to marriage which has subsisted for four years or more'. This requirement can be problematic for couples on two levels. First of all, it can necessarily be extremely difficult for the nationals of two countries to continue to pursue a relationship for a period as long as four years without either member of the couple having the right to live in the other's home country. While a heterosexual couple can meet and marry within a matter of weeks or months and then take advantage of the immigration rules which permit the foreign partner in a married couple to apply to enter or remain in the UK, unmarried partners must somehow manage to maintain the relationship for four years even though they may not have the right to live in the same country.

6.13   Furthermore, the instructions require that the term ' living together' be applied very strictly. The instructions as issued in August 1998 state:

'The intention of this concession is to allow *genuine long term relationships to continue*. It is not an open door to couples who are in the early stages of a cohabiting relationship, but to provide an opportunity for those couples who are *already living together* in a committed relationship akin to marriage to enter or remain in the UK on this basis alone. It will not benefit those couples who claim they are unable to live together because there is no provision in the Immigration Rules either of the UK or the partner's home country.

In order to assess whether a couple are in a genuine long-term relationship we would expect to see evidence of cohabitation for the preceding four-year period. Short breaks apart would be acceptable for good reasons, such as work commitments, or looking after a relative which takes one partner away for a period of up to six months where it was not possible for the other partner to accompany and it can be seen that the relationship continued throughout that period by visits, letters etc.

Where a couple claim that they have maintained their relationship during the four-year period by merely visiting each other as often as they can, this will not be sufficient to show that they have been living together in a relationship akin to marriage which has subsisted for four years or more. However where a couple have been *living together* in a committed relationship for the preceding four-year period, barring short breaks of up to six months as set out above, but have been dividing their time between countries and may, for example, have used the "visitor" category, then this will be sufficient to meet the requirement.'

6.14 This 'four year rule' has proved very onerous to large numbers of genuine couples seeking to remain in the UK on the basis of the concession. During the first year of the concession's operation, many of such couples have been unsuccessful in their applications simply because their relationships fall short of these numerical requirements. As a result of continuing lobbying by the Stonewall Immigration Group and those affected, the Home Office is carrying out a review of the operation of the concession. It is hoped that this may result in a lessening of the length of relationship requirement currently imposed, perhaps to a more reasonable two-year period.

6.15 In addition to the four-year rule, the concession requires that 'any previous marriage or similar relationship by either partner has permanently broken down'.

6.16 It further requires that 'there will be adequate accommodation for the parties and any dependants without recourse to public funds in accommodation which they own or occupy exclusively' and that 'the parties will be able to maintain themselves and any dependants adequately without recourse to public funds'. Public funds for these purposes include income support, housing benefit and various other specific welfare benefits. It should be noted, however, that if the British-based partner is already receiving public funds in his/her own right, the application should not fail if it can be shown that there will be no *additional* recourse to public funds by allowing the foreign partner to enter or remain in the UK. With respect to the accommodation requirement, exclusive occupation of one bedroom with shared use of the remainder of the premises should suffice to satisfy the accommodation rule, since that is how a similar requirement has been interpreted in the context of the immigration rules relating to marriage.

1 Making an application under the concession

6.17 If the requirements of the concession can be satisfied, an application should be made with all the supporting evidence to the nearest British Consulate if the partner is outside the UK, or to the Home Office if the foreign partner is already lawfully in the UK. To be lawfully in the UK, the applicant needs to have leave to enter or remain in the UK which has not expired and which was not obtained by deception.

6.18 An application from outside the UK is made by completing forms IM2A and IM2B, available from the British Consulate and by paying a fee of £250. If the application is successful, the foreign partner will be given entry clearance (a visa) as an unmarried partner and, on entry to the UK, will have a stamp placed in his or her passport granting leave to enter for an initial period of twelve months.

6.19 Individuals who are lawfully in the UK should apply before their current leave to enter or remain expires by completing the current version of Form FLR(0) and submitting it to the Home Office with supporting documentation. No fee is payable. If an application is successful, the applicant will be granted further leave to remain for twelve months.

6.20 At the end of the twelve-month period, if it can be demonstrated that the relationship is continuing, that the parties intend to live together permanently and that they are still able to support and accommodate themselves, an application can be lodged on Form SET(0) for indefinite leave to remain in the UK which, if granted, gives the individual concerned the right to remain permanently in the UK.

6.21 At the time of the initial application, a couple needs to demonstrate through documentary evidence that they have indeed been living together for the required period. Evidence of cohabitation is best shown by correspondence which links the couple to the same address and any official records of this address such as doctor's records, national insurance records, bank statements and other such documentation.

6.22 Evidence also needs to be submitted confirming the couple's ability to support and accommodate themselves. This should include bank statements and wage slips covering the preceding three-month period.

6.23 Further documentation confirming the existence of the couple's relationship may also be relevant. This can include letters written by the couple themselves, family and friends, photographic evidence, evidence of joint commitments (joint bank account, investments, rent agreements, wills, pension agreements, etc) and evidence of the couple's communication during any periods of separation.

6.24 With respect to applications made to the Home Office, it is very important that the relevant form and required supporting documentation are submitted at least two weeks before the end of the applicant's current leave to remain in the UK. While, technically, the application need not be submitted until the last day of the applicant's current leave, the Home Office may send back by second class post any application form which has been improperly completed or lacks the requisite supporting documentation. In such cases, it is essential that the corrected application package be re-submitted before the end of the applicant's current leave and also before the applicant will become an 'overstayer' and any right of appeal against a refusal of the application will be lost.

2   Cases where requirements of the concession have not been met

6.25   Practitioners will often be requested to advise in cases where the relationship in question clearly does not meet the requirements of the concession. In such cases, it is essential that the adviser have a very strong grounding in general immigration law so that other possibilities may be explored for the couple to remain together in the UK or in another country until such time as they meet the concessionary requirements.

6.26   It may be possible, for example, for the foreign partner to come and live in the UK under some other category of the immigration rules. Relevant categories would include students, commonwealth working holidaymakers (a category reserved for commonwealth citizens aged 27 or less), work permit employment (usually only available for senior positions or where there is a skill shortage or for particular training or work experience schemes) and other categories limited by occupation. It may also be possible for foreign partners to establish themselves in business in the UK, although the capital require-ments for qualification under this heading are very high (£200,000), unless the applicant comes from one of the eastern European countries which is party to an association agreement with the European Community.

6.27   It may also be worth investigating the ancestry of a foreign partner since the existence of parents or grandparents born in a European country may entitle the individual to citizenship or qualify the individual for an ancestry based concession. In the context of the UK, for example, a UK born grandparent of a commonwealth citizen gives such a citizen the right to live and work in the UK for four years leading to permanent residency thereafter.

6.28   It may also be possible for the UK-based partner to consider living in the foreign partner's country for the required period. If one of the partners is British or the national of another EEA country, the couple could also consider living together in another EEA country which recognises same-sex relationships of a lesser duration, such as the Netherlands or one of the Scandinavian countries in the EEA.

6.29   There will always be cases, however, where individuals find that there are no options for remaining together either within the terms of the immigration rules or by seeking to live together in another country. Sometimes, because of the legal position of homosexuality, it may be impossible for a couple to even consider spending time together in the foreign partner's home country. For such couples, the only option may be to make an application in any event under the terms of the concession, even though the four-year cohabitation requirement is not satisfied. So long as an application is made before the foreign partner's current leave to remain in the UK expires, the applicant will have the right to appeal against the negative decision which is likely to follow. So long as an appeal is lodged, the foreign partner will be entitled to remain lawfully in the UK until the appeal is disposed of. At the time of writing, it is taking the Home Office some months to make initial decisions and the Immigration Appellate Authority some months to list appeals for hearing. It is likely to take at least one year from the date of application to the date of appeal hearing, by which time the four-year requirement may be satisfied. Anyone considering pursuing this course, however, should only do so with expert legal advice and assistance.

6.30 Individuals contemplating making an application under the concession may already be living in the UK unlawfully. They may be people who entered the country illegally or overstayed their leave to enter or to remain. One year after the commencement of the concession, the Home Office had not yet decided how to deal with applications made by persons in these categories. Again, specialised legal advice from an immigration practitioner is essential.

6.31 At the time of writing, only a very few appeals have proceeded with respect to people refused under the terms of the concession. Immigration adjudicators have tended to be sympathetic to the appellant in such cases. In virtually all cases which have been decided up to October 1998, adjudicators have made a 'recommendation' that the Secretary of State rethink his approach to the concession and grant individuals successive periods of one year's leave until they have accumulated the necessary four years of cohabitation.

6.32 To date, however, there has not been an appeal allowed on a purely legal basis although various legal arguments are being developed. One interesting argument is that the unreasonable terms under the concession make it ultra vires because it is inherently 'a snare and a delusion' and 'indeed but a mirage'. In making this argument, the lawyers have cited the case of *Monshoora Begum* [1] in which Simon Brown J declared an immigration rule unreasonable and ultra vires which required that, on the one hand, sponsors seeking to bring relatives to the UK had to demonstrate that the relative was poorer than the average members of his or her community and yet, at the same time, had to demonstrate that the British sponsor was sending financial support to that relative.

1   [1986] Imm AR 385, QBD.

6.33 If a person who does not qualify under the concession is faced with removal or deportation from the UK, it is arguable that such a removal would breach the UK's obligation under the European Convention on Human Rights. In *X v United Kingdom* [1] the Commission found that a deportation order requiring the foreign partner in a same-sex relationship to leave the UK could constitute an interference with both partners' right to respect for their private life under art 8. However, it appears that there will only be an interference if it can be established that there are obstacles to, or special reasons why, the couple's private life could not be established in the foreign partner's country. If it can be established that there will be an interference, it will be necessary for the Home Office to show that the interference is necessary in democratic society for one of the specified aims set out in art 8(2). The Commission has held that where the aim of legislation is 'to protect the family', that is a legitimate aim justifying an interference with the right to a private life [2]. It is arguable, however, that the aim of the four-year concession is not to 'protect the family' but to preserve the 'special position of marriage'. That is how the minister has justified it. It is arguable that the interference caused by the four-year requirement is not in proportion to the aim pursued. It is possible to give a 'special position to marriage' without imposing the high hurdle that is the four-year rule. If an applicant can point to an alternative to secure the stated aim, that may be evidence, although not necessarily decisive evidence, of disproportion.

1   App 9369/81 (1983) 5 EHRR 601.
2   *S v United Kingdom* App 11716/85 (1985) unreported.

6.34   If it can be demonstrated that art 8 is engaged, but no interference can be shown on the facts, it may still be possible to argue that the four-year requirement is discrimination on the grounds of marital status and in breach of art 14 of the Convention. It would be for the Home Office to justify why they treat unmarried and married couples differently for immigration purposes.

6.35   Where the foreign partner is in a relationship with an EEA national and the four-year requirement cannot be satisfied, it is at least arguable that to remove or prevent the entry of the foreign partner creates an obstacle to the mobility of the EEA national. Regulation 1612/68 requires that 'obstacles to the mobility of workers shall be limited particularly as regards to the worker's right to be joined by his family'. Article 10 of the regulation gives the right to the spouse of an EEA national to join a national in another member state and creates an obligation that member states facilitate the admission of any other 'member of the family' if they are dependent on the worker or live together. It is at least arguable, that 'the member of the family' should include same-sex partners. There is, however, no authoritative case law to date.

C   APPLICATION FOR POLITICAL ASYLUM BASED ON SEXUAL ORIENTATION

6.36   As already noted, the fact that individuals cannot live openly as gay men or lesbians in their own country may be a relevant factor in supporting an application by such individuals for leave to remain in the UK with a British-based partner. It is also possible for individuals coming from a country where there are legal or other difficulties for gay men and lesbians to consider the possibility of making an application for political asylum in the UK on the basis that they would face a 'well-founded fear of persecution' if returned to their home country because of their sexual orientation.

6.37   Thus far, the record of the UK in recognising refugees on this basis is a poor one. The authors of this chapter are, at the time of writing, aware of only two successful cases clearly based upon sexual orientation, both decided in 1998, one relating to an Algerian and the other to a Romanian. This contrasts with a very different record in many other countries, such as the United States where, apparently, hundreds of such cases have been recognised.

6.38   An initial hurdle to be overcome in pursuing such cases is the collection of information confirming the persecution of homosexuals in the country concerned. Aside from the usual sources of information, such as Amnesty International, Human Rights Watch, the Refugee Legal Centre Documentation Centre, and the United Nations High Commission for Refugees etc, a specialised collection point for documentation is:

International Gay and Lesbian Human Rights Commission Asylum Project
1360 Mission Street #200
San Francisco
CA 94103
USA
Tel 001 415 255 8680 Fax 001 415 255 8662.

This organisation produces country bundles relating to the situation of gay men and lesbians in various countries for a relatively modest fee.

6.39   Several important legal issues relevant to such cases remain unsatisfactorily unresolved. One particular difficulty is the current muddled state of UK law regarding the question of whether sexuality can define a 'social group' for purposes of the 1951 Convention Relating to the Status of Refugees. There is a growing chain of authorities from the Immigration Appeal Tribunal confirming this position including *Apostolov* [1], *Vrachiu* [2], *Seuleanu* [3] and the minority determination in *Sadegh* [4]. At the same time, there have been other less helpful Immigration Appeal Tribunal determinations reaching an alternative conclusion.

1   18547.
2   11559.
3   14292.
4   11324.

6.40   The Home Office itself, however, seems less inclined to suggest that homosexuals do not constitute a 'social group' for these purposes. Gay and lesbian asylum seekers found an unlikely ally in this regard in the then Home Office immigration minister Ann Widdecombe who, in a letter to David Alton MP dated 31 January 1996, wrote:

'We interpret this provision in the Convention as follows:
(i)   the group is defined by some innate or unchangeable characteristic of its members analogous to race, religion, nationality or political opinion, for example their sex, linguistic background, tribe, family or class which the individual cannot change or should not be required to change; and
(ii) there must be real risk of persecution by reason of the person's membership of the group.
Whilst claims based on homosexuality might satisfy (i) within this definition, the requirements set out in (ii) would also have to be met in the individual case.'

6.41   At the time of writing, the House of Lords is about to hear the cases of *Shah* and *Islam* which, while dealing with the issue of women as a social group, will no doubt define standards which will further illuminate the issue of homosexuals as a social group.

6.42 The Refugee Legal Centre has produced (under the authorship of Simon Russell) a useful memorandum on this subject entitled 'Sexual orientation and refugee claims based on membership of a particular social group under the 1951 Refugee Convention'. There is also an interesting European Legal Network on Asylum (Elena) research paper published in June 1997 by the European Council on Refugees and Exiles.

6.43 A further legal issue arising in cases relating to gay men and lesbians claiming refugee status is whether or not 'prosecution' for homosexual acts can constitute 'persecution'. In the case of *Vraciu*, for example, the Immigration Appeal Tribunal suggested that 'prosecution may amount to persecution depending on the focus of the prosecution', suggesting for example, the distinction between prosecution aimed at preventing consensual homosexual acts in private and prosecution for other reasons. In another case, *Secretary of State v S* [1], a majority of the Immigration Appeal Tribunal (the legally qualified chair dissenting) found that there was no persecution where a gay man from Iran was being prosecuted and faced execution if convicted, holding that this was a matter of law for the Iranian authorities. In this case, however, when leave to appeal to the Court of Appeal was granted, the Home Office conceded the case, although on a disingenuous basis that the appellant faced persecution for 'political' reasons.

1   13124.

D   ISSUES RELATING TO HIV AND AIDS

6.44 The attitude of the British government with respect to immigration issues relating to HIV and AIDS has been, in many ways, a commendable one. Unlike many other countries, including notably the USA, the UK government has always maintained that HIV infection (including AIDS) should not in itself be considered justification for a recommendation on public health grounds to refuse leave to enter the UK. This policy was first set out in a letter from the Chief Medical Officer quoted in the *New Scientist* of 6 July 1991 and subsequently reconfirmed by the Department of Health. The only constraint on this policy—a constraint which applies similarly to all medical conditions—is that immigration officers must, under certain circumstances, consider whether individuals will be in a position to pay for medical treatment which may be required because of HIV-related illness during the course of their stay in the UK. This applies only to certain categories of individuals who are coming for a limited stay in the UK and, in fact, is rarely invoked.

6.45 Nor should an individual's HIV status be relevant to an individual's application to extend leave to remain in the UK unless the individual wishes to raise the issue as a compassionate factor to encourage the Home Office to exercise discretion favourably in cases which might otherwise not fall neatly within the current immigration law and practice.

6.46 Thus, for example, in applications made with respect to same-sex partners wishing to remain together in the UK, discretion has fairly regularly been exercised positively in cases which do not fit squarely within the terms of the concession where there are compassionate HIV-related factors affecting the health of either the foreign or British-based partner. Similarly, in some cases, where an asylum seeker has failed to be recognised as a refugee but is able to present compassionate evidence relating to HIV-related illness, the Home Office has been willing to grant such individuals exceptional leave to remain in the UK. Indeed, in some instances, it may be possible to base a claim for political asylum specifically on persecution which an individual may if returned to a country, face because of HIV status.

6.47 In making representations, an individual's representative should present substantial documentation regarding the state of the individual's health, information regarding treatment they are receiving and the availability of such treatment in their home country and frank information about their life expectancy, the likelihood of their needing to rely on public funds and other related issues. Detailed reports from doctors, social workers and others familiar with such cases should be submitted. Solicitors working in the Advice Centre at The Terrence Higgins Trust are an excellent source of guidance regarding the approach to be taken in such cases.

6.48 In 1995, the Immigration and Nationality Department issued two sets of guidelines, one relating to 'AIDS and HIV+ cases' and the other relating to 'Enforcement Action in AIDS and HIV+ cases'. The guidelines make clear that 'the fact that a person suffers from AIDS or is HIV positive is not grounds for refusing entry clearance or leave to remain if the person concerned otherwise qualifies under the Immigration Rules'.

6.49 They go on to state, however, that 'equally, the fact that an applicant has AIDS or is HIV positive is not in itself sufficient grounds to justify the exercise of discretion where the requirements of the rules are not met'. The guidelines rather inconclusively suggest that decision makers must perform a difficult balancing act in each case. The experience of practitioners working in the area is that it is essential to document as fully as possible the compassionate nature of a particular case in order to be successful in obtaining exceptional leave to enter or remain.

6.50 With respect to asylum cases, of particular relevance are the Asylum Directorate instructions relating to the granting of exceptional leave [1] and available on the Home Office website. Paragraph 2.1 of these instructions states that:

> 'Ele/r[exceptional leave to enter or remain] may be granted to asylum applicants *only* if they fall under one of the following criteria…

> Where there is *credible* medical evidence that return would result in substantial damage in the physical/psychological health of the applicant or his dependants. In cases of doubt, a second opinion should be sought from a credible source.'

1   Ch 5, s 1, March 1998.

6.51 The Home Office has been resisting the application of this guideline to failed asylum cases where practitioners have argued that exceptional leave should be granted because the asylum seeker has, while in the UK pursuing the asylum claim, started a course of combination therapy which would necessarily be interrupted resulting in a rapid deterioration of health if the asylum seeker were returned to a home country where such combination therapy was unavailable. At the time of writing, two High Court challenges have been launched challenging the failure by the Home Office to follow its own guidelines in this respect.

6.52   Further, para 2.2 of the policy states that a grant of exceptional leave to enter or remain would be appropriate where the return of the asylum seeker to his or her home country would be in breach of art 3 of the European Convention on Human Rights. In this regard, the European Court of Human Rights decision in the case of *D v United Kingdom* [1] is directly relevant because, in that case, the court held that to return someone to a place where there was no treatment and where the applicant would die a hastened death without support would constitute a breach of art 3.

1   (1997) 24 EHRR 423.

6.53   In August 1998, in Ch 17, s 2 of the Immigration Directorate's instructions, a new policy on 'carers' was announced permitting 'applications from persons here in a temporary capacity seeking leave to remain to care for a sick relative or friend who is suffering from a terminal illness, such as cancer or AIDS'. Such applications are to be granted on a discretionary basis 'on the individual merits of the case' and the guidelines make clear that this is meant to be 'only a temporary capacity and that once alternative arrangements have been made or if the patient should die then the "carer" will be expected to return home.' These guidelines are accessible on the Home Office website.

E   CONCLUSION

6.54   While the policies of the UK government are far from ideal in the areas covered by this chapter, they do reflect a willingness by decision makers to be swayed in at least some cases by the effective presentation of compassionate factors. An important responsibility on those representing individuals is to ensure that cases being pursued are extremely well documented and that, in particular, the 'human face' of the legal problem being addressed is clearly portrayed.

6.55   The advances made with respect to the unmarried partner concession particularly demonstrate the fact that a successful campaign to accomplish change involves not only legal argumentation and litigation but also carefully organised and calibrated political lobbying and a responsible press policy. Ultimately, however, the most crucial factor is the existence of a client base which clearly illustrates the highly compassionate nature of the problem and which is either articulate in its own right or has legal and/or organisational advocates prepared to state their case in the most efficacious manner.

6.56   Those who have been working in the field of immigration rights relating to gay men and lesbians have felt themselves particularly fortunate to be blessed with a highly motivated, multi-skilled client base which has propelled in many ways the positive changes which have occurred. The risks which those clients have taken and continue to take in pursuing cases which are, on their face, unpopular to the public at large and media unfriendly, should make the situation of the next generation of gay men and lesbians facing these issues an easier one, as well as inspiring others who are fighting similar but as yet unwon battles for just and equitable change.

Chapter 7

Crime

A SEX

1 Consensual offences

7.01 The criminal law has almost nothing to say about the regulation of consensual sexual activity between lesbians. By default the age of consent for sexual activity for gay women is 16. Apocryphally, this silence on lesbian sexuality originates from the legislators' reluctance to broach the subject with Queen Victoria when the offences regulating gay male sexuality were first considered as part of the Criminal Law Amendment Act 1885. More realistically, the silence on lesbian sexuality has more to do with the manner with which women's sexuality is ignored by the law in general. In this particular case the oversight is something to be welcomed rather than challenged.

7.02 Gay men, on the other hand, have been the specific target of criminal law for a least a century (the precise genesis of specific gay male sexual offences is the subject of some debate). The 'classic' charges brought against gay men engaging in consensual sexual offences are buggery, gross indecency and importuning. These last two are either way offences and the former is indictable only. For gay men who were the subject of gross indecency or importuning charges in the 1960s and 1970s, the typical scenario was a brief and shameful court appearance, a guilty plea, a stiff financial penalty and humiliating publicity. The targets of much of this prosecution work were men caught allegedly abusing the facility of public lavatories (cottages) or engaging in sexual activity at night in deserted parks or wasteland (cruising grounds).

7.03 In the 1980s, with gay politicisation, an increasing number of men charged with such offences chose to fight the allegations—often citing the fabrication of evidence or homophobia by the police. The typical venue for contested cases became the Crown Court where juries showed an increasing willingness to acquit defendants facing such charges. Two factors seemed to be at play—first, a growing readiness amongst juries to accept that the police did fabricate evidence against what were seen as 'easy targets' and second, an apparent 'collective disapproval' that police time and energy were being expended on pursuing ostensibly victimless offences when the victims of 'real' crimes like robbery, car theft or burglary were given little assistance beyond a crime report number.

7.04   Unfortunately, the collective cynicism displayed by juries towards the 'classic offences' was not shared by lay and stipendiary magistrates in the lower criminal courts.

7.05   From experience as a practitioner looking after a large number of gay male defendants in the 1980s, the author would put the acquittal rate in the Crown Court at about 80% whilst the corresponding rate in the magistrates' court during the same period was about 20%.

7.06   Consequently in the late 1980s there was a distinct shift in prosecution policy, particularly within London, away from the 'classic' either way offences and towards the use of summary only offences—including an extensive reliance on local byelaws, the Public Order Act 1986, s 5, the Town Police Clauses Act 1847, s 48 and, ironically, outraging public decency. Irony is mentioned in respect of the last matter because it is in fact indictable only as a common law offence—a fact simply not appreciated by many charging police officers. On occasions this prosecution strategy took on the semblance of an undignified scrabble—as soon as a defendant indicated that they were electing trial at the Crown Court the prosecution would ferret around for and substitute some unlikely summary only offence.

This section looks at the 'classic' triumvirate of gross indecency, buggery and importuning and at the more recently employed summary offences.

(i)   Gross indecency and buggery

7.07   Sections 12 and 13 of the Sexual Offences Act 1956 confirmed the criminalisation of sexual activity between men. Section 12 made it an offence to engage in the act of buggery (more commonly known as anal intercourse). The section covered not just buggery between men but also a man and a woman or a man and an animal. Section 13 of the Sexual Offences Act 1956 rendered it an offence for men to engage in acts of gross indecency (basically sexual activity short of anal intercourse). The Sexual Offences Act 1967 partially decriminalised sexual activity between men providing that the relevant acts were in private and between men who had attained the age of 21. The Criminal Justice and Public Order Act 1994 lowered the age of consent for gay men to 18. In August 1998 the House of Commons passed an amendment to the Crime and Disorder Bill equalising the age of consent for gay male sexual activity to 16 (the age of consent for heterosexual activity). The amendment was, however, defeated by the House of Lords and the government allowed the amendment to lapse promising to introduce new legislation in the autumn of 1998 to effect equality.

7.08   The Sexual Offences Act 1967 is sometimes seen as 'legalising' gay male sexual activity. It does not do so. Rather, it decriminalises such sexual activity within a very small window. The conditions for legality are that any such acts are in private and both parties have attained the age of 18.

7.09 'Private' has a particular definition. Section 1(2) of the SOA 1967 provides that an act is not in private when:

(*a*)   more than two persons take part or are present;

(*b*)   the act is in a lavatory to which the public have or are permitted to have access whether on payment or otherwise.

7.10   Thus any group sexual activity between men is automatically unlawful as is activity between two men with another merely observing person. Similarly any activity in a public lavatory, even within a locked cubicle, is automatically unlawful.

7.11   The courts have also given consideration to the question of privacy, particularly in relation to outdoor locations which might ordinarily be considered public but where sexual activity takes place late at night.

7.12   In *R v Reakes* [1], R was indicted for committing an act of buggery other than in private and without the consent of his sexual partner. The act took place in an enclosed unlit private yard at about 1am. There was a gate from a public road into the yard and in the yard was a 'water closet' used by patrons of two neighbouring restaurants and the employees of a taxi service. Someone came to use the WC shortly after the act. R's defence was that the act was done in private and with his partner's consent. The judge directed as to privacy 'you look at all the surrounding circumstances, the time of night, the nature of the place including such matters as lighting and you consider further the likelihood of a third person coming upon the scene'. On appeal the direction as to privacy was held to be clear and wholly satisfactory. The appellate court rejected submissions that the test of privacy was subjective and that regard should only be had to the moment when the act took place: all the circumstances had to be looked at and considered.

1   [1974] Crim LR 615.

7.13   The direction appears to concede that the public or private nature of a place can vary from time to time. The act done in a public bar or public library would presumably be done in private if it occurred when all the patrons had gone home, the doors were locked and only the two participants were present.

7.14   In *R v Ghik* [1], G was indicted for committing an act of gross indecency with C in a public place, namely the underground car park at Euston station. The act was alleged to have taken place on stairs inside the NCP at 0035. The station shut at 0100 hours. The case was before the Central Criminal Court and at the end of the prosecution case the defence submitted that the onus of disproving privacy lay upon the prosecution and that there had to be at least some evidence of the likelihood of a third person coming upon the scene. The fact that the place was ordinarily a public place was not conclusive since Parliament in the 1967 Act, by specifically excluding from its provisions acts done in private in a public lavatory, clearly envisaged that privacy could be found and relied on in other public places.

1   [1984] Crim LR 110.

7.15   The court accepted that there was no evidence of the likelihood of anyone coming on the scene nor even that the car park was open at the time and directed a verdict of not guilty.

7.16 There exists a great myth within the gay community (one of several relating to the operation of the law) that sexual activity between two men in a hotel room is de facto unlawful as it breaches the 'privacy' condition. There is absolutely no authority for this proposition and indeed, the analysis offends against what authorities do exist.

7.17 The directions on privacy do leave some questions unanswered however.
(a) If an act takes place on, for example, a piece of parkland late at night and is observed by police officers specifically tasked to detect such activity, can those police officers be considered to be 'persons likely to come upon the scene', thereby losing the parkland its otherwise private status?
(b) If an act takes place on a piece of parkland late at night which is notorious for gay male sexual activity (a 'cruising' ground) and there is evidence that whilst no third parties were directly present many other people were around can those others, apparently there for similar purposes, be held to be persons likely to come upon the scene?

7.18 The author has been confronted by both scenarios and has sought to argue that the purpose of the 'privacy' provisions in the legislation is to protect 'innocent' members of the public not police officers or other gay men. Such arguments have not met with much success although the adverse decisions were taken at a low level within the criminal justice system and do not therefore constitute authorities.

What is gross indecency ?

7.19 Buggery (anal penetration) is a self-explanatory activity (although it should be noted that both the penetrator and the receiving partner are guilty of the offence) but gross indecency is not specifically defined. Through prosecution practice it has come to cover a variety of sexual activity between men—oral sex and mutual masturbation being the most obvious examples. However gross indecency has also been held to cover the activity of two men masturbating themselves in conjunction with no actual physical contact [1]. The offence is not committed unless both men actually participate in the indecency— 'with another man' cannot be construed as meaning 'against' or 'directed towards' a person who did not consent [2]. More recently attempts have been made to argue that the meaning of gross indecency must be seen as changing with changing mores and that 'grossly indecent' acts should be confined to exceptional activities. This argument was used in particular in the Bolton seven case—a well-publicised group sex prosecution from 1997.

1   *R v Mount* (1934) 24 Cr App Rep 135, CA.
2   *R v Preece and Howells* [1977] QB 370, 63 Cr App Rep 28, CA.

Time limits

7.20 There is a very frequently overlooked provision contained in s 7 of SOA 1967 which places a time limit of a year from the commission of the relevant act for a prosecution to be brought in any case of:
(a) gross indecency;
(b) buggery not amounting to an assault and not being an offence involving a boy under 16 years of age.

Therefore for any group sexual activity and for any sexual activity involving a consenting 16 or 17-year-old, a prosecution must be commenced (ie charge made or information laid) within a year.

7.21 This is, as stated, an important but frequently overlooked provision—particularly by the police and prosecution. In group sexual activity, detection of the offence is rarely by way of one of the parties complaining but by the police discovering some record (most typically photographs or a video) ancillary to another investigation. Such records may be dated but frequently are not. The issue then arises as to when the activity took place. The onus is on the prosecution to prove that the activity took place within the last year. Without such proof a prosecution will fail. A defence lawyer confronted with overwhelming photographic records of group sexual activity may feel compelled to advise his client to plead to an offence, or even worse, may advise his client in the police station to answer questions about the date of the activity.

7.22 In *R v Lewis* [1] where it was unclear upon the evidence given at trial whether the offence charged had been committed within the year prior to the commencement of proceedings, the court quashed the conviction. The court held that a judge need not in every case to which SOA 1967, s 7 applied, direct the jury to be sure about the date of the offence but must do so where the issue was raised by the defence or where it clearly arose on the evidence at trial.

1   (1978) 68 Cr App Rep 310.

7.23 It is also becoming increasingly common for male victims of sexual abuse in their teens to complain about such activity during adulthood even when those acts were, on the face of it, consensual. If the acts complained of occurred when the complainant was 16 or 17 (or indeed if there is uncertainty about whether the complainant had achieved such an age) then s 7 may provide a defence or a bar to any proceedings. Section 7 does not, however, have any application in cases of sexual assault, however old.

Powers of arrest and punishment

7.24 Gross indecency is an either way offence. Buggery is indictable only. Gross indecency is punishable with a maximum of five years' imprisonment in cases of underage sexual activity but with a maximum of two years' imprisonment for group or other non-private sexual activity. This means that 'underage' gross indecency is an arrestable offence under the Police and Criminal Evidence Act 1984, but 'non-private' gross indecency is not. Again this may be a point of some significance since the police invariably purport to arrest someone accused of committing non-private gross indecency—especially someone arrested in a public lavatory ('cottaging'). The police may seek to justify their arrest by relying on PACE, s 25 which allows arrests for non-arrestable offences when one or more stated conditions (general arrest conditions) are satisfied. The conditions most commonly relied on in gross indecency arrests are that:

(*a*)   the name of the relevant person is unknown and cannot readily be ascertained;

(*b*)   the constable has reasonable grounds for believing that an arrest is necessary to prevent the relevant person committing an offence against public decency.

The latter condition can only be relied on however when members of the public going about their normal business cannot reasonably be expected to avoid the person to be arrested [1].

1   PACE 1984, s 25(5).

7.25 It would be fair to say that the police regularly fail to abide by the arrest requirements set out in PACE 1984, ss 24 and 25. Frequently they purport to arrest for gross indecency simpliciter. When challenged on the issue, reference may be made to the s 25 general arrest conditions—particularly the prevention of an offence against public decency. However in many cases the idea that a man approached by a police officer and obliged to give his name and address will then continue 'cottaging' is inconceivable. Furthermore the police tend to rely on this exemption even in situations where there is not a member of the public going about his or her normal business present—eg where an 'arrest' takes place on a late night cruising ground.

7.26 One of the most notorious cases of a mass arrest of gay men for gross indecency took place in the village of Hoylandswaine in 1993. Thirty-six men were arrested after the police raided a private party purportedly looking for stolen goods. None of the men were engaged in any form of sexual activity and indeed all were fully clothed. The allegation made by the police was that the men were conspiring (planning) to commit acts of gross indecency in the sense of engaging in group sexual activity. All 36 men were interviewed and all declined to answer police questions on legal advice. The Crown Prosecution Service advised taking no action against the men through lack of evidence. Sixteen of the men subsequently sued South Yorkshire Police for wrongful arrest and false imprisonment relying on the fact that gross indecency is not an arrestable offence. The police settled the case without admitting liability—paying out some £42,500 in damages.

7.27 The situation regarding sentencing (and thus powers of arrest) for buggery is rather more complex. The maximum penalty for buggery with a person under the age of 16 is life imprisonment (thus this is an arrestable offence); if the accused is over 20 and the other person under 18, five years (again, arrestable); otherwise two years (not an arrestable offence).

Procuring

7.28 There is a specific secondary offence with respect to buggery enshrined in the Sexual Offences Act 1967, s 4. It is an offence for a man to procure another man to commit an act of buggery with a third man even where the act procured is entirely lawful. The maximum penalty is two years' imprisonment. The offence is either way. The provision has led to fears within the gay community that the introduction of two friends in the hope that they will 'get on' and possibly enter into a sexual relationship will be sufficient for the commission of this offence. In reality 'procuring' quite clearly requires more effort than this—'you procure a thing by setting out to see that it happens and taking the appropriate steps to produce that happening.'[1]

1 *A-G's Reference (No 1 of 1975)* [1975] QB 773, [1975] 2 All ER 684, CA, per Lord Widgery CJ.

(ii)   Importuning

7.29 Under the Sexual Offences Act 1956, s 32 it is an offence for a man persistently to solicit or importune in a public place for immoral purposes. This is an either way offence punishable in the Crown Court with up to two years' imprisonment. This is not therefore an arrestable offence and the same comments made about the police arrests for gross indecency (see paras **7.24** and **7.25**) also apply to importuning arrests.

7.30 Importuning and gross indecency were the two most common gay male sexual offences used against men frequenting public lavatories (cottages) or cruising grounds. If the police did not allege sexual activity between two or more men (gross indecency) then the allegation would invariably be that a single male was making overtures to one or more other men.

7.31 Although the offence can only be committed by a man, the target of the importuning may be another man or a woman [1] and thus it is not specifically a gay sexual offence. However in practice the charge is one laid almost exclusively against men soliciting other men and might only be used against a man soliciting a woman for unlawful sexual purposes—eg if the woman is under 16 years of age.

1   *R v Goddard* (1990) 92 Cr App Rep 185, CA.

7.32 The element of persistence means that either the same person has to be solicited more than once or at least two different people solicited. The period between the solicitations may be substantial—even 24 hours [1].

1   *Dale v Smith* [1967] 1 WLR 700, DC.

7.33 The immoral purpose requirement has to be some form of sexual activity [1]. In the case of gay men it has been held that importuning for a lawful sexual purpose (eg sex between two men over the age of consent in a private location) may still be immoral—it is a matter for a jury to decide [2]. In practice if the contention is that what was being solicited was lawful sexual activity, then it must be worth arguing that no offence has been committed.

1   *Crook v Edmondson* [1966] 2 QB 81, DC; *R v Kirkup* (1993) 96 Cr App Rep 352, CA.
2   *R v Ford* (1977) 66 Cr App Rep 46, CA and see *R v Kirkup* [1993] 1 WLR 774 where the authorities are reviewed.

(iii)   Prostitution and brothels

7.34 The charge of importuning is one that is commonly laid against men engaging in gay male prostitution. The police have sought to use the equivalent but summary only offence of soliciting for the purposes of prostitution under s 1 of the Street Offences Act 1959 against male prostitutes but it has been held that this provision applies only to women [1].

1   *DPP v Bull* [1995] QB 88.

7.35 British law does not render the act of prostitution—selling sexual services for a commercial reward—a criminal offence. However most of the activities surrounding the central act of prostitution are unlawful. The sexual services are not limited to sexual intercourse for an act of prostitution to occur, but include 'any form of lewdness' eg masturbation or oral sex [1].

1   *R v De Munck* [1918] 1 KB 635, 13 Cr App Rep 113, CA; *R v Webb* [1964] 1 QB 357, [1963] 3 All ER 177, CCA.

Soliciting

7.36 Section 32 of the Sexual Offences Act 1956 makes it an offence for a man persistently to solicit in a public place for immoral purposes (see para **7.29**). If proved, the offence is punishable by up to two years' imprisonment in the

Crown Court and six months' imprisonment and/or £5,000 fine in the magistrates' court.

7.37 Section 1 of the Street Offences Act 1959 makes it an offence for a 'common' (female) prostitute to loiter or solicit in a public place for the purposes of prostitution. The offence is punishable in the magistrates' court only by way of fine up to £1,000.

Pimping

7.38 It is an offence for a man knowingly to live wholly or partly on the earnings of (female) prostitution—Sexual Offences Act 1956, s 30. The offence is normally alleged where it is believed that a man is operating as a pimp. If proved, the offence is punishable by up to seven years' imprisonment in the Crown Court and six months' imprisonment and/or £5,000 fine in the magistrates' court. The producer of a directory of female prostitutes has been found guilty under this provision[1].

1   *Shaw v DPP* (1961) 45 Cr App R 113.

7.39 It is an offence for a woman for the purposes of gain to exercise control, direction or influence over a (female) prostitute's movements in a way which shows she is aiding or compelling her prostitution[1]. If proved, the offence is again punishable by up to seven years' imprisonment in the Crown Court and six months' imprisonment and/or £5,000 fine in the magistrates' court.

1   Sexual Offences Act 1956, s 31.

7.40 It is also an offence for a man or a woman to live wholly or partly on the earnings of male prostitution. If proved, the offence is punishable by up to seven years' imprisonment in the Crown Court and six months' imprisonment and/or £5,000 fine in the magistrates' court.

Managing a brothel

7.41 It is an offence for anyone to keep, manage or assist in the management of a brothel[1]. The brothel may be male, female, gay or straight. It is also an offence to let or permit your premises to be used as a brothel[2]. All these offences can only be dealt with in the magistrates' court and are punishable with up to six months' imprisonment and/or £2,500 fine.

1   Sexual Offences Act 1956, s 33.
2   Sexual Offences Act 1956, ss 34–35.

7.42 The offences of managing a brothel and living off immoral earnings are the charges invariably brought against those engaged in running gay male brothels or massage parlours. The management offence is drafted widely to include those who assist and can catch, inter alia, a receptionist or cashier who derives no profit share.

Kerb crawling

7.43 Kerb crawling (male crawler and female prostitute only) and persistently soliciting a woman for the purposes of prostitution are offences under the Sexual Offences Act 1985. Both matters can only be dealt with in the magistrates' court and are punishable with a fine up to £1,000.

Outreach work and the supply of condoms

7.44 Understandably, outreach workers and agencies involved in the promotion of safer sex which liaise with male and female prostitutes may be involved in the provision of condoms to their clients. Whilst it is extremely difficult to envisage the distribution of condoms placing the outreach worker at any practical risk of investigation or prosecution for a (secondary) criminal offence, the carrying of condoms by male or female prostitutes can increase the risk of prosecution for them. This factor should be carefully considered by condom providers and it may be considered appropriate to advise the recipients about the risks.

7.45 The carrying of condoms by an individual is, by itself, clearly not sufficient to establish one of the criminal offences mentioned at paras **7.36–7.37**, for example, soliciting. However the carrying of condoms has been used by the police as corroborative evidence to support an allegation before the courts that an individual is operating as a prostitute. Such strategies have been the subject of attacks by, amongst others, the English Collective of Prostitutes, as it discourages the carrying of condoms by prostitutes and consequently encourages the practice of unsafe penetrative sexual intercourse.

7.46 Similarly in police prosecutions of brothels, gay saunas and the like, the presence and availability of quantities of condoms on the premises have been used as evidence to indicate that unlawful sexual acts and/or prostitution are taking place. Again, using the presence of condoms as evidence in this manner has led to sauna/brothel mangers restricting the availability of condoms on their premises with the consequent increased risk of the spread of infection.

(iv) Other offences

Outraging public decency

7.47 All open lewdness, grossly scandalous behaviour and whatever openly outrages decency or is offensive and disgusting, or is injurious to public morals by tending to corrupt the mind and destroy the love of decency, morality and good order, is an offence indictable at common law. Like many common law offences this offence is indictable only and punishable by an unlimited fine and an unlimited term of imprisonment.

7.48 The charge has been used against gay men in cottaging or cruising situations where an offence of gross indecency or importuning might not be sustainable—eg an allegation that a man is standing in a public cruising area simply masturbating himself in order to attract attention but not actually directing his actions towards any specific person.

7.49 It must be proved that the act complained of was committed in public— that is in a place, public or private, where there exists a real possibility that members of the general public might witness it [1]. It is sufficient however if only one person actually sees the act [2]. It must also be established that the act was of such a lewd, obscene or disgusting character that it must constitute an outrage on public decency.

1   *R v Walker* [1996] 1 Cr App Rep 111, CA.
2   *R v Mayling* [1963] 2 QB 717, 47 Cr App Rep 102, CCA.

Public Order Act 1986, s 5

7.50 Section 5 of the Public Order Act renders it an offence punishable by fine only to use threatening, insulting or abusive words or behaviour, or disorderly behaviour in the presence of a person likely to be caused harassment, alarm or distress thereby.

7.51 The offence is summary only and in the late 1980s/early 1990s became a very common substituted offence for original charges of gross indecency or importuning. The allegation was typically put as one of 'insulting' or 'disorderly' behaviour. The typical facts alleged would be that the defendant was masturbating openly in a public lavatory or cruising ground.

7.52 In such cases invariably the police alone give evidence although the requirement for the presence of a person likely to be caused harassment, alarm or distress usually led to police witnesses 'creating' a visibly offended member of the public who left the scene without giving or refusing to give personal details to the police. It may be possible to argue that evidence of a third party's distress given in that party's absence is unfair evidence which falls to be excluded under PACE 1984, s 78.

7.53 A police officer him or herself is capable of being caused harassment, alarm or distress although arguably should be expected to be somewhat more thick-skinned than an ordinary member of the public[1]. Furthermore, in the case of police officers specifically tasked to monitor a cottage or cruising ground it may well be possible to argue that it is inconceivable that they should be caused harassment, alarm or distress when they observe what they had been expecting to see all along.

1   *DPP v Orum* (1988) 88 Cr App Rep 261, DC.

7.54 If the prosecution choose to characterise the behaviour as insulting then a question also arises as to whether masturbating towards another person can properly be characterised as 'insulting' when the intention of the masturbator is to make a positive overture towards another man, not to insult him. The issue was considered but not fully resolved in the case of *Parkin v Norman*[1] which was a case under the Public Order Act 1936. There is no requirement however that the alleged insulting behaviour should be deliberately directed at anyone[2].

1   [1983] QB 92, DC
2   *Masterson v Holden* [1986] 1 WLR 1017, DC.

Town Police Clauses Act 1847, s 28

7.55 This is another summary only offence which is frequently used in preference to the classic either way offences. It is an offence under this provision to 'wilfully and indecently expose one's person [penis] in a street to the annoyance of passengers'. The meaning of 'street' for the purposes of s 28 of the 1847 Act was extended by the Public Health Acts Amendment Act 1907, s 81 by the following words:

> 'Any place of public resort or recreation ground belonging to, or under the control of, the local authority, and any unfenced ground adjoining or abutting upon any street in an urban district...shall be deemed to be a street.'

Thus 'street' is not given its strict meaning and may, most significantly, include a local authority public lavatory.

7.56 However, the most significant ruling on s 28 and one which is frequently overlooked, is the case of *Cheeseman v DPP* [1]. This held that the word 'passenger' in relation to a place of public resort such as a lavatory meant anyone resorting in the ordinary way to that place for one of the purposes for which people would normally resort to it. In the particular case where police officers were 'staking out' the lavatory in question it was held that they were not passengers.

1   (1991) 155 DP 469, DC.

7.57 Police officers observing a lavatory in this fashion is a very common scenario and the judgment is therefore of considerable value in defending such cases. It should be noted, however, that *Cheeseman* also confirmed that it was not essential for an annoyed genuine lavatory user to be called to give evidence. Annoyance of such a party could be shown or suggested by other evidence and the facts of a particular case might be such as to allow an inference of annoyance to be readily drawn.

Byelaws

7.58 There are a plethora of local byelaws which regulate indecent behaviour in public places. Byelaw 14 of the London Borough of Waltham Forest Byelaws, for example, states:

> 'No person shall in any street or public place to the annoyance of residents or passengers commit any nuisance contrary to public decency or propriety.'

7.59 In the late 1980s the author was involved with a number of legal challenges to the use of local authority byelaws in cottaging situations. There were two principal sets of challenges. First, it was contended that many local byelaws were passed ancillary to the enabling provisions in the Local Government Act 1933 [1]. The whole of the 1933 Act was repealed by the Local Government Act 1972 [2]. There is no explicit provision saving byelaws passed under the 1933 Act and thus, it was argued, all such byelaws ceased to have validity.

1   Local Government Act 1933, s 249.
2   Local Government Act 1972, s 272.

7.60 The issue was considered by the Divisional Court in the case of *DPP v Jackson* [1] where, in an extraordinarily convoluted judgment which defies summary, the court found that byelaws of 1933 remained valid under and were preserved by the Local Government Act 1972.

1   (1990) 154 JP 967, QBD.

7.61 The second challenge, put succinctly, was that local byelaws are supplemental to and not a substitute for national statutory provisions. Section 235(3) of the Local Government Act 1972 provides:

> 'Byelaws shall not be made under this section for any purpose as respects any area if provision for that...area is made by, or is or may be made under, any other enactment.'

Section 249(4) of the 1933 Act similarly provides:

> 'Where by or under any enactment in force in any area provision is made for the prevention and suppression in a summary manner of any nuisance, power to make byelaws under this section for that purpose shall not be exercisable as respects that area.'

7.62 This, it was further argued, meant that if an individual's alleged criminal behaviour was covered by a national statutory provision then, as a matter of law, a charge under a similar byelaw could not be brought. Consequently, withdrawing a charge of gross indecency and substituting a local byelaw offence, or indeed, charging a byelaw offence if the alleged behaviour amounted to gross indecency was not permissible. The argument was considered by the Divisional Court in October 1993 and dismissed.

Ecclesiastical Courts Jurisdiction Act 1860, s 2

7.63 Under this provision it is an offence to engage in, inter alia, any riotous, violent or indecent behaviour in England or Ireland in any church or in any duly certified place of religious worship or in any churchyard or burial ground. The offence is summary only and is punishable with a level 1 fine or two months' imprisonment.

7.64 The provision has been used in respect of sexual behaviour in churchyards which have become late night cruising grounds. In such cases it is the 'indecency' limb of the provision which is relied on.

(v) Shifts in policing strategy

7.65 In May 1990 the lesbian and gay direct action group, OutRage, was founded in the wake of the murder of Michael Booth. Booth was found dead in an open area popular with gay men in West London. The killing focused attention on the failure of the police to take anti-gay violence seriously whilst they simultaneously devoted considerable resources to policing arguably victimless sexual activities taking place in public lavatories and open cruising areas.

7.66 Later in 1990, under considerable pressure from the media and the gay community, the metropolitan police set up a consultative forum to promote liaison between London's community and the police. The metropolitan police's forum was followed by similar regional schemes; many forces appointed specific gay community liaison officers; a lesbian and gay police officers group emerged; anti-gay violence monitoring schemes were established and instructions were issued by the metropolitan police requiring restraint in cottaging operations.

7.67 Yet despite the advances, these policing initiatives were initially greeted with suspicion, cynicism and downright hostility by certain sections of the gay community. In August 1993, OutRage withdrew from the umbrella metropolitan police/London gay community liaison group, LLGPI, on the basis that two years of liaison had produced very little of substance for London's gay community and because the group was in danger of being used by the police as public relations exercise only.

7.68   The situation was well illustrated by police cottaging operations. In April 1993 the metropolitan police produced a set of instructions regarding such operations which were clearly influenced by representations made by the LLGPI and which set out a step-by-step approach to be adopted by police divisions in dealing with complaints about cottages. The directions required, inter alia, that: all complaints from members of the public regarding cottages should be recorded so that verification that the police were not acting on their own initiative could be provided; that the initial police response to genuine complaints should be to discuss alterations to the lavatory (for example, improved lighting or the provision of an attendant) with the relevant local authority; failing this, patrols by identifiable uniformed officers should be tried and, ultimately, if the preceding steps were unsuccessful, a senior officer could authorise an undercover surveillance operation, providing such operations were publicised in advance in the gay press.

7.69   The directions also made it clear that no arrests should take place if an offence of importuning (trying to pick another man up) was directed at a plain clothes police officer and that consideration should always be given to cautioning an arrested person rather than prosecuting him.

7.70   The directions provided a model policing practice. Initially however they were honoured in their breach. Nevertheless, it would be fair to say that since about 1995 the directions have been largely adhered to within the London area and this has led to a substantial decrease in the number of prosecutions for 'cottaging' and 'cruising' offences.

7.71   Outside of the capital, operations targeting both cottages and cruising grounds are still common. Additionally it should be noted that operations are still mounted within the London area by British Transport and Parks police.

Agents provocateurs

7.72   Allegations from within the gay community of the use of police officers to entrap men into committing offences of indecency are widespread and long-standing. The use of such agents provocateurs was so common in the 1970s and 1980s that the officers engaged in such operations earned themselves their own description of 'pretty policemen'. With the general decrease in cottaging operations within the London area, the use of agents provocateurs has also decreased to the point of non-existence. Outside of London however, allegations of the employment of pretty policeman are still common.

7.73   For example, in 1995 and again in 1997, one particular officer engaged in operations based around a lay-by near Falmouth in Cornwall. His particular modus operandi was to engage another single male in conversation and then arrest the male for indecent assault (contrary to SOA 1956, s 15) when his target touched him.

7.74   Reproduced below is an excerpt from the police evidence relating to one of the men who was arrested and charged with indecently assaulting the police officer in 1995. The excerpt is reproduced in full as it neatly illustrates the degree of encouragement which prompted the commission of the 'offence'.

Police constable: 'Have you arranged to meet anyone here?'

Defendant: 'No. Have you?'

Pc 'I'm waiting for Bob but he hasn't turned up yet. I haven't seen you here before'

D   'I don't get here very often but I had a job in Falmouth so I thought I would drop in here on my way home'

Pc 'It's very quiet here tonight'

D   'Is it? I wouldn't know, I don't get out much'

Pc 'Are you looking for anything in particular?'

D   'No I'm not fussy. I don't want anything too deep'

Pc 'What had you in mind?'

D   'Oh I don't know'

Pc 'Well where do you normally start?'

D then placed his hand at the top of the officer's leg.

Pc 'That's where you start is it? What do you do then?'

D then moved his hand to the front of the PC's trousers and was arrested for indecent assault.

7.75   Leaving aside the issue of agent provocateur, it is submitted that the defendant facing an indecent assault allegation arising out of such circumstances should be able to avail himself of the defence set out in *R v Kimber* [1]. This confirmed that no offence of indecent assault is committed where the person committing the alleged assault believes that his target was consenting to his conduct, whether that belief was based on objectively reasonable grounds or not. *Kimber* is actually a case on an assault by a man on a woman under the Sexual Offences 1956, s 14 rather than by a man on a man but it is submitted that the principle must hold good for both scenarios.

1   (1983) 77 Cr App Rep 225.

7.76   It has been established for some time that the fact that a defendant would not have committed an offence if it were not for the activity of an agent provocateur is not defence in English law [1]. Section 78 of PACE, however, may be of assistance when use of an agent provocateur is alleged. The section provides that in any proceedings a court may refuse to allow evidence, on which the prosecution proposes to rely, to be given if it appears to the court that, having regard to all the circumstances, including the circumstances in which the evidence was obtained, the admission of the evidence would have such an adverse effect on the fairness of the proceedings that the court ought not to admit it.

1   *R v Sang* [1980] AC 402, HL; *R v Birtles* (1969) 53 Cr App Rep 469, CA; *R v Mealey and Sheridan* (1974) 60 Cr App Rep 59, CA.

7.77   What authorities there are on the issue are not positively helpful [1] but they certainly do not preclude the exclusion of evidence obtained via an agent provocateur. In the case of *Teixera de Castro v Portugal* before the European Court of Human Rights [2] it was held that entrapment may amount to a breach of the right to a fair trial under art 6 of the European Convention on Human

Rights. Whether the entrapment was unfair appears to depend on whether there was evidence that the defendant was predisposed to crime. Presumably in the case of men arrested at certain locations the prosecution would seek to rely on the alleged notoriety of the location to establish predisposition. It is unclear whether previous convictions can be relied upon to establish predisposition.

1   *R v Smurthwaite* (1993) 98 Cr App Rep 437, CA; *R v Morley and Hutton* [1994] Crim LR 919, CA; *DPP v Marshall* [1988] 3 All ER 683, DC; *R v Mann* [1995] Crim LR 647, CA.
2   [1998] Crim LR 751.

(vi)   Cautions and bind overs

7.78   For the more minor offences of indecency, the prosecution may propose or accept a bind over or even a caution. The latter resolution will entail the matter being referred back to the police for the caution to be administered.

7.79   A caution entails the admission of the commission of a criminal offence by the defendant. Furthermore, the caution is formally recorded (currently for a period of three years) and may be referred to in subsequent proceedings. A bind over does not entail any formal admission of guilt. Indeed the charge against the defendant is invariably withdrawn so conviction of any offence is an impossibility. Despite this a bind over is often treated (and even recorded) as a finding or admission of guilt.

(vii)   Disorderly houses—'backroom' sex

7.80   The early 1990s saw a rapid increase in the number of commercially run establishments that allowed their gay male customers to have sex on the premises. These were typically clubs, public houses or saunas—collectively referred to as 'backrooms'. Both participants and the managers of backrooms risk prosecution. As already described at para **7.09**, the Sexual Offences Act 1967, which only partially decriminalised gay sex between men, specifically states that sexual activity between men is not 'in private' and not, therefore, lawful if more than two men are present or taking part. The resulting offence of gross indecency is punishable with a maximum of two years' imprisonment.

7.81   Managers of premises with backrooms risk prosecution for an offence of 'keeping a disorderly house'. This is a common law offence, which technically carries an unlimited penalty. A 'disorderly house' is one which is not regulated by the restraints of morality and which is so conducted as to violate law and good order. There must be an element of open house but it does not need to be open to the public at large [1].

1   *R v Berg* (1927) 20 Cr App Rep 38, CA.

7.82   Arguably there are other charges which could be brought against backroom managers and, in particular, charges of aiding, abetting, counselling or procuring offences of gross indecency. In practice, an allegation of keeping a disorderly house seems to be preferred—possibly because the potential penalties are higher. And, certainly, there is a risk of a backroom manager receiving a prison sentence. Keeping a disorderly house, unlike many other common law offences, is triable either way rather than on indictment only.

7.83 In 1995 a prosecution was brought against the licensee of a backroom bar in London for using the premises as an unlicensed sex encounter establishment contrary to the provisions of Sch 3 to the Local Government (Miscellaneous Provisions) Act 1982. The case was dismissed (albeit only at magistrates' court level) on the basis that there was no element of a 'performance', required by the definition of a sex encounter establishment [1], in a group of gay men engaging in sexual activity in a public house.

1   Local Government (Miscellaneous Provisions) Act 1982, Sch 3, para 3A.

7.84 Within the London area there again seems to have been a discernible shift in policing policy with respect to regulating backrooms since the mid-1990s. After some expensive failed prosecutions of managers (including London bars the Pride of Stepney in 1994 and Attitude in 1995) the policing of gay bars has typically shifted to attacking the venues' liquor licences. The ultimate achievement is often the same—the closure of the bar in question—but the method is less onerous for the police and apparently less well scrutinised by the courts.

7.85 Attacks on liquor licences by the police ultimately led to the closure of Attitude several months after its prosecution and to the closure of a South London bar, the Anvil, in 1997. There is also convincing anecdotal evidence that other (allegedly backroom) bars throughout the capital have had their licenses threatened unless the behaviour of their customers is better regulated.

7.86 Although any person can object to the grant or renewal of an on-licence, in the vast majority of cases it is the police alone who participate in the proceedings. Licences once granted typically last for up to three years and are usually routinely renewed. The regular licensing hours are 11am to 11pm and on Sundays 12 noon to 10.30pm [1]. These hours can be extended by making an application for a special hours certificate for music and dancing. This enables alcohol to be served up until 2am and, in central London, 3am [2]. It is a requirement of such a certificate that the bar is actually used to provide music, dancing and substantial refreshment. Lip service seems to be paid by many bars to the dancing and food requirements and this in turn may provide an easy avenue of challenge to a late licence if a bar is considered to be unduly unrestrained.

1   Licensing Act 1964, s 60.
2   Licensing Act 1964, s 77.

7.87 It is also possible for the police to apply to have a bar's licence revoked altogether on the ground that the licensee is not 'a fit and proper person' or that the premises have been 'badly conducted'. It was the former provision that resulted in the loss of the licenses for both Attitude and the Anvil.

7.88 Police actions to revoke or restrict a licence can be difficult to challenge. Quite often the misbehaviour complained of by the police does not take place in the presence of the licensee or their staff and yet licensing law renders the licensee effectively strictly liable for such behaviour.

7.89 There also seems to be a less rigorous approach adopted by magistrates in considering such cases. This may be prompted by the notion that the licensee is 'only' losing their licence and is not actually being convicted of a criminal offence or being punished directly—even though the closure of the bar and the loss of income are indirect consequences.

2   Non-consensual offences

(i)   Rape

7.90   The Criminal Justice and Public Order Act 1994 introduced an amendment to s 1 of the Sexual Offences Act 1956 rendering the act of non-consensual buggery committed on either a man or a woman an act of rape equivalent to non-consensual intercourse with a woman per vaginam. Such an act was, of course, previously an offence of buggery under the Sexual Offences Act 1956, s 12. The offence is punishable with up to life imprisonment and is triable on indictment only. It should be noted that a consensual act of buggery with a person under the age of consent for homosexual acts is still charged as buggery and not rape.

(ii)   Indecent assault

7.91   Under the Sexual Offences Act 1956, s 15 it is an offence to indecently assault a male person. This is an either way offence punishable on indictment with up to ten years' imprisonment.

7.92   It should be noted that consensual sexual activity, short of buggery, between two men at least one of whom is below the age of homosexual consent but at least 16 is charged as gross indecency and not indecent assault. Consensual sexual activity between two men where the 'victim' is under the age of 16 is charged as indecent assault. This anomaly will disappear if the age of consent for gay male sexual activity is lowered to 16, as expected.

7.93   An indecent assault is an assault accompanied by circumstances of indecency. For a full exposition of the ingredients of the offence see *R v Court* [1]. The principle set out in *R v Kimber* [2] may be of relevance in such cases.

1   [1989] AC 28, HL.
2   (1983) 77 Cr App Rep 225. See para **7.75**.

3   Sadomasochism

7.94   On 19 February 1997, after a decade of litigation and campaigning, the Operation Spanner case finally reached its conclusion with the delivery of a unanimous judgment by the European Court of Human Rights. This ruled that the United Kingdom authorities had been right to prosecute and convict a group of gay men for engaging in consensual sadomasochistic sexual activities [1].

1   *Laskey v United Kingdom* Case No 109/1995 (18 January 1995, unreported).

7.95   The Operation Spanner investigation started in 1987 with the accidental discovery by police of a number of homemade videos showing adult gay men participating in clearly consensual sadomasochistic activities. The investigation resulted in 42 people being arrested, dozens more being interviewed and 16 men being prosecuted for offences of assault (under both ss 47 and 20 of the

Offences against the Person Act 1861) and aiding and abetting assaults—the latter charges being brought against those in the group who had asked to be spanked, beaten or pierced.

7.96   The prosecutions led to a preliminary hearing at the Old Bailey in December 1990 where Rant J, having ruled that the mens' consent did not constitute a defence in law, sentenced several of them to lengthy terms of imprisonment.

7.97   Rant's ruling was first challenged before the Court of Appeal in February 1992. The three judges unanimously upheld Rant's interpretation of the law although they substantially reduced the longest sentences of imprisonment. It was made clear, however, that this was only because the men may not have understood at the time that they were committing criminal offences and that no practitioners of sadomasochism apprehended in the future should expect to be treated so leniently.

7.98   It was the Court of Appeal that produced the classic justification for the state's interference in consensual sadomasochistic practices.

> 'It is not in the public interest…that people should try to cause, or should cause, each other actual bodily harm for no good reason…what may be good reason it is not necessary for us to decide. It is sufficient to say…that the satisfying of sadomasochistic libido does not come within the category of "good reason".'[1]

1   *R v Brown* [1994] 1 AC 212, HL.

7.99   An unsuccessful appeal (3:2 majority) to the House of Lords then followed [1]. Lord Templeman, one of the majority, ruled:

> 'There can be no conviction for the summary offence of common assault if the victim has consented…Even when violence is intentionally inflicted and results in…wounding or serious bodily harm the accused is entitled to be acquitted if the injury was a foreseeable incident of lawful activity in which the person injured was participating. Surgery…is a lawful activity…ritual [male] circumcision, tattooing, ear piercing and violent sports including boxing are lawful activities. Similarly, in the old days, fighting was lawful provided that the protagonists consented…The brutality of knuckle fighting however, caused the courts to declare that such fights were unlawful even if the protagonists consented…The question whether the defence of consent should be extended to the consequences of sadomasochistic encounters can only be decided by considerations of policy and public interest…The violence of sadomasochistic encounters involves the indulgence of cruelty by sadists and the degradation of the victims. Such violence is injurious to the participants and unpredictably dangerous. I am not prepared to invent a defence of consent for sadomasochistic encounters which breed and glorify cruelty and result in offences under sections 47 and 20 of the Act of 1861.'

1   *R v Brown* [1994] 1 AC 212, HL.

7.100 Three of the men, Tony Brown, Roland Jaggard and Colin Laskey, decided to challenge the British courts' rulings by making an application to the European Commission of Human Rights on the basis that there had been an unjustifiable interference with their right to a private life contrary to art 8 of the European Convention on Human Rights. Colin Laskey was to die whilst the case was still outstanding before the European Court. In January 1995, the Commission referred the case to the ECHR.

7.101 In the ECHR judgment the judges agreed that the prosecutions brought against the Spanner men were, fundamentally, an interference with their private lives but asserted that interference was justifiable on the grounds of protecting health and morals[1]. Like the English courts before them, the European tribunal condemned the applicants for what they might have done rather than what they actually did—effectively censuring sadomasochists because the court would not accept that they could possibly display sufficient self-discipline or concern for each other to remove the risk of serious harm occurring. This was despite the fact that no evidence of such consequences was presented before any of the tribunals considering the case.

1   *Laskey v United Kingdom* Case No 109/1995 (18 January 1995, unreported).

7.102 One of the judges, the Italian representative Pettiti, additionally questioned whether the Spanner mens' behaviour could truly be classified as 'private' given the degree of alleged organisation within the group. Pettiti characterised sadomasochism as a form of 'unrestrained permissiveness, which can lead to debauchery, paedophilia or…torture'.

7.103 The rulings of the Court of Appeal and the House of Lords in the Spanner case sit ill with the later ruling of the Court of Appeal in *R v Wilson* [1] in which the court held that nothing said in the Spanner judgments prevented a wife from validly consenting to the branding of her husband's initials on her buttocks. The court sought to categorise the branding as more akin to tattooing rather than an act of sadomasochism. Sadomasochistic branding had been considered and condemned in the Spanner case. Lord Russell in the *Wilson* case maintained that *Brown* (the Spanner case) was distinguishable on the basis that the Spanner defendants had engaged in 'sadomasochism of the grossest kind involving physical torture and the danger of serious physical injury and blood infection'. The court in *Wilson* also ruled that 'consensual activity between husband and wife in the privacy of the matrimonial home is not, in our judgment, normally a proper matter for criminal investigation let alone criminal prosecution.'

1   [1996] 2 Cr App Rep 241.

7.104 The judgment in *Wilson* seems to highlight the fact that the Spanner case was a prosecution targeted specifically on homosexual sadomasochistic activities rather than sadomasochism in general. Even *Blackstone's Criminal Practice* wryly comments that *Wilson* 'appears to take liberties with the law as stated in *Brown*'.

7.105 Since the Spanner case there have not been any further prosecutions of gay men or lesbians for consensual sadomasochistic activities. However the Spanner prosecution has certainly marginalised gay sadomasochism as an activity beyond the pale and that marginalisation has had certain consequences.

In the area of pornographic material (see paras **7.123**ff) the depiction of sadomasochistic activities will invariably lead to seizure and prosecution. Furthermore, gay clubs run for the benefit of those interested in sadomasochistic activities have, since Spanner, attracted a disproportionate level of interest from the authorities. This interest has led to what might be termed 'extra-legal' sanctions being applied.

7.106 In January 1996 for example, officers from the Area One Clubs and Vice Squad based at Charing Cross Police Station in London visited Club 180 in Earls Court when it was hosting the rubber and fetish club Gummi.

7.107 The two officers spent an hour at the premises observing no illegal activity but becoming evidently perturbed by a number of tubes and hoses which had been draped over electrical fittings and which were to be used in a safer sex cabaret later in the evening. The officers explicitly (and rather imaginatively) suggested that the equipment was to be used for electrical torture.

7.108 Subsequently the licensees of the premises (employees of Bass Taverns who own Club 180) were required to attend a meeting at Charing Cross. A Gummi representative also sought to attend the meeting with a view to answering questions and providing reassurance but was barred from doing so. The agenda of the meeting consequently remains a mystery although it is understood that one outcome was a decision by the Clubs Unit to issue guidance on 'unacceptable' practices in gay clubs. In February 1996, Bass Taverns, the owner of the premises, informed Gummi, Sadie Masie (the sadomasochistic dance club) and SM Gays that they could not hold events at any Bass premises.

B DRUGS

7.109 The law regulating the possession and distribution of controlled drugs (the Misuse of Drugs Act 1971) applies equally, of course, to gay men, lesbians and heterosexuals. Here is not the place to review the law relating to controlled drugs in full.

7.110 The general law is worth mentioning however, if only for the reason that within London there have been a number of concerted police operations which have targeted gay venues and which have resulted in clubbers being routinely stopped and searched for drugs on leaving the club premises.

7.111 The Misuse of Drugs Act 1971 divides drugs into classes. Almost all of the drugs prevalent on the gay scene fall into either Class A or B and the vast majority of these into Class A. Ecstasy, speed, heroin, LSD and cocaine are all Class A drugs. Cannabis is a Class B drug.

7.112 There has, for many years now, been an acknowledged policy of cautioning someone arrested for their first offence of possessing a Class B drug. More recently, there has been a tacit extension of this policy on the part of the police to include first-time Class A drug 'possessors', providing that the quantity was small and clearly for personal use. Second-time possessors may expect a prosecution leading to a financial penalty. Further prosecutions may result in community penalties and custody. The supply of either Class A or B drugs invariably attracts an immediate custodial penalty unless the supply can truly be characterised as a purely 'social' supply—eg the sharing of a small jointly purchased amount.

Alkyl nitrites (poppers)

7.113   The use of 'poppers' within the gay (male) community is widespread. The drug is used as a stimulant both in sexual activity and on the dance floor. Inhalation of the drug, which is invariably in liquid form, causes a dilation of the blood vessels and a characteristic pounding of the heart and dizzying 'rush' or 'buzz'.

7.114   Alkyl nitrites is the proper term for poppers and covers amyl and isobutyl nitrites—the most common forms of poppers. The product was originally used for the treatment of heart conditions although its usage in this respect appears nowadays to be uncommon.

7.115   The simple possession of alkyl nitrites is not a criminal offence nor is their importation since they are not controlled drugs within the Misuse of Drugs Act 1971. The only restrictions on alkyl nitrites in the UK are on their sale and those restrictions are set out in the Medicines Act 1968.

7.116   This piece of legislation makes it an offence to sell or supply 'medicinal products' unless licensed to do so (that is, basically, unless you are a pharmacist, nurse, doctor, dentist or veterinary surgeon [1]). The offence is either way and is punishable with up to two years' imprisonment and an unlimited fine. A 'medicinal product' is defined by the Act as something taken for a 'medicinal purpose'[2]. That, in turn, is defined as the treatment, prevention or diagnosis of disease; contraception; anaesthesia or the 'interference with the normal operation of a physiological function'[3]. Given the well-established side-effects of inhaling poppers (including light-headedness and an increased heart rate) establishing an interference with the normal operation of a physiological function should be an easy hurdle to overcome.

1   Medicines Act 1968, s 37(1).
2   Medicines Act 1968, s 130(1).
3   Medicines Act 1968, s 130(2).

7.117   The requirements of the Medicines Act 1968 can best be summarised by the statement: 'If any form of alkyl nitrite is sold for human consumption then it will be considered to be a medicinal product within the Medicines Act.' If it is sold other than by a licensed distributor, then an offence will be committed. The 'human consumption' qualification means that many UK vendors frequently try to disguise the products as 'room odorisers' or 'vinyl cleaners'. These facades arguably do not assist since alkyl nitrites have no acknowledged usage apart from being used for human consumption—either as a legitimate medicine or though substance abuse.

7.118   In addition to almost certainly being a medicinal product amyl nitrite has also been classified as a 'prescription only' medicine. This means that if a retailer were selling amyl nitrite then, as well as committing an offence of selling a medicinal product, they would also be committing an offence of selling a prescription only medicine.

7.119   Prosecutions under the Medicines Act 1968 are brought by the Royal Pharmaceutical Society of Great Britain. In 1995 the RPSGB commenced a campaign against the sale of alkyl nitrites on the basis that usage of the substances was detrimental to health. The evidence for this assertion is suspect. Only one questionable death has been traced back to usage of alkyl nitrites. The RPSGB has also cited concern that the usage of poppers may be linked to the incidence of Kaposi's sarcoma (one of the defining conditions for AIDS) although the clinical evidence for such a contention appears to be weak or non-existent.

7.120   The most notorious example of the RPSGB's campaign against the sale of alkyl nitrites was the prosecution of the gay owned company Millivres in 1996. The company publishes the magazine *Gay Times* and also owns the retail outlet Zipperstore in London. It was from this store that RPSGB investigators made a test purchase of 'poppers' which formed the basis of the subsequent prosecution .

7.121   Although the company pleaded guilty to the offence and were fined a nominal £100 the RPSGB were heavily criticised by the sentencing judge for their conduct of the prosecution and were obliged to bear their own legal costs—estimated at some £50,000. Millivres' plea also meant that there was no detailed judicial consideration of the law and that, contrary to the RPSGB's subsequent insistence, no test case was established. The RPSGB were criticised in particular for not warning the retailers to desist in the sale of the alkyl nitrites before commencing a prosecution. This in turn followed controversy over whether the substances did or did not fall within the ambit of the Medicines Act 1968.

7.122   Since the prosecution, the RPSGB has continued with a campaign of warning importers, manufacturers, wholesalers and retailers of alkyl nitrites of the possibility of prosecutions being brought although such cases have yet to be brought.

C   PORNOGRAPHY

7.123   Gay men and, to a lesser extent, lesbians have frequently fallen foul of the criminal law over the importation, distribution, sharing and in some limited circumstances, simple possession of erotic imagery (photographs, magazines and videos).

7.124   Additionally, a number of agencies, including the Terrence Higgins Trust, have been concerned to promote information about safer sex practices amongst the gay community by using sexually explicit text and images. The rationale behind such a strategy is to ensure that the information is clear and does not rely upon ambiguous metaphors and also to make the information as attractive as possible to a target audience.

7.125 British law, however, places controls on the use and distribution of sexually explicit material. The principal piece of legislation is the Obscene Publications Act 1959, as amended by the Obscene Publications Act 1964.

1 The Obscene Publications Act 1959

7.126 Section 2 of the Act makes it an offence to publish an obscene article or to have an obscene article for publication for gain. The latter prohibition may have limited relevance to the distributors of safer sex information as the vast majority of such information is distributed free rather than as a commercial exercise. An offence under s 2 is punishable with up to three years' imprisonment on indictment. The offence is either way.

7.127 An 'article' is defined as anything containing material to be read, looked at or listened to[1]. 'Publishing' includes distributing, circulating, selling, hiring , showing, playing, giving, lending and offering for sale or hire [2].

1   OPA 1959, s 1(2).
2   OPA 1959, s 1(3).

7.128 The test of obscenity is contained in s 1 of the Act. The effect of the article taken as a whole must be to 'tend to deprave and corrupt [a significant proportion of] persons who are likely...to read, see or hear the matter contained or embodied in [the article]'.

7.129 There have been attempts to define 'deprave and corrupt', but such definitions have been largely tautological. In the case of *Lady Chatterley's Lover* [1], 'deprave' was defined as 'to make morally bad, to pervert, to debase or corrupt morally'. 'Corrupt' was defined as 'to render morally unsound or rotten, to destroy the moral purity or chastity of, to pervert or ruin a good quality, to debase, to defile'.

1   *R v Penguin Books Ltd* [1961] Crim LR 176.

7.130 These appear to be strong words—the suggestion is that what is being prohibited is something which might destroy the fabric of society. However, in the 1960s, 1970s and 1980s, prosecution policy almost rendered the phrase 'deprave and corrupt' largely devoid of any real meaning. In practice the legislation was applied by having an effective blacklist of forbidden images. Text is, since a number of unsuccessful prosecutions, left largely untouched. The blacklist is not static however, but is constantly changing as publishers seek to push the boundaries of permitted images forward and the prosecuting authorities seek to reimpose what they feel to be the appropriate limits.

7.131 For example, it was considered until relatively recently, that an image of an erect penis was not permissible. The early 1990s, however, have seen an explosion of sexual guidance videos, which contain such images and yet have been certificated by the British Board of Film Classification and have, to date, not been the subject of any prosecutions under the Obscene Publications Act. At the time of writing it would appear that there is some consensus amongst authorities that scenes of implicit oral and anal penetration will be tolerated but not explicit scenes of such acts.

7.132 These constant shifts in what is and what is not permissible make it difficult to give certain advice on what is obscene. The publishing of text is certainly less at risk from prosecution than that of images.

7.133 With respect to advising the producers of safer sex promotional material there are also certain concepts within the Act which may be of assistance. Some of these concepts may also assist commercial producers or retailers of gay and lesbian pornography and erotica.

7.134 First, it is arguable that careful targeting of a specified audience (for example, only distributing safer sex material for gay men at gay venues) will lessen the risk of prosecution since the Act requires the corruption of persons who are 'likely to', as opposed to 'conceivably might', see the article. Consequently, it might be argued that if the target audience has regularly experienced such imagery then there is no risk of corruption. However, in *DPP v Whyte* [1], the House of Lords held that the Act was not merely concerned with the once and for all corruption of the wholly innocent, it equally protected the less innocent from further corruption and the addict from feeding or increasing their addiction.

1   [1972] 3 All ER 12, HL.

7.135 Second, in the case of *R v Calder and Boyers* (the prosecution of *The Last Exit to Brooklyn*),[1] the Court of Appeal added the requirement that a 'significant proportion' of the likely readership would tend to be corrupted. This requirement was imposed to protect the publisher from speculation by a jury as to the possible adverse effect of an article on a young person who might just happen to see it. Targeting safer sex information is, again, therefore advisable. The 'significant proportion' test does not, however, require the prosecution to prove that a majority, or substantial number of readers or viewers would be adversely affected.

1   [1969] 1 QB 151.

7.136 Third, the article in question must be viewed as a whole [1]. Any isolated items of an apparently offensive nature must be viewed in their context. This may be of significance if safer sex material uses an explicit sexual image to attract the interest of its intended recipient, but otherwise contains text.

1   *R v Penguin Books Ltd* [1961] Crim LR 176.

7.137 Finally, even if a prosecution is brought under s 1 of the Act there would, with safer sex material, be a chance of a 'public good' defence succeeding under s 4 of the Act. This states that the publication may be justified as being for the public good on the grounds that it is in the 'interest of science, literature, art or learning, or other objects of general concern'. It is possible to call expert evidence on the merits of a publication.

7.138 Some of the case law on this section appears to be unhelpful to the application of the 'public good' defence to sexually explicit material. In the case of *A-G's Reference (No 3 of 1977)* [1] (following *DPP v Jordan* [2]) the Court of Appeal considered the relevance of calling expert evidence to establish that certain magazines contained material which had merit in the field of sex education or had value in teaching about sexual matters, with a view to founding the 'public good' defence. The court ruled that expert evidence was not appropriate in such a case and that the provision of information about sexual matters did not fall within the scope of the 'public good' defence.

1   (1978) 67 Cr App Rep 393, CA.
2   [1977] AC 699.

7.139   However, it is arguable that the ruling was largely expedient and sought principally to control pornography dressed up as sex education material. Safer sex information may still be regarded as possessing scientific interest if it extends an existing body of knowledge or presents known facts in a systematic way. It would certainly be arguable that safer sex information should be within the scope of the 'public good' defence.

7.140   The Act contains not only provisions to prosecute obscene material but also to seize it without prosecution [1]. This power is frequently used because its use effectively places the onus upon the loser of the material to take action for its recovery. However the power of seizure only applies to material which is kept for publication for gain and freely distributed safer sex information should, consequently, be exempt. Such material may still, unfortunately, be the subject of a speculative seizure.

1   Obscene Publications Act 1959, s 3.

7.141   Curiously the police often seek to suggest that there is a lesser standard of obscenity applying to seized material than to articles which fall to be prosecuted. Thus one often hears the remark 'this doesn't warrant prosecution but we are going to seize it'. This, of course, is incorrect—the same standard of obscenity applies throughout the Obscene Publications Act 1959.

7.142   Although a precise meaning of 'obscene' is never going to be established there is one particular argument that is worth considering in respect of the seizure or prosecution of gay erotica. This relies in part on the 'targeting' and 'significant proportion' points mentioned above. With respect to a specifically gay retail outlet it may be possible to argue, first, that the vast majority of customers will be adult gay men or lesbians, second, that such persons may perfectly lawfully engage in certain acts of intercourse and, finally, that images of such lawful acts cannot sensibly be described as corrupting.

7.143   This argument was successfully applied in respect of material seized from the gay-run retail outlet Clone Zone in Earls Court, London. Officers from Kensington Police Station seized magazines worth approximately £7,000 from the shop in December 1994 and purported to forfeit the material under OPA 1959, s 3. A stipendiary magistrate sitting at Horseferry Road Magistrates' Court ordered the return of the stock in 1995, after accepting the aforementioned analysis. However, the court declined to award costs on the basis that such seizures were an inevitable part of a risky trade.

2   Other relevant legislation

7.144   There are a number of other statutory provisions which may cause difficulties with the distribution and display of safer sex information or to the distribution of erotica and pornography. It should be noted that with respect to some of these provisions the test adopted is whether the material is 'indecent' rather than 'obscene'. Indecency is accepted to be a lower standard than obscenity and therefore more articles will be prohibited under legislation containing this test [1]. Furthermore, such legislation typically does not contain provisions parallel to the 'public good' defence and the material would be, consequently, viewed in isolation rather than in the context of its overall purpose.

1   *R v Stanley* [1965] 2 QB 327, a case under the Post Office Act 1953.

(i)   Video Recordings Act 1984

7.145 This legislation established a system for the classification by the British Board of Film Classification of videos supplied to the public. Any new video has, therefore, to be submitted to the Board before its release. Certain videos are exempted from the Act—principally educational videos or videos concerned with sport, religion or music [1]. However the exemptions do not extend to any video dealing with human sexual activity or human excretory functions.

1   VRA 1984, s 2.

7.146 Certain supplies of videos are also exempted from the Act—namely supplies which are neither for reward nor in the course of a business [1]. Thus lending a video on a friend-to-friend basis will not be caught by VRA 1984 although if the article is obscene, OPA 1959 may still be of relevance.

1   VRA 1984, s 3.

7.147 Since the early 1990s, the Board, under the leadership of the now-retired James Ferman, has taken a liberal attitude to the certification of sex education videos containing explicit sexual imagery. This extended to the *Gay Men's Guide to Safer Sex*, which was published in association with the Terrence Higgins Trust in 1992 and which received an 18 certificate from the Board. The Board did not even impose an 18R (restricted) classification which is traditionally used for sexually explicit material and which confines the sale of such items to licensed sex shops.

7.148 Certification by the Board does not , however, preclude a prosecution under the Obscene Publications Act 1959 since the two pieces of legislation are not linked in any manner.

7.149 Sections 9 to 14 of the Act establish various offences. These were all originally summary only and punishable only by fines. However the Criminal Justice and Public Order Act 1994, s 88 made the most serious offences under ss 9 and 10 of the Act indictable and punishable with up to two years' imprisonment and also introduced the possibility of up to six months' imprisonment for the remaining summary offences. The offences under the Act are as follows:
(*a*)   supplying a video recording of an unclassified work [1];
(*b*)   possessing a video recording of an unclassified work for the purposes of supply [2];
(*c*)   supplying a video recording of a classified work to a person who has not attained the age stated in the classification [3];
(*d*)   supplying an 18R video other than from a licensed sex shop [4];

(e)   failing to comply with the labelling requirements set out in the legislation [5]; and
(f)   supplying a video containing a false indication as to classification [6].

1   VRA 1984, s 9.
2   VRA 1984, s 10.
3   VRA 1984, s 11.
4   VRA 1984, s 12.
5   VRA 1984, s 13.
6   VRA 1984, s 14.

7.150   It is a defence to an allegation under s 10 (possession for the purposes of supply) for the accused to prove:
(a)   he had reasonable grounds for believing the video contained exempted or classified work(s);
(b)   he had reasonable grounds for believing any supply would be an exempted supply; or
(c)   that he did not intend to supply until a classification certificate had been issued.

7.151   Since the introduction of the punishment of imprisonment in CJPOA 1994 the authorities have shown a distinct preference for prosecuting retailers of erotic videos under VRA 1984 rather than OPA 1959 as this avoids the increasingly problematic issue of establishing 'obscenity'.

(ii)   Importation of pornographic or erotic material

7.152   The Customs Consolidation Act 1876, s 42 prohibits the importation of any obscene or indecent articles. Section 170 of the Customs and Excise Management Act 1979 renders an importation flouting this prohibition an offence punishable with up to seven years' imprisonment. Again, Customs have the power to seize as well as to prosecute material. One consequence of EEC legislation has been that Customs are prevented from using the lower indecency test for material imported from other EEC countries—the obscenity test contained in the Obscene Publications Act must still be applied although the 'public good defence' may not be relied on [1]. Conversely material imported from for example the United States can be seized and may be the subject of a prosecution for being simply indecent. This can lead to the thoroughly anomalous situation of articles being legitimately on sale within this country but the subject of seizure when imported from a non-EEC country. This happened with the Tom of Finland Retrospective (which contained gay erotic drawings) when it was re-imported by the gay artist Philip Core on a personal basis from the US in 1989.

1   *R v Bow Street Magistrates' Court, ex p Noncyp Ltd* [1990] 1 QB 123, CA.

7.153   On 20 December 1994 the group Gay Men Fighting Aids (GMFA) were notified by British Customs that a video containing their two highly praised safer sex commercials and other prize-winning material from the San Francisco AIDS Foundation's International Gay Safer Sex Video Awards had been seized. Customs officers claimed that the material was obscene. GMFA's adverts were produced in this country, had been certificated by the British Board of Film Classification, and were shown on Channel 4 several times during 1994. The seizure was challenged but upheld by magistrates at Stratford Magistrates' Court in East London. The court declined to allow any expert evidence to be called on the merits of the material in accordance with the *Noncyp* judgment [1].

1   *R v Bow Street Magistrates' Court, ex p Noncyp Ltd* [1990] 1 QB 123, CA.

(iii)   Post Office Act 1953

7.154   This makes it an offence to send any indecent or obscene article through the post. Section 11 of the Act defines obscene as 'offending, shocking, lewd or indecent', which is a clearly different test from that contained in the Obscene Publications Act 1959. The legislation does not apply to alternative distribution systems such as Red Star.

7.155   The offence is triable either way. The maximum penalty is 12 months' imprisonment on indictment or a fine not exceeding the statutory maximum summarily.

(iv)   Unsolicited Goods and Services Act 1971

7.156   It is an offence under s 4 of the Act for a person to send any book magazine or leaflet which they know or ought reasonably to have known was unsolicited and which describes or illustrated human sexual technique. The sending of advertising material may be an offence even if that material does not itself describe or illustrate human sexual techniques [1]. Safer sex material or material promoting erotic articles should only, therefore, be sent when requested and not unsolicited. The offence is summary only and punishable by way of a fine up to the statutory maximum.

1   *DPP v Beate Uhse Ltd* [1974] QB 158.

(v)   Indecent Displays (Control) Act 1981

7.157   It is an offence under s 1 of this legislation to display, in public, any indecent matter. This is an either way offence punishable with up to two years' imprisonment. Unlike OPA 1959, there is no requirement to consider the totality of any 'matter' on display [1]. Thus under ID(C)A 1981, a book may truly be judged by its cover.

1   ID(C)A 1981, s 1(5).

7.158   This provision may cause problems with, for example, a safer sex road show, which is displaying posters containing sexual imagery. Films, plays, television programmes and art or museum exhibitions are excluded from the ambit of the legislation [1].

1   ID(C)A 1981, s 1(4).

(vi)   Public Order Act 1986

7.159 Section 5 of the Public Order Act renders it an offence, punishable by fine only, to use threatening, insulting or abusive words or behaviour or disorderly behaviour; or to display any threatening, insulting or abusive writing, sign or visible representation in the presence of a person likely to be caused harassment, alarm or distress thereby.

7.160   The provision was used, in 1993, to bring a prosecution against two of the managers of an AIDS information service based in Leamington Spa for displaying, in the window of the service's offices, a Terrence Higgins Trust safer sex poster which depicted a man kissing the inner thigh of another person. The prosecution was brought by the local police but was discontinued by the Crown Prosecution Service.

7.161   If the case had gone to trial the defendants would have made use of a defence stemming from s 6(4) of the Public Order Act, which specifies the mental element that the prosecution must establish to prove that an offence under s 5 has been committed. Section 6(4) provides that a person is guilty of a s 5 offence only if they intend their words, behaviour, sign or writing etc, to be threatening, insulting or abusive or is aware that it may be so.

7.162   In *DPP v Clarke* [1] the Divisional Court ruled that the 'awareness' limb of s 6(4) was a subjective awareness and that defendants who gave evidence that they lacked the requisite intention or awareness and were believed on such points should be acquitted. The facts of *Clarke* neatly illustrate the stringency of the subjective awareness rule. The relevant events took place outside an abortion clinic. The respondents, who were opposed to abortions, demonstrated outside the clinic displaying pictures of an aborted foetus. The magistrates found that on an objective analysis the pictures were abusive and insulting, but accepted the respondents' evidence that they personally did not intend and were not aware that the pictures were threatening, abusive or insulting, and acquitted them.

1   (1991) 156 JP 267, 94 Cr App Rep 359, CA.

3   Child pornography

7.163   The Criminal Justice Act 1988 made it an offence, for the first time, simply to possess (as opposed to create or distribute) indecent photographs or videos of children (under the age of 16) [1]. When the legislation was introduced the offence was punishable with a fine only. The Criminal Justice and Public Order Act 1994 however, increased the possible penalty to six months' imprisonment and also extended the definition of photograph to include 'pseudo-photographs' or electronically manipulated images which appear to be of children. Since the penalties changed in February 1995 the courts have shown a clear willingness to use their new powers. The offence is summary only.

1   CJA 1988, s 160.

7.164   Child pornography is the only type of pornography which it is an offence to possess. Pornographic videos involving adults (aged 16 years and over) are legitimate to own although it may be an offence under OPA 1959 (depending on their content) to lend or show or sell them to others—even on an informal basis.

7.165   The suppliers of pornographic videos are at risk of prosecution under OPA 1959 or under the Protection of Children Act 1978 if the material involves children. The latter enactment makes it an offence to:

(a)   take or permit to be taken or to make any indecent photograph of a child;
(b)   distribute or show such photographs;
(c)   have in one's possession such photographs with a view to their being distributed or shown;
(d)   publish an advertisement suggesting that the advertiser distributes or shows such photographs [1].

'Photograph' includes a video [2].

1   PCA 1978, s 1(1).
2   PCA 1978, s 7(2).

7.166   The offences are either way and punishable with up to three years' imprisonment. The penalties for any form of distribution are quite severe and invariably involve a prison sentence.

7.167   Whether an offence is committed by merely possessing pornography in photographic form depends, therefore, on the ages of the actors or models. There is material which involves very young children whose ages are undoubtedly below 16 and, equally, there exists material involving adults who are evidently over that age. Unfortunately, there are also a substantial number of 'grey area' videos or magazines which involve young or young looking actors who are teenagers but who may or may not be below the lawful age.

7.168   Section 2(3) of PCA 1978 (as amended by CJPOA 1994) provides that 'a person is to be taken as having been a child at the material time if it appears, from the evidence as a whole, that he was then under the age of 16.' It is submitted that the onus still lies on the prosecution to prove beyond a reasonable doubt that a particular actor or model is under the age of 16 but that that onus may be discharged by simply showing the video or photograph in question and inviting the relevant tribunal to be sure that the participant is below the statutory age. There is no onus to produce a birth certificate or such like or indeed the model himself.

7.169   It may of course be very prejudicial although unavoidable for the video or magazine to be shown. Whilst looking at explicit sexual activity between young people a tribunal may find it difficult to concentrate on the issue of age.

7.170   What may assist a defence case is the obtaining of expert paediatric evidence on the likely ages of any participants. This may emphasise how difficult it is to assess age based on bodily development alone and cast doubt over the ages of specific participants. Any doubt about age must of course be resolved in a defendant's favour.

7.171   In the mid-1990s a large number of gay men found themselves prosecuted for offences under CJA 1988, s 160 as a result of their contact with video distribution companies called AVN (Adult Video News) and Man Alive. Both were based in Amsterdam and operated by having agents based in the UK distributing pirated pornographic videos. The police managed to acquire mailing lists for both the companies and used these to conduct a series of raids, seizures and prosecutions.

7.172 Both companies assured their customers that they did not handle material involving under 16s although it would appear that these assertions were untrue. The problematic videos typically originated from Germany and the Czech Republic, were pirated by the two companies and sold within the UK. In the case of AVN the company's brochure even included a lengthy and accurate statement of UK law as well as the assurance that the videos contained no illegitimate material.

7.173 Unfortunately the written reassurances provided by the video distribution companies that their material only involved actors of 16 and over did not provide any defence to the allegations of possession of child pornography. A defendant to a charge under CJA 1988, s 160 does have a defence if he can prove that he had a legitimate reason for having the photograph; that he had not seen the photograph and did not know or suspect it to be indecent, or that the photograph was sent to him unsolicited and he did not keep it for an unreasonable time [1]. None of these defences apply however to a defendant misled into acquiring an indecent photo of a child—the point goes to mitigation only.

1   CJA 1988, s 160(2).

4   The Internet

7.174 Pornography on the Internet has, in the mid-1990s, been the subject of a seemingly endless stream of articles in both the tabloid and broadsheet press. The police have not been slow to adopt this new popular concern—the announcements of the most recent 'smashings' of 'paedophile rings' have been accompanied by the news that suspects are using the Internet to trade child pornography and to meet young people.

7.175 Pornography, including child pornography, is undoubtedly available on the Internet—although you have to look reasonably hard to find it. Most sexual images are contained within newsgroups. Newsgroups are locations on the Internet where like-minded individuals can share information on favourite topics. There are about 18,000 (and increasing) newsgroups on the Internet covering subjects from animation to zen. With such a vast number of groups the subject matter gets esoteric. The vast majority of the groups, however, simply involve an exchange of written as opposed to pictorial information.

7.176 By the author's calculation, about 0.002% of the newsgroups contain sexual images. Most of these are found in the alt.binaries area. 'Alt' is an abbreviation for 'alternative' and 'binaries' suggests pictures rather than just words. For example, the 'alt.binaries.nude celebrities' group contains just what it suggests—shots of nude 'celebrities'. The vast majority of the material can hardly be described as hardcore. Most of the pictures are scanned from mainstream magazines like *Playgirl* or 'grabbed' off videos—items that are readily available over the counter in this country.

7.177 The incidence of child pornography on the Internet reflects its incidence in society as a whole—arguably it is minuscule. Unfortunately, commentators on the subject don't seem to be too keen to acknowledge this point or very keen to distinguish between adult soft pornography and the material involving children.

7.178 Comments on pornography on the Internet are often accompanied by calls for new legislation on the basis that such material is, in effect, totally unregulated. The calls for new legislation are ill-founded because not only is there no substantial problem to tackle but also because a wealth of relevant legislation already exists.

7.179 The Obscene Publications Act 1959, for example, has already been amended by the Criminal Justice and Public Order Act 1994 so that 'publication' now includes the transmission of electronically stored data which, upon decoding or resolution, is obscene. Arguably, this places at risk not just the sender of obscene material over the Internet but also Internet service providers—the agencies providing access to the Internet.

7.180 The CJPOA also amended legislation relating to child pornography so that it is now an offence to create, distribute, publish or simply possess (including on a hard drive) not only an indecent photo of a child (under 16) but also an indecent 'pseudo-photo' of a child. A pseudo-photo is something that appears to be a photo and appears to show a child—even if it is not based on a child or indeed a real person. This means that electronically manipulated or created images will be caught. Yet again Internet service providers will be placed at risk of prosecution if they 'channel' such images.

7.181 The investigation of criminal offences relating to pornographic and other offensive material on the Internet seems to have fallen by default to the clubs and vice unit at Charing Cross police station in London. The vice unit was hived off from the former obscene publications squad at New Scotland Yard and principally has the responsibility for regulating clubs, brothels and the distribution of pornography. In 1995 and 1996 the vice unit developed something of a notoriety within London's gay community for the degree of interest they showed in the capital's gay clubs (see paras **7.106ff**).

7.182 In August 1996, a standard letter was sent from the vice unit to some 140 companies providing access to the Internet (Internet service providers) detailing 133 newsgroups that the police wanted ISPs to block. The list was arranged so that the first half page consisted of explicitly and unpleasantly titled paedophile newsgroups. The consequent reaction was typically distaste followed by support for the police action. It was only the persistent reader who would realise that the police also wanted to restrict access to newsgroups which dealt with adult consensual sexual activities—many of them lesbian and gay interest groups.

7.183 The police action also failed to acknowledge the transient nature of many sites on the Internet—even by the time the list was issued some were defunct (and doubtless others similar in nature had sprung up). The censorship demand also failed to take into account the technical difficulties of such action. The 60-strong Internet Service Providers Association (ISPA) responded to the police letter by assuring co-operation with the police but also by pointing out the total impracticality of monitoring 18,000 newsgroups.

7.184   Nevertheless the police action has been reinforced with a clear threat that if ISPs do not co-operate over the proposed censorship then legal action against ISPs for publishing obscene and indecent material will be considered. Effectively ISPs are being press-ganged into policing the Internet on behalf of the police. No legal action has been taken yet and late 1996 saw a period of consultation taking place between the police and groups like ISPA and the British Computer Society (BCS). The feedback from these meetings however was less than positive with one of those attending a BCS meeting describing the clubs and vice squad as 'wishing to assume the role of lawmaker as well as law enforcer'.

7.185   The pressure from the police also had a negative effect on the adoption of a coherent and united response by ISPs. In September 1996, Peter Dawe, formerly ISPA's political officer, resigned from the group to form the Safety Net Foundation—the concept of which was akin to the government's benefit fraud hotline, with Internet users being invited to 'tell' on the posters and providers of pornography.

7.186   At the start of 1996, officers from the clubs and vice squad also commenced an investigation into the Lesbian and Gay Christian Movement (LGCM) for allegedly assisting in the publication of a 'blasphemous libel'. The law on blasphemous libel criminalises slurs on the Christian religion but does not extend to any other faiths. In the case of LGCM the allegation was that they had provided a link from their web page to another website containing the James Kirkup poem *The Love that Dares to Speak its Name*. That poem, which describes a Roman centurion's lust for the figure of Christ on the cross, was held to constitute a blasphemous libel by the House of Lords in 1977 as the result of a prosecution brought against the now defunct *Gay News* [1].

1   *Whitehouse v Gay News Ltd* [1979] AC 617, HL.

7.187   It is believed that the investigation was instigated after pressure from a senior level within the Church of England. The investigation was halted after more than a year through lack of evidence. Since that date the poem has been reprinted in full—most notably in the book *The Justice Game* by Geoffrey Robertson QC—without any action being taken. The dropping of the investigation into LGCM has meant that the issue as to whether the provision of a website link constitutes a 'publication' remains untested.

7.188   The Telecommunications Act 1984 makes it an offence to use a public telecommunications system to send grossly offensive, threatening or obscene material [1] and this would seem to cover data sent via the Internet. The 'public telecommunications service' requirement is likely to mean that offensive messages sent by one work colleague to another over an internal network (intranet) would not be caught by this provision. The offence is summary only and punishable with up to six months' imprisonment.

1   TA 1984, s 43.

7.189   The Public Order Act 1986 also renders it an offence to use or to display threatening, insulting or abusive words or behaviour etc in the presence of a person likely to be caused harassment, alarm or distress thereby (see paras **7.50–7.54**). The provision could be applied to malicious communications sent via e-mail. This would not catch harmless teasing however because the legislation provides that a person is guilty of an offence only if they intend their behaviour to be threatening, insulting or abusive or is aware that it may be so.

7.190   In May 1998, magistrates in Lincolnshire found a 28-year-old male teacher guilty of possessing indecent photographs of male children after repair staff at PC World discovered a number of images on his malfunctioning computer. Although prosecutions under the Criminal Justice Act 1988 for possessing indecent photographs or videos of children (under the age of 16) are quite common, this case was unusual for the manner in which the man came into possession of the photographs.

7.191   The brief facts of the matter were that in mid-1997 the man had taken his malfunctioning PC into PC World for repair. The staff there had 'discovered' a number of files on the hard drive of the machine which contained the indecent photographs. They had called the police and the teacher was arrested in the store. When interviewed by the police the man indicated that he did not understand how the image files got on to his hard drive. He accepted browsing the Internet and also, out of morbid curiosity, visiting some of the more extreme sites on the Internet but adamantly denied deliberately downloading any such images on to his computer's hard drive.

7.192   What neither he nor the police (nor, indeed, it would appear, PC World's staff) were aware of at the time of that first police interview was the caching function of the browser software. This 'snatches' a copy of whatever is being looked at on the Internet, including images and stores it in the cache directory of the browser software. The reason for this is not to facilitate the downloading of material from the Internet but to speed up the browsing system. If you revisit a particular site then the browser software takes most of the information from the cache and only downloads any new material from the Internet site to display the contents of the current site.

7.193   By the time the case was ready for trial the police had obtained their own detailed forensic evidence which explained the function of browser software. The evidence also indicated that because of the location of the particular image files (in the netscape cache) it was extremely unlikely that these images were deliberately downloaded—rather they were almost certainly there as a result of an automatic function of the browser software. Despite their own evidence on this point, the authorities decided to proceed with the prosecution and the matter came before the teacher's local magistrates' court for hearing in April 1998.

7.194   Because of the forensic evidence obtained by the police, the Crown Prosecution Service chose to put their case on three mutually exclusive bases:
(*a*)   that, despite the location of the image files in the cache directory, the defendant had deliberately downloaded the images and then put them there to conceal his actions;
(*b*)   that the defendant must have been aware that the browser software had the function of automatically downloading material from websites into

a cache directory and consequently must have been aware that by simply looking at such material on the Internet he would thereby come into possession of it;

(c)   that even if he was not aware of the automatic function of the browser software he nonetheless could be held to have been in possession of such material because the image he looked at on the Internet had been on his computer screen and he had consequently at that point been 'in possession' of the image.

7.195   The defendant contested the case on two bases.

(a)   To 'possess' something requires an element of knowledge of possession— in other words you can only be deemed to be in possession of an article if you are aware of its presence. The classic example is that of a person who unknowingly has something slipped inside their pocket or handbag. On a strict interpretation that person might be viewed as being in possession of the article on the basis that they have it about their person. The courts, principally in considering drugs possession cases, have held that such a strict interpretation would have obviously unfair consequences and that, in such a scenario, the individual could not be held to be in possession because they did not know the article was there [1]. There are limits to such a principle however—it is not a defence to claim that you had forgotten you were in possession of something you initially knew about. It may also not assist to say that you were mistaken as to the nature of the article you possess—so for example if you are given a sealed package to carry and told it is cannabis but it later turns out to be heroin you could be found guilty of possessing the latter substance [2].

(b)   The 'statutory' defence set out in CJA 1988, s 160(2): that the photograph was sent to him without prior request and he did not keep it for an unreasonable time. The browser software had, effectively, sent the images to the defendant—he had not requested them and, because he did not know they were even there, the question of not keeping them longer than was reasonable did not arise.

1   *Warner v Metropolitan Police Comr* [1969] 2 AC 256.
2   *R v McNamara* (1988) 87 Cr App Rep 246.

7.196   The court rejected both these submissions and found the defendant guilty of possession. The matter was appealed and the verdict overturned by the Lincoln Crown Court in August 1998—the court accepting both points set out at para **7.195**.

Chapter 8

Equality 2000

8.01 Over the years and decades of campaigning along the slow road to equality, the basic objective of all those involved has been that of equality before the law and equality before the courts. Positive discrimination has never been asked for, neither have special rights, nor preferential treatment. Sexuality is only one aspect of a person's life—just as the colour of a man's skin is only one aspect of his life. All that is asked for is for judgment on the way lives are lived and jobs are done, not on what happens in bedrooms.

A NEW HOPE

8.02 The same theme was taken up by Angela Mason when she launched Stonewall's Equality 2000 campaign shortly after the 1997 general election:

> 'The election of a new Labour government on 1 May with an inclusive agenda for change has inspired thousands of lesbians, gay men and bisexuals with new hope. We want to be part of a new Britain where discrimination does not deny opportunity, where we are all equally respected and valued. There is a widespread desire for a way of life that is fairer and more tolerant, where individuals are judged on their merits, not outdated stereotypes. Lesbians and gay men are more and more determined to live openly and freely, able to contribute equally in every area of life.'[1]

1 Equality 2000: The Stonewall Lobby Group, June 1997.

8.03 That new hope was based on the rhetoric of the new government and its leaders when in opposition. Speaking as Shadow Home Secretary in the age of consent debate on 21 February 1994, Tony Blair argued that 'a society that has learned, over time, racial and sexual equality can surely come to terms with equality of sexuality'[1]. In his first conference speech as leader of the Labour party at Blackpool in October of that year he proclaimed that 'responsibility and opportunity require fairness, justice and the right to be treated equally as citizens. That means a strong stand against discrimination on grounds of race, sex, creed or sexuality.' In the 1997 election manifesto the Labour Party committed itself 'to ending unfair discrimination wherever it exists'.

1 HC Official Report (6th series) cols 97–100, 21 February 1994.

8.04 But equality is absolute and indivisible. Partial equality is—by definition—inequality. There must always be a heavy burden of proof upon those who argue for inequality, for discrimination, against any minority: 'The way in which a society treats unpopular minorities is a litmus test of the extent of its civilisation.'[1] An equal age of consent of 16 which was for the first time approved by the Commons—but not by the Lords—in the summer of 1998 will be but a single step towards equality. In practical terms the importance of an equal age of consent has almost certainly been overrated. Stephen Fry, at the first Equality Show at the London Palladium in October 1993, asked anyone in the audience to put their hands up if they had waited until they were 21. He received, of course, a totally negative response. And in 1994—when the age of consent was still 21—the BMA reported that the average age of first homosexual encounter was 15.7 and that extensive recent research did not indicate that young men aged 16–21 were in need of special protection. Evidence also suggested that reducing the age of consent to 16 would be unlikely to affect the number of men engaging in homosexual activity either in general or within specific age groups.

1   HL Official Report (5th series) col 398, 6 March 1996, Lord Lester of Herne Hill.

8.05 In moving her age of consent amendment Ann Keen MP had said:

> 'By agreeing to the new clause, we shall signal once again that we have a House of Commons that will deliver equality and justice. We must take a positive step forward in creating a culture in which all law abiding citizens are given the opportunity to live their lives openly and freely, confident that they will not be discriminated against.'[1]

And Gerald Kaufman MP said:

> 'When [the new clause] is passed it will be a moment of achievement in which we should all take satisfaction. However when we pass it the House should not be smug or congratulate itself. Although the new clause will be a belated act of reparation, many more injustices will remain to be put right.'[2]

1   HC Official Report (6th series) col 761, 22 June 1998.
2   HC Official Report (6th series) col 775, 22 June 1998.

B CONTRADICTIONS AND INCONSISTENCIES

8.06 The age of consent is essentially a political symbol—an important symbol certainly—but still only a symbol. When it comes, as it will, it will be but a small step towards the ultimate objective in this area, namely equality before the criminal law. It will be only another example of piecemeal change. The lack of any comprehensive debate and coherent reform of sexual offences law in modern times—which was explored in Chapter 1—has resulted in a body of law which is still riddled with contradictions and inconsistencies, inequalities and injustices. The examples are legion.

- Gay sex is still unlawful if it takes place at home and more than two people are present—even if all are over 18 years old [1]. There is no such restriction on heterosexual sex.

- Gross indecency [2] is an offence only a man can commit with another man and is thus an exclusively gay offence.
- Soliciting for an immoral purpose [3] is an offence only a man can commit and is almost exclusively used against gay men.
- The statutory defence to 'unlawful sexual intercourse' with a girl over 13 years of age but under 16 [4] is not available to a man charged with having sex with any youth under the age of consent.
- A girl under 16 years of age commits no offence if she has sexual intercourse [5]. Young men who have sex when under the age of consent are committing an offence and frequently prosecuted to conviction, as in the case of the Bolton seven.
- The maximum penalty for consensual gay sex, other than in private, even when both partners are over the age of consent is two years' imprisonment and there is no requirement that it should outrage public decency. Heterosexual sex in public is usually prosecuted—if at all— under the common law offence of 'outraging public decency' and on conviction the penalty is usually a small fine.
- The maximum penalty for 'soliciting for an immoral purpose' by a man is two years' imprisonment, even when the soliciting is non-commercial. The maximum penalty for heterosexual prostitution and kerbcrawling is a level 3 fine.
- The maximum penalty for an age of consent offence by a gay man over 21 is five years' imprisonment even if the boy is aged 17. For a heterosexual age of consent offence it is two years' imprisonment unless the girl is under 13.
- Consensual sadomasochistic homosexual activity, over the age of consent and in the privacy of the home, which causes no permanent injury or need for medical attention is unlawful [6] whereas ritual circumcision, tattooing, boxing, religious flagellation, even heterosexual branding [7] are all lawful.
- A 'rent boy' is not, in law, a 'common prostitute' and so cannot be prosecuted under the Street Offences Act 1989 [8].
- The privacy provisions of the Sexual Offences Act 1967, s 1(2) apply to consensual homosexual buggery but not to consensual heterosexual buggery.
- The DPP has to give his or her consent for a prosecution for homosexual buggery where either party is under 21 years of age [9]. No such consent is required for heterosexual buggery.
- There is a limitation period of a year for prosecutions for consensual homosexual buggery, gross indecency and soliciting for immoral purposes where both parties are over 16 years of age [10] whereas there is no such limitation period for consensual heterosexual buggery.

1   Sexual Offences Act 1967, s 1(2).
2   Sexual Offences Act 1956, s 13.
3   SOA 1956, s 32.
4   SOA 1956, s 6(3).
5   *R v Tyrrell* [1894] 1 QB 710.
6   *R v Brown* [1994] 1 AC 212.
7   *R v Wilson* [1996] 2 Cr App Rep 241.
8   *DPP v Bull* [1995] 1 Cr App Rep 413.
9   SOA 1967, s 8.
10 SOA 1967, s 7.

C   REFLECTING SOCIETY

8.07   What is needed is an entirely new approach to sexual offences law incorporating the concepts of sexual equality and equality of sexuality across the board. Against that background a new Sexual Offences Act must provide protection and penalties against all sexual assaults, however minor, however grave. It must protect the vulnerable and those under the age of consent, wherever it is set. The law must also, of necessity, provide adequate protection for members of the public against public indecency. But that, it is suggested, is a matter of public order and public sexual activity—both homosexual and heterosexual—should be dealt with by amendment and extension of ss 4A and 5 of the Public Order Act 1986. The common law offence of 'outraging public decency' and the statutory offences of 'gross indecency' [1] and 'buggery' [2] would be abolished. At least some of the terrible words which for centuries have been used by legislators and journalists, priests and pundits, judges and courts to demonise the homosexual man, will at last be expunged from the statute book. Prostitution should be dealt with separately under an amended Street Offences Act. It should cover both heterosexual and homosexual activity and soliciting for an immoral purpose would be abolished [3].

1   Sexual Offences Act 1956, s 13.
2   SOA 1956, s 12.
3   SOA 1956, s 32.

8.08   Having argued the case for such reform for nearly four years [1], it was pleasing to read in *The Times* [2] that the government has decided to undertake a comprehensive review of the current legislation and penalties for sexual offences. Alun Michael, Minister of State at the Home Office, was reported as saying: 'This area of law is ripe for reform, but needs careful consideration. Any laws should reflect the society in which we live today. Our review will ensure that the framework of sexual offences and penalties is coherent and effective.'

1   Stonewall lecture, 8 December 1994 (General Council of the Bar).
2   16 June 1998.

8.09   In the course of the age of consent debate on 22 June 1998, speaking to an amendment which would have repealed the privacy provisions of s 12(1B) of the Sexual Offences Act 1956 and s 1(1) of the Sexual Offences Act 1967, Alun Michael added:

> 'I am sympathetic to the intention behind the new clause and the amendments and to the strong feeling on the part of many people that the law in this area is discriminatory. There are inequalities and those inequalities need to be addressed. There are many anomalies in the existing legislation which in many respects reflects attitudes and views that are no longer acceptable in modern society. The review of this area of legislation is long overdue.' [1]

1   HC Official Report (6th series) col 791, 22 June 1998.

8.10   One area which has always received too little attention is that of secondary legislation. There is a multitude of council and transport byelaws, most made under the powers given by the Local Government Act 1972, s 235, which criminalise acts of public indecency. For example byelaw 23 of the City of Westminster provides that:

'Every person who in any street or in any public place to which the public have access for the time being shall commit or attempt to commit any act of indecency with any other person or shall to the annoyance of residents or passengers commit any act of indecency...shall be guilty of an offence.'

8.11 The phraseology is not untypical and such byelaws have too often been used by police and prosecuting authorities to evade the complexities—and safeguards—of proceeding under primary legislation. Amending individual byelaws would be a monumental and ultimately impracticable task. But byelaws are an integral part of the debate and, as part of any package of reform, they will have to be brought into line with any new sexual offences legislation which emerges from the government's review.

1 Equality at work

8.12 If equality before the criminal law is largely—if not entirely—a matter of concern for gay men, equality in the workplace affects every single member of the lesbian and gay community. As the law stands today, deciding not to appoint someone because of their sexuality is not unlawful; nor is treating someone less favourably because of their sexuality; nor is harassing someone because of their sexuality, nor is sacking someone because of their sexuality. The decisions of the UK's Court of Appeal and of the European Court of Justice in *Grant v South-West Trains Ltd* [1] have confirmed that it is not unlawful to pay someone less because of their sexuality. The decision of the Court of Appeal in *R v Ministry of Defence, ex p Smith* [2]—the first 'gays in the military' case—approved a policy of sacking all known gays and lesbians. The protection provided—but only after two years' employment—by the Employment Protection (Consolidation) Act 1978 is in the case of homosexuals largely illusory since most tribunals—led by the Employment Appeal Tribunal— have readily and habitually found that dismissal on grounds of sexual orientation constitutes a substantial reason for rendering that dismissal not unfair. The EAT has even held that employers may dismiss homosexuals on the grounds of potential client prejudice, even where that prejudice has not been proved to exist.

1   [1998] IRLR 206.
2   [1996] QB 517, CA.

8.13 In this context there must surely be an unanswerable case for legislation at the earliest opportunity along the lines of Lady Turner's Sexual Orientation Discrimination Bill (see para **1.36**) which she has now introduced into the Lords three times in three years. The short title defines its aims as 'to render unlawful certain kinds of discrimination on the grounds of sexual orientation'.

8.14 It is a short Bill, containing only eight clauses and should not take up too many hours of parliamentary time. It would make a real difference to the working lives and conditions of every lesbian and gay man in the country. The Bill completed its passage through the Lords in July 1998, but at such a late stage in the session its chances of making any real progress in the Commons, were non-existent.

8.15 Although—as reported in the opening chapter—Lady Blackstone for the government was unable to support the Bill, her words were not entirely unfriendly. She certainly felt able to say 'I can promise that the government are committed to giving serious consideration to the issues raised by the Bill...in the context of the wider review of equality legislation.'

8.16   The review to which she referred is that of the Equal Opportunities Commission which is currently consulting on proposals for extensive changes to the Sex Discrimination Act 1975 and the Equal Pay Act 1970. Their present consultation proposes a new right to equal treatment encompassing sexual orientation protection. Similar legislation has already been approved in Denmark, Finland, France, Ireland, Holland, Sweden, Spain and New Zealand. As Lord Rea said during the second reading debate in 1996: 'Why should not Britain follow these eminently civilised countries and enact this extremely simple and fair piece of legislation?'[1] Some idea of the current absurdities in this area of law can be gauged from the Court of Appeal decision in *Smith v Gardner Merchant*[2] where the gay appellant, who was complaining of harassment aimed at his sexuality, was told that he could only succeed if the same behaviour would not have been directed at a lesbian. If the facts showed that the alleged harasser had 'a rooted aversion to homosexuals of either sex and would have subjected a female homosexual to the same harassment' the appellant's claim would inevitably fail, because then the discrimination would be on the ground of sexual orientation and not of sex.

1   HC Official Report (6th series) col 395, 6 March 1996.
2   [1998] IRLR 510.

2   Penetrating the military

8.17   In the field of employment law the issue of gays in the military is, to the SOD Bill, rather what the age of consent is to a new Sexual Offences Bill in the field of criminal law. To those who are personally affected by the ban there are degrading and intrusive searches and interrogations. Lives and careers continue to be ruined. But the numbers involved are still comparatively small. To them the issue is central. To the rest it is like the age of consent, largely symbolic. The government's position was set out by Lady Blackstone in her SOD Bill speech on second reading:

> 'The government have committed themselves in the course of this Parliament to reviewing the position [as regards homosexuality in the Armed Forces]. We will take account of the weight of the evidence, of the UK's laws and of the views of the European court and of the Armed Forces themselves. The review will start with the position agreed in the last Parliament and will look in detail at the findings of the thorough survey which was undertaken by the Ministry of Defence in 1995–96. A way forward will then be established.'[1]

1   HC Official Report (6th series) col 654, 5 June 1998.

8.18   Remembering that the Labour Party, in opposition, allowed a free vote on the issue when it was last debated in May 1996 the logic must be that the Labour government will also allow a free vote when the Armed Forces Bill comes up for review and renewal before the end of the current Parliament—perhaps in 2001.

8.19 Bearing in mind that British troops regularly serve alongside openly gay personnel from many NATO and Commonwealth countries and that there is no such comparable ban in Canada, Norway, Denmark, Holland, Belgium, Spain, France, Germany, Australia, New Zealand, Iceland, Israel, Sweden, Austria and Switzerland, it is difficult to see how the average Labour backbencher could vote against Edwina Currie's 1996 amendment that:

'(1)   sexual conduct, whether heterosexual or homosexual, shall not constitute an offence against any provision of [the Armed Forces] Act unless that conduct—

(a)   is prejudicial, or may be prejudicial, to good order or discipline; or

(b)   undermines, or tends to undermine, command relationships; or

(c)   involves the use of rank or position to obtain sexual favours or to coerce or encourage another person or persons to take part in sexual activity; or

(d)   constitutes a civil offence.'

8.20 Applied equally across the board to all relationships, heterosexual as well as homosexual, it should surely answer all reasonable concerns. As Mrs Currie said in the course of moving the new clause:

'It would apply to all inappropriate sexual behaviour, whether heterosexual or homosexual. It would protect women as well as men. It would protect young people and it would protect those in junior ranks who might be at risk of sexual harassment. The ban against homosexuals is the only blanket ban that the armed forces currently operate. Heterosexual misconduct, drug taking, alcoholism, bullying, and even serious criminal convictions in the civil courts are treated as discretionary disciplinary matters…the ban is based on prejudice, pure and simple, and as such it is offensive, impractical and expensive.'[1]

1   HC Official Report (6th series) col 482, 9 May 1996.

3   Immigration, housing and adoption

8.21 If a new Sexual Offences Bill and SOD Bill should be the main priorities for the current Parliament there are other issues where lesbian and gay law reformers will look for positive movements towards equality before the next election. Even after the changes announced in October 1997, the immigration rules still discriminate against same-sex couples. Four years prior committed cohabitation across the board sounds fair enough, but the equality is more apparent than real. A straight couple always has the option of marriage. That is not open to the gay couple, for whom the strictly applied four-year rule is an almost insuperable hurdle. Hopefully, in time, the discretion will be further refined either by reducing the qualifying period to, perhaps, two years, or by allowing partners to enter for a limited period, reapplying for further permission to remain until a sufficient period of cohabitation has been established.

8.22 One thing that is virtually certain is that s 28 of the Local Government Act 1988 will be repealed in this Parliament. This has already been confirmed by Hilary Armstrong, the Local Government Minister; by Jack Straw the Home Secretary in a letter to the author dated 11 June 1998 and by Lady Blackstone in her SOD Bill speech where she said:

'The government have stated their intention to repeal s 28 as soon as a suitable legislative opportunity arises. The section has been widely perceived as discriminatory, and we believe that it serves no useful purpose.'[1]

1   HC Official Report (6th series) col 654, 5 June 1998.

8.23   There can be less certainty of success for attempts to identify homophobic assaults as hate crimes. The government opposed amendments to this effect from Richard Allan MP during the committee stage of the Crime and Disorder Bill in June 1998 on the grounds that it would be seen to weaken the government's commitment to crack down on racially motivated assaults. On the contrary, it would be seen to confirm its commitment to oppose all crimes motivated by prejudice and bigotry. It was in the same month that the government also opposed attempts by Robert Maclennan MP to include sexual orientation as a specific ground for non-discrimination in art 14 of the European Convention on Human Rights when that Convention is incorporated into UK law by the Human Rights Act 1998.

8.24   On the other hand in her SOD Bill speech Lady Blackstone clearly indicated the government's sympathy with people in Martin Fitzpatrick's predicament (see *Fitzpatrick v Sterling Housing Association* [1]) when she said

'In housing, at present certain succession rights to tenancies are given to the surviving member of a heterosexual partnership but not of a same-sex partnership. The government have undertaken to consider, in the light of comments made in the course of a Court of Appeal judgment how far that legislation may be amended, but this must be done carefully.'[2]

As far as adoption is concerned all she would say is that:

'Currently non-married couples are excluded from jointly adopting a child as marriage is seen as an indication of permanence and commitment of the couple. It also helps the child's legal status if the adoption breaks down. These are not systems to be dispensed with lightly.'[3]

1   [1997] 4 All ER 991.
2   HC Official Report (6th series) col 657, 5 June 1998.
3   HC Official Report (6th series) col 656, 5 June 1998.

8.25   Surely the logical answer—always remembering that in this area of the law the interests of the child must be paramount—would be to allow all couples, straight or gay, married or unmarried, to adopt provided they had demonstrated both 'permanence and commitment', possibly by cohabiting in a committed and loving relationship for, perhaps, four years. If that is a proper protection for society under immigration law, are our children entitled to anything less?

D   THE CENTRAL ISSUE

8.26   So far the law reforms proposed are, in the parliamentary and political time scales, at the very most medium-term objectives. In the longer term—and that probably means at least two full Parliaments, if not more—there is the important question of gay marriage or, as it is preferable to put it: of civil domestic partnerships with the same rights and responsibilities and legal consequences as a civil marriage and open to all couples, straight or gay. For the time being and arguably for the foreseeable future, gay marriage is not on the political agenda of any of the major parties. In his letter of 11 June 1998 Jack Straw MP said:

'We understand that the present position, where the law does not recognise long-standing relationships between members of the same sex, is less than satisfactory to those concerned. However, we have no plans to introduce legislation to permit same-sex marriages.'

8.27 We are constantly being lectured, by leaders of a variety of religions, by politicians of all parties, by 'social commentators' and journalists, on the importance of the family and of the marriage contract as the cement which holds society together. On almost every issue where gays wish to establish rights as equal citizens they are faced with the 'family' argument. In his negative speech on the 'age of consent' debate Sir Norman Fowler MP from the Opposition front bench found it necessary to make this contrast:

'I need no persuasion that the rights of gay people must be protected and that this is a legitimate concern of the House. Equally I am strongly in favour of family life. I shall continue to advocate the importance of the family, and my belief that it must continue to be at the centre of national life.'[1]

In the same debate Stuart Bell MP, speaking for the Church of England, said:

'In Paris yesterday 20,000 people marched for civil marriage for homosexual couples and for the legal right to adopt children. This is a further undermining of family life, which has been and will continue to be the basis of our society for years to come.'[2]

1 HC Official Report (6th series) col 780, 22 June 1998.
2 HC Official Report (6th series) col 796, 22 June 1998.

8.28 In her speech from the government front bench in the House of Lords on the SOD Bill, Baroness Blackstone gave as her first reason why the government opposed the Bill:

'The importance that this government places on the family and the need to consider how all our policies impact on the family. We recognise the central value of the family and marriage.'

Conceding that 'there are strong and mutually supportive families and relationships outside marriage' she still felt compelled to say:

'We must tread a careful path between taking account of social reality and at the same time ensuring that we do not undermine the family.'[1]

1 HC Official Report (6th series) col 655, 5 June 1998.

8.29 Common to all these speeches and those of almost everyone who speaks as 'the party of the family' in support of 'traditional family values' is the implicit statement that the only valid family unit is the nuclear family of mother, father and 2.4 children. None of them is prepared to provide any more profound analysis of the family and the reasons why society has supported the family as a social structure for so long. All of them imply that procreation is an essential prerequisite for a family and family life. But the family, as an institution, is constantly evolving and changing. Just compare the family of a century ago, which was extended in terms of numbers but very narrow geographically, with the family of the late twentieth century, which is extended geographically, but narrow in numbers. It was refreshing to hear Lord Williams of Mostyn, Parliamentary Under-Secretary of State at the Home Office, speaking in the House of Lords:

> 'We are not in the business of preaching or prescribing. Families in our society vary infinitely. We live in a diverse society. People are entitled to diverse views about the way in which they wish to run their lives. It is not for me or the government to define precisely what is a family unit. The mark of a civilised society is to accommodate diversity in others.'[1]

1   HC Official Report (6th series) cols 2–3, 9 December 1997.

1   Defining the family

8.30   The most perceptive analysis of the family for a long time is contained in Lord Justice Ward's minority judgment in *Fitzpatrick v Sterling Housing Association* [1]:

> 'There being no dispute but that the appellant and the deceased were living together, it is necessary to go on and ascertain, in so far as this is possible, the manner in which they were living together in the same household. If asked why, would not both they and the heterosexual couple equally well reply "because we love each other and are committed to devote comfort and support to each other"? When asked "In what manner do you, a gay couple, live together?" would their answer be any different from that given by the heterosexual couple save only in the one respect that in their case their sexual relations are homosexual not heterosexual? No distinction can sensibly be drawn between the two couples in terms of love, nurturing, fidelity, durability, emotional and economic interdependence—to name but some and no means all of the hallmarks of a relationship between a husband and his wife [2]…The test has to be whether the relationship of the appellant to the deceased was one where there is at least a broadly recognisable de facto familial nexus. I would not define that familial nexus in terms of its structures or components: I would rather focus on familial functions. The question is more what a family does rather than what a family is. A family unit is a social organisation which functions through linking its members closely together. The functions may be procreative, sexual, sociable, economic, emotional. The list is not exhaustive. Not all families function in the same way. Save for the ability to procreate, these functions were present in the relationship between the deceased and the appellant.'[3]

1   [1997] 4 All ER 991.
2   [1997] 4 All ER 991 at p 1022.
3   [1997] 4 All ER 991 at p 1023.

8.31   One can only hope that it is against an intellectual analysis of this rigour that the marriage/partnership debate can be conducted. In that debate there will be much prejudice, even more hot air and very little light. It will need to be very clear what is being argued and why this is wanted. Above all we must start by going back to first principles.

8.32   For centuries state and society have provided a whole range of rights and benefits, both financial and social, to encourage the institution of marriage and the family. Why are those rights and benefits provided? It cannot have anything to do with any religious ceremony, as they are given to those who go through both civil and religious marriages and, in the UK at least only a minority of marriages are religious. It cannot have anything necessarily to do with procreation, as many are given from the moment of marriage—regardless of the intention or ability of the parties to have children—and continue long after any children cease to be dependent. And in many cases those rights and benefits are not extended to unmarried couples who do have children. If this analysis is correct they are given by state and society to encourage long-term committed relationships in the—arguably correct—belief that such relationships are important in maintaining the stability of state and society.

2   Rights, responsibilities and recognition

8.33   There is then a powerful sociological argument for extending those rights and benefits to all long-term committed relationships, both same-sex and opposite-sex, whether they accept or reject the concept of legal marriage, whether they can or cannot be married. But the debate is not just about rights. It is much more about responsibilities. If the same-sex couple is prepared to take on the responsibilities of family life, then surely they should be entitled to receive the rights and the public recognition which society gives to the family, perhaps through a public ceremony of commitment. We must accept that the consequences of such changes would not be all one way. In the social security system, for example, the concept of mutual support would result in both gains and losses.

8.34   Until comparatively recently there had been very little real debate in this country on these issues. In the USA it has been driven very largely by the Hawaiian gay marriage case, *Baehr v Milke,* the Marriage Project of the Lambda Legal Defence and Education Fund and its director Evan Wolfson. Gay marriage cases are currently pending in both Vermont and Alaska. But the backlash was the enactment in September 1996 of the federal Defence of Marriage Act and in the passage in at least 25 of the 50 states of legislation restricting marriage to opposite-sex couples or denying recognition to same-sex couples.

8.35   In Europe, especially in Scandinavia, the debate has gone down the very different track of legally binding domestic partnerships providing much the same rights and responsibilities as heterosexual civil marriage. They include the right to use each other's names, the responsibility of mutual support, the right to a half-share of all joint possessions and the right of inheritance to the survivor should one of the partners die. The conditions for dissolving the partnership are the same as for heterosexual divorce. If a partnership breaks down, shared possessions must be divided equally unless the couple have signed a pre-partnership agreement. In Scandinavia, where the process started as long ago as 1989, domestic partnerships are reciprocally enforced in the other jurisdictions. And the movement is extending across Europe to Germany, Holland, France, Spain and even Hungary.

8.36 In this country the lesbian and gay community is still undecided as to whether to follow the American or the Scandinavian route. Some, for deeply held and very personal reasons of religious belief, would settle for nothing less than the right to marry. Others argue that only the recognition of gay marriages will satisfy the basic human rights case for equality before the law. On the other hand there are those who believe that marriage is a fundamentally flawed heterosexual institution with an alarming rate of divorce, domestic violence and child abuse and that gay people should be seeking to develop alternative models of relationship recognition. At least the debate is now very much part of the current social and legal—if not yet political—agenda. It began with the publication of Andrew Sullivan's book *Virtually Normal* [1] which was closely followed by a leading article in *The Economist* entitled Let Them Wed [2]. There have been major pieces arguing the case in *The Independent*, *The Guardian* and *The Times* and debates on a variety of television channels. A leader in *The Times* [3] argued that long-term same-sex committed relationships were just as entitled to the benefit of reforms in the law of matrimonial property as opposite-sex unmarried partnerships.

1   Sullivan A *Virtually Normal* (1995) Picador.
2   *The Economist* January 1996.
3   Happy Families *The Times*, January 1998.

8.37 When, in his letter of 11 June 1998, the Home Secretary conceded that the current law is 'less than satisfactory to those concerned' he was not overstating the position. The inequalities in both immigration and adoption law which have already been referred to, flow directly from the inability of a gay couple to marry. The great majority of public sector pension schemes do not provide the equivalent of a widow's or widower's pension to a gay partner. The estates of same-sex couples are charged Inheritance Tax at 40% on anything they leave each other over £223,000 and Capital Gains Tax on any property transferred from one to another. Married couples can transfer as much as they like and leave as much as they wish to each other without attracting Capital Gains or Inheritance Tax. If a lesbian or gay man dies intestate then property does not automatically go to their partner, as it would if they could marry. Same-sex couples are not automatically deemed to be each other's next of kin.

8.38 So far little is known about the state of public opinion in this country on these issues either in the homosexual or heterosexual communities. It would be interesting to see the results of an opinion poll which asked the question 'Do you approve or disapprove of those in long-term committed same-sex relationships being entitled to the same rights and responsibilities as those provided for by the traditional marriage contract?' The issue must be kept in the public eye and it must be explained to the general public that gay marriage is not the only possibility. A forum must be found—perhaps the Law Commission—where the implications of such changes can be examined and the experiences of other jurisdictions can be explored. Most importantly political leaders must be convinced that the legal recognition of long-term committed same-sex partnerships can only strengthen the social fabric and that is the experience of those Scandinavian countries which have already followed this route.

E BACK TO EUROPE?

8.39 So far this chapter has been concerned only with legislative reform. But the litigation route should not be forgotten, especially after the passage of the Human Rights Act 1998 incorporating into domestic law the rights and freedom guaranteed under the European Convention on Human Rights. When the provisions of that Act will be implemented is still uncertain. Before they are, there will have to be a major educational programme for the judiciary at every level. At the time of writing, the Judicial Studies Board is already falling behind with its training timetable for the Woolf civil justice reforms. It may well be that the provisions of the Human Rights Act 1998 will not be implemented until, perhaps, late in 2000. Until then Strasbourg remains a very real option and Luxembourg will always be a possibility.

8.40 In his wide-ranging second Stonewall lecture: *A Case for Equality* delivered on 4 December 1997, Peter Duffy QC identified a number of areas where progress may still be made through the European courts or in the domestic courts through the Human Rights Act 1998. On the adoption issue he said:

'After enactment, I see scope for challenge to whether s 14 of the Adoption Act can be construed as extending to stable gay couples on the basis that they are de facto married and, if the court concludes that this construction is not possible, then arguments over a possible incompatibility declaration.'

In relation to the *Fitzpatrick*[1] case he argued that:

'Such discrimination is contrary to art 8 of the Convention which protects home and family, read with art 14 which, we have seen in *Sutherland* was construed powerfully as protecting homosexuals against discrimination on grounds of sex or status.'

On the future of s 28 of the Local Government Act 1988 he suggested that:

'Access to information and ideas is protected under art 10 of the Convention; there is a duty not to disseminate in relation to any functions assumed in relation to education and teaching under protocol 2.1, art 2 read with art 14. A Court of Human Rights judgment [*Campbell and Cosans v United Kingdom*[2]] indicates that the UK reservation to protocol 2.1, art 2 will not oust human rights review of a provision like s 28. Challenges to any use of s 28 look very likely indeed.'

1 [1997] 4 All ER 991.
2 (1982) 4 EHRR 293, para 37.

8.41 In addition, the conviction of the Bolton seven and the privacy provisions of the Sexual Offences Acts 1956 and 1967 are certain to be challenged under arts 8 and 14 unless pre-empted by the government's review and reform of sexual offences legislation. A case, known only as *AT v United Kingdom*, on the same issue is already well on the way to Europe. The emphasis may swing back to legislation as the most effective means of achieving equality of sexuality but the litigation route remains a very real and, potentially, very important way forward.

8.42   In many ways and in many areas the attitudes of the senior judiciary are well in advance of the attitudes of senior politicians. In *R v Ministry of Defence, ex p Smith* [1]—the first gays in the military case—in the Divisional Court, Lord Justice Simon Brown said: 'The tide of history is against the ministry. Prejudices are breaking down; old barriers are being removed.' In the same case, in the Court of Appeal, Lord Justice Henry said:

> 'Over the years, since the passing of the Sexual Offences Act 1967, there can be no doubt that public opinion has moved a very long way towards tolerance and acceptance of homosexuals. We have seen a greater and greater acceptance of homosexuals together with a greater personal openness in acknowledging it.'

Lord Bingham—then Master of the Rolls, now Lord Chief Justice—said: 'There has in this country been a discernible trend, over the last half century or so, towards greater understanding and greater tolerance of homosexuals by heterosexuals, and towards greater openness and honesty by homosexuals.'

1   [1996] QB 517, CA.

8.43   For many years the radical left in this country has been fearful of a reactionary judiciary when issues of human rights have been raised. In the past their fears were too often justified. On the basis of these dicta—and those in *Perkins* and *Fitzpatrick* and *Re W*—there must be good ground for optimism that the Human Rights Act will open a new era in the fight for the basic human right of equality of sexuality, and that the higher judiciary will be in the vanguard of that battle.

8.44   Closing this chapter are two quotations: first, from a speech by Gerry Studds—then an openly gay member of the US House of Representatives—in the House debate on the Defence of Marriage Act in September 1996:

> 'We are going to prevail and we are going to prevail just as every other component of the civil rights movement in this country has prevailed. In the words of Dr Martin Luther King, this country is going to rise up and live out the true meaning of its creed. There is nothing any of us can do today to stop that. We can embrace it warmly as some of us do. We can resist it bitterly as some of us do. But there is no power on earth that can stop it.'

The second is from Sedley J's introduction to the author's Stonewall lecture in December 1994:

> 'This is a significant time in the struggle for acceptance of all the varieties that make up the totality of sexual choice in our society. The depth of prejudice is not to be underestimated, nor its capacity to endure. But although anger and intolerance are alive and well fortunately it isn't necessary to fight fire with fire. It is very much better to fight it with reasoned argument and in a spirit of intelligent understanding.'

Precedents

NOTES FOR GUIDANCE

The following precedents aim to provide a framework for advisers asked to draw up cohabitation agreements and declarations of trust by same-sex (or hetrosexual) cohabitants. The cohabitation agreement includes suggested clauses for a variety of situations, whereas the declaration of trust is limited to one situation. Some texts are now devoted exclusively to precedents of this nature and acknowledgment is given to two of these: Bowler et al, *Living Together Precedents*, Waterlow, 1989 and Lush, *Cohabitation and Co-ownership Precedents*, Family Law, 1993, to which the author is indebted in achieving the frameworks below and to which advisers are referred for precedents suitable for a wider variety of situations.

Advisers should note that the author cannot guarantee or accept any responsibility for the legal enforceability of the suggested precedents, which must remain a matter for the individual adviser's own judgment. The framework cohabitation agreement is not intended to be comprehensive and other issues not covered here can be added in. Clauses used in the cohabitation agreement in relation to the family home could equally be used in a declaration of trust relating to the family home where no cohabitation agreement as such is being entered into.

Please note that possible alternatives are given in square brackets and advisers need to carefully consider the appropriateness of each alternative in the light of their instructions. Instructions and notes to advisers are given in italics and contained in round brackets.

Appendix I

FRAMEWORK COHABITATION AGREEMENT (FOR OWNER OCCUPIERS)

This Cohabitation Agreement is made this   day of   19

BETWEEN

(*insert name*) of (*insert address*) (hereinafter called 'X') of the one part

and

(*insert name*) of (*insert address*) (hereinafter called 'Y') of the other part

WHEREAS:

(1) The parties [are cohabiting] [intend to cohabit]

(2) The parties wish to enter into an agreement regulating their rights and obligations towards each other and [any children of the relationship and] in relation to their family home and other property

(3) The parties intend this agreement to be legally binding upon them and have each [taken] [been advised to take] independent legal advice as to the effect of this agreement

(4) Full and frank disclosure has been made by each party to the other of the material facts relating to their respective financial circumstances [and a statement of each party's assets, income and liabilities is set out in Schedule 1 hereto]

(5)(a) The parties presently have [no][*insert number*] child[ren] of their relationship[, who is [are] [a] minor[s][, namely]—]

(*set out names, dates of birth and details of parental responsibility*)

AND/OR

(b) X has [number] child[ren] by a previous relationship[, who is[are] [a] minor[s]]

(*set out names, dates of birth and details of parental responsibility*)

AND/OR

(c) Y has [*number*] child[ren] by a previous relationship[, who is[are] [a] minor[s]]

(*set out names, dates of birth and details of parental responsibility*)

The family home—legal title

(6) The parties are presently living at (*insert address*) ('the family home') which is a [free][lease]hold property purchased in the [sole][joint] name[s] of (*insert name(s)*)

OR

(6) The parties (*or name of one of them as appropriate*) intend[s] to purchase as [their joint residence][the joint residence of the parties] a [free][lease]hold property at (*address*) ('the family home') in the [joint] [sole] name[s] of (*insert name(s)*)

The family home—beneficial ownership

(7) The parties [intend to enter][have entered] into a deed of trust [dated (*insert date*)] which reflects their express common intention [to share][not to share] the beneficial interest in the family home as set out below. Furthermore they shall enter into a new deed of trust in respect of any other family home they may acquire in the future for their residence. [In default of any such deed of trust and subject to any contrary intention expressly included in the Conveyance, Transfer, Lease or Assignment or in any variation of or substitute for this agreement made between the parties, any replacement family home bought by the parties hereto shall be held in the same proportions as set out herein.]

IT IS HEREBY AGREED:

(Choose appropriate option from following possibilities)

Sole beneficial ownership

1 That the family home [has been][will be] purchased in the sole name of (*name*) and irrespective of any direct or indirect contributions made towards the purchase price, mortgage repayments, maintenance or improvement of the home made by (*name of non-owning party*) he/she [has not and] will not acquire any beneficial interest in the family home.

(In this situation, independent legal advice for both parties and particularly the non-owner is imperative.)

OR

Equitable joint tenancy [converting to equitable tenancy in common]

1 That the beneficial interests of the parties in the family home are held as joint tenants in equity [unless and until severance of the joint tenancy occurs, whereupon they shall hold as tenants in common in equity in the shares specified below].

(In this case one of the following clauses relating to beneficial tenancies in common as may be appropriate from instructions should follow.)

AND/OR

Equitable tenancy in common in fixed shares

1(a) That irrespective of their direct or indirect contributions made towards the purchase price, mortgage and mortgage-related repayments, maintenance or improvement of the family home made by either party, their beneficial interests in the property are held as tenants in common in equity in the following shares calculated with reference to the [net proceeds of sale as at the date of sale or transfer defined as (*insert definition agreed, eg the gross sale price less, sum required to redeem mortgage, estate agent's fees, legal expenses incurred in the sale*)] *or* [gross proceeds of sale as at the date of sale or transfer, with each party undertaking to redeem their share of the mortgage, estate agent's fees and legal expenses in the same proportion (*or specify other proportions agreed*)]:

X (*insert percentage*) and Y (*insert percentage*)

OR

Equitable tenancy in common in floating shares proportionate to direct contributions to the purchase of the family home

1(a) That their beneficial interests are held as tenants in common in equity in shares proportionate to their respective direct contributions towards the purchase of the family home calculated in the first instance as a percentage of the [gross] proceeds of sale as at the date of sale or transfer (*define or adapt if legal or estate agency expenses are to be deducted prior to calculation of proportions*) [but subject to each party redeeming their share of the mortgage redemption figure as at that date, to be calculated in the same proportions as their agreed contributions to the mortgage instalments [and linked endowment policy premiums] set out in clause 2, and subject also to account being taken of any lump sum capital repayment of the mortgage in accordance with clause 3].

1(b) For the avoidance of doubt, direct contributions to the purchase of the family home include (*specify as appropriate and indicate whether it is intended the list should be exhaustive*):

[capital contributions (including right to buy/acquire or other discount) to the purchase price] (*where the home was originally the home of just one partner, the value of their unencumbered share at the outset of cohabitation could be inserted as their capital contribution*).

[lump sum repayment of mortgage capital pursuant to clause 3]

[payment of mortgage instalments] [pursuant to clause 2]

[payment of endowment policy premiums linked to mortgage] [pursuant to clause 2]

(Consideration should be given and instructions taken as to whether the following should be specifically included or excluded and the position clarified in the agreement.)

[AND DO NOT INCLUDE]

[contributions to the cost of repairs and/or improvements to the family home]

[legal expenses incurred on purchase and/or sale of the home]

1(c) A statement of the direct contributions made by each of the parties at the date hereof is set out in Schedule 2 hereto.

General note: The effect of this option is to create an express resulting trust which crystallises at the date of sale or transfer of the property at which point the beneficial interests can be calculated. Parties will need to ensure that records and receipts are kept of all contributions and this is a possible disadvantage of such a clause. Note also that the clause is looking at the contributions themselves and not at the effect of the contributions on any change in value of the property, which may be appropriate especially in respect of payment for improvements. If this is required, this should be made clear. Floating share calculations are of necessity complicated and to some extent cumbersome as will be seen. However, the advantage is that this is a method which may well commend itself to parties as being as fair as possible, both when entering into the agreement and on relationship breakdown. Thought needs to be given, however, to the position of a party who cannot make contributions due to changed circumstances. Do the parties want this to reduce that party's beneficial interest? Is this fair? In a situation where the inability to pay is triggered by child care undertaken on behalf of both parties, parties may wish to protect the beneficial interest of that party. See clause 10(b).

Method of calculation

The proportionate shares of each partner are calculated by determining the separate proportion of each partner for each relevant heading (eg capital contributions and mortgage) as a percentage of the combined contributions made by both parties under that heading and adding the percentages calculated for each partner for each heading together to arrive at their total proportion of the gross proceeds of sale from which their respective agreed proportions of the mortgage redemption figure should be deducted. The aim of using the gross proceeds of sale rather than the net proceeds of sale is to ensure that any increase or decrease in value is passed on on sale in proportion to the contributions originally made to the purchase price either by way of capital or mortgage.

A simple illustration may assist:

Assuming X and Y bought a property ten years ago for £100,000 with a mortgage advance of £75,000 and have agreed to sell it for £120,000 on relationship breakdown, with a mortgage redemption figure of £65,000 in respect of an ordinary repayment mortgage:

Capital contributions on purchase were:

X – £10,000 (ie 10,000/100,000 = 10%)

Y – £15,000 (ie 15,000/100,000 = 15%)

Mortgage contribution arrangements in respect of repayment of the advance of £75,000

X – 75% of the mortgage (ie (75% x £75,000) ÷ (£100,000) = 56.25%)

Y – 25% of the mortgage (ie (25% x £75,000) ÷ (£100,000) = 18.75%)

Total shares subject to mortgage

X = 66.25%

Y = 33.75%

Mortgage redemption liability

X – (75% x £65,000) = £48,750

Y – (25% x £65,000) = £16,250

Thus total share of gross proceeds of sale (£120,000) but subject to mortgage redemption liability (£65,000) is:

X – (66.25% x £120,000) – £48,750 = £30,750

Y – (33.75% x £120,000) – £16,250 = £24,250

(subject to payment of expenses related to the sale in the proportion agreed).

In a negative equity situation the calculation would result in a negative share for one or both parties. Although it would not affect the joint and several liability of joint mortgagors to the mortgagee, it would indicate the agreed proportions in which the resultant debt to the mortgagee should be paid.

If felt appropriate, the commentary on the method of calculation of the shares set out above could be included in the clause and a step by step guide to calculation could be detailed in a schedule by means of a formulaic example. This approach has been adopted in the Schedule to the declaration of trust, see page 210.

For a discussion of a net proceeds of sale calculation in respect of floating shares see Lush, 1993, pages 32–42.

Contributions to mortgage, mortgage-related payments and other outgoings in respect of the family home

2(1) The mortgage repayments [and mortgage-related endowment policy premiums] shall be paid by (*insert name of paying party*) alone.

OR

2(1) [Subject to clause 10(b)] (*This should be inserted where the parties have agreed floating shares and a reduction in contributions to the mortgage during a period of child care suggested in clause 10(b)*) the parties shall contribute to the mortgage repayments [and mortgage-related endowment policy premiums] in the following proportions—

X (*insert percentage*)

Y (*insert percentage*).

OR

2(1) The parties shall contribute to the mortgage repayments [and mortgage-related endowment policy premiums] in proportions to be agreed from time to time between the parties [and [subject to clause 10(b)] their respective beneficial interests in the family home shall be calculated by reference to the payments actually made by each party].

Failure to pay

2(2) If, other than [by agreement in writing,] [or] [by virtue of one party having reduced their income in order to undertake child care of a child or children of the [parties] [family]] [or] [by virtue of any practical arrangement whereby one party undertakes instead to make a greater contribution than agreed to the payment of other outgoings [or debts] in respect of the family home on behalf of] [both parties][the other party], one party fails to make his/her agreed contributions to the mortgage repayments [and mortgage-related endowment policy premiums], the calculation of the respective shares of the parties attributable to mortgage-related contributions [shall be adjusted to reflect the actual payments made] OR [shall not be thereby affected] [but in the event that these repayments are made in full or in part by the other party, unless otherwise agreed, such payments shall be treated as a loan to the party in default (*insert any terms with regard to interest*) by the other party. It is further agreed that on sale or transfer of the family home any sums outstanding in respect of such a loan be deducted from the defaulting party's share of the net proceeds of sale (*define here if not previously defined*) and paid to the other party without prejudice to their right to recover any further balance of the loan debt]. (*Carefully consider instructions on the various options and delete as appropriate. Note this will not affect each party's joint and several liability to the mortgagee.*)

Capital lump sum mortgage repayments

3 In the event that either party makes a capital payment in discharge or part discharge of any mortgage secured on the family home, that party's beneficial interest in the home shall be adjusted to reflect such a payment. [Calculation of the adjusted share shall be made as a percentage of the value of the family home at the date of the capital payment, which if not agreed between the parties shall be determined by an independent valuer appointed jointly by the parties or in default by a valuer to be appointed by the President of the Royal Institution of Chartered Surveyors (RICS).] [A note of such variation shall be endorsed hereon in accordance with clause 12 hereof.]

Improvements and repairs

4(a) Unless previously agreed between the parties, improvements which may change the value of the family home shall not be undertaken. [Where such an agreement is reached, the parties' respective contributions to the cost of the improvements will be in the proportions agreed between them (*or specify the proportions here if appropriate*) and any necessary adjustments to their respective shares in the family home [which will reflect the change in value of the home] shall be calculated with reference to the value of the home at the date the work is commenced (*or insert other date if considered more appropriate*)] [as agreed by the parties or as determined by an independent valuer appointed jointly by the parties or in default by a valuer to be appointed by the President of the RICS]. [A note of such variation shall be endorsed hereon in accordance with clause 12 hereof.]

4(b) Repairs to the property which are reasonable and necessary shall be paid for in the proportions

X (*insert contribution*)% and

Y (*insert contribution*) %,

save that any major repairs exceeding the cost of (*insert agreed threshold*) shall not be undertaken unless at least two (*or insert agreed number*) independent estimates have been obtained. Any other repairs shall not be undertaken without the prior agreement of the parties.

Non-monetary contributions

5 Unless previously agreed in writing and noted as a variation in accordance with clause 12, non-monetary contributions to the property shall not affect the parties' beneficial interests in the family home. [Nothing in this clause shall affect the agreement reached in clause 10(b) hereof.] (*Clause 10(b) considers changed contributions where one party gives up work to care for children and it is agreed that this will not affect the parties' beneficial interests.*)

Outgoings

6 Payment of [the ground rent and service charge due under the Lease of the family home], [building insurance premiums][contents insurance premiums] [all household bills including council tax, water rates, other utility bills (*define and/or add to these as appropriate, eg telephone, television rental and licence, food, joint holidays, decorating costs, minor repair costs etc*) shall be made by the parties in the proportions

X (*insert contribution*) %

Y (*insert contribution*) %.

(*General note: Where parties are sharing the beneficial interest in the home, contributions to items relating to any lease or insurance of the property are likely to be made in the same proportions as those in which the beneficial interests are held. All parties will need to decide how the living expenses should be shared. There is no reason (other than lack of simplicity) why parties should not agree to pay bills in proportions specified by individual item. If this is decided, a schedule annexed to the agreement may be most appropriate.)*

Personal property and contents of the family home

7(a) All personal effects intended for the personal use of one party acquired prior to this agreement (*or specify other date such as when cohabitation began as appropriate*), or subsequently belong to that party and shall remain their separate property regardless of who acquired them or how they were acquired. (*This is aimed at items such as clothing, jewellery, personal computers etc which may have been purchased, inherited or given as gifts. Any exceptions such as a family heirloom of the other party should be detailed and examples of items included may be specified or included in a Schedule.*)

7(b) All other personal property acquired by X prior to this agreement (*or specify other date such as when cohabitation began as appropriate*), whether by gift, inheritance or purchase [and listed in Schedule (*insert appropriate number*)] shall also remain the property of X, even though intended for the joint use of the parties during their period of cohabitation. (*This may include furniture, motor car, rugs, kitchen equipment etc. Provision for the running costs of a car could be set out here if appropriate.*)

7(c) All other personal property acquired by Y prior to this agreement (*or specify other date such as when cohabitation began as appropriate*), whether by gift, inheritance or purchase [and listed in Schedule (*insert appropriate number*)] shall also remain the property of Y, even though intended for the joint use of the parties during their period of cohabitation. (*This may include furniture, motor car, rugs, kitchen equipment etc. Provision for the running costs of a car could be set out here if appropriate.*)

Jointly acquired contents or other property and property acquired on credit

8 All property acquired after the date of this agreement (*or specify other date such as when cohabitation began inserted in clause 7*) and during the period of cohabitation, for the joint use and/or benefit of the parties in their home (including furniture, household or garden equipment) shall be owned jointly and in equal shares (*or specify shares agreed*) by the parties regardless of which of the parties acquired them, SAVE THAT any items acquired by one party by means of any loan, credit agreement or arrangement (other than a credit or charge card in the name of one party on which the other party is a second cardholder) shall [until such time as the full debt has been repaid] be owned solely by the party liable under such a loan, credit agreement or arrangement who shall retain sole liability for all repayments in respect of the credit obtained. Where items are acquired jointly on credit, by means of a joint bank loan, overdraft, joint credit or charge card (including a second cardholder arrangement), or other joint credit facility (other than a loan secured on the family home), these shall be jointly owned in equal shares (*or specify as appropriate*) and the parties shall be jointly responsible for making all the repayments in equal shares (*or specify as appropriate*).

(Note: If loans are or may be taken from friends or relatives on an informal basis, it may be appropriate to except these from the above clause and make provision in a separate clause indicating where responsibility for repayment lies.)

Bank and building society accounts

9(a)   Any bank or building society account or other capital asset (not previously referred to in this agreement) in the sole name of either party shall remain the sole property of that party.

9(b)   Any bank or building society account or other capital asset (not previously referred to in this agreement) vested in the joint names of the parties shall belong to the parties in the proportions

(insert percentage) to X and

(insert percentage) to Y

notwithstanding the proportions of their respective actual contributions made to the account or to acquisition of the asset.

Children/child care

[10(a) The parties agree that they will share responsibility for the care of their children.] [This includes their intention to apply for a shared residence order in respect of any children of the relationship and to share in the costs of the birth of any child.] [Where both parties are working, they will take turns in staying at home with the children if they are ill or on holiday and no other child care arrangements can be made or are appropriate.]

(Note: Children of the relationship should be defined in the same-sex context.)

AND/OR

[10(b) If [whilst the parties are cohabiting] one party [gives up work] [reduces their hours of work] to care for the children of the relationship, the other party will pay them [50% *(or specify percentage or figure as appropriate)*] of their disposable income *(insert definition)*] until the youngest child [attends nursery/ primary school] [reaches the age of 5 *(or specify other age agreed)*]. [During this period, the party undertaking the child care [shall continue to make their contributions to the mortgage and other outgoings previously referred to] [shall make reduced contributions to the mortgage and other outgoings namely *(either specify the new contributions if these can be agreed or in most cases indicate that these will be reduced in proportion to the carer's new share of the family's joint gross income, or as agreed between the parties)*]. Nothing in this clause will act to proportionately reduce the beneficial interest in the family home of the party undertaking the childcare.] *(This aims to protect the beneficial interest of the partner undertaking child care where the parties have agreed to the floating share method of calculation. Cross reference needs to be made to this clause in other relevant clauses.)*

[10(c)   Any child support or maintenance received for the benefit of a child(ren) of one of the parties from a previous relationship shall be used for the benefit of [that][those] child(ren).]

Review

11 The parties agree to review this agreement every two years (*or specify other appropriate period*) and whenever there is a major change in their financial or personal circumstances including but not limited to the birth of a child, serious illness or injury, loss of employment, significant reduction or increase in either party's income or capital, with the intention of considering whether any variation of the agreement should be undertaken.

Variation

12 Any variation of this agreement shall be in writing and executed by both parties in the form of a deed. The variation shall be noted and endorsed upon each party's copy of this agreement.

Termination

13   This agreement will be terminated on the happening of any of the following events:

(i) The death of either party;

(ii) Mutual agreement of the parties that cohabitation shall cease whereupon the Separation Provisions set out below shall apply;

(iii) The expiry of (*insert number*) month[s] notice in writing by one party to the other that they wish to cease cohabiting and terminate the agreement whereupon the Separation Provisions set out below shall apply;

(iv) The voluntary abandonment of the family home by one party for a period of (*insert number*) weeks, whereupon the Separation Provisions set out below shall apply.

The separation provisions

The family home

14(a) As soon as possible on termination, each party should notify the other in writing whether or not they wish to remain in occupation of the family home [and, if not previously severed, will serve notice severing the joint tenancy in equity of the family home]. An independent open-market valuation of the property will be obtained by a valuer agreed by the parties or in default appointed by the President of the RICS. If only one party wishes to remain, they will be given a period of (*insert number*) months from the date of termination of the agreement in which to complete the purchase of the other party's share of the family home, calculated on the basis of the independent valuation and in accordance with the provisions of this agreement.

14(b)   If both parties wish to remain, preference shall be given [to the party with whom the children of the relationship will reside] [the party in whom the legal title is vested] [the party who is in a position to complete first] the purchase of the other party's interest as evidenced by a mortgage offer and or cleared funds sufficient for this purpose].

14(c)   If neither party wishes to remain in the home, or if the party wishing to remain fails to complete within the specified period, the home shall be sold for the best price obtainable as agreed between the parties or in default of agreement certified by [the jointly instructed Selling Agent] [an independent valuer appointed by the President of the RICS].

Mortgage-related payments by occupier

15   Pending sale of the family home, [the mortgage repayments [and mortgage-related endowment policy premiums] shall [be made wholly by the party in occupation in satisfaction of any claim for an occupation rent] [continue to be paid by the parties in the proportions set out in clause 2 hereof]] *AND/OR* [where one party has excluded the other party from the family home against their will and without reasonable cause, the party remaining in occupation shall pay to the other party an occupation rent of a sum to be agreed or advised by an independent valuer].

(Which option is appropriate will depend on who has made the major capital and mortgage contributions to the property and the reasons for the other party leaving the property.)

Other outgoings

16 The parties agree to notify the relevant authorities and utility companies of the date on which cohabitation ceased and remain liable for their share of the outgoings up until that date. Thereafter, [the party in occupation shall make payment of all the outgoings specified in clauses 4(b) and 6] [the parties shall continue to make payments [in the same proportions] [in the following proportions *(specify proportions agreed)*] [in proportions which reflect the parties' ability to pay]] pending sale of the home].

Bank and building society accounts, other capital assets, credit cards etc

17 On termination of the agreement, other than by reason of death of one of the parties, the parties agree—

(i) to notify the banks and building societies concerned and close all accounts held in their joint names, destroying all cheques and cheque cards, cancelling standing orders and dividing the credit balances equally *(or state proportions)* between them or remaining liable in respect of any overdraft in the same proportions with each party being responsible for repayment and interest and charges on their allocated share of the debt and keeping the other party indemnified against the consequences of failure so to do.

(ii) to notify all credit and charge card companies where the parties are joint or first and second cardholders, cancelling and destroying all relevant credit and charge cards and allocating responsibility for the debts at the point of closure in accordance with which of them is to retain the goods thereby purchased or enjoyed the benefit of the services thereby obtained, with each party being responsible for repayment and interest on their allocated share of the debt and keeping the other party indemnified against the consequences of failure so to do.

Other capital assets

(iii)   that any other capital asset jointly owned by the parties will be sold and divided between the parties equally (*or state appropriate proportions*) with incidental sale costs being borne in the same proportions. (*Where there is an endowment mortgage, consideration can be given to whether the endowment policy is to be surrendered on breakdown and the sum obtained divided or whether it may be possible to sell or transfer it to one of the parties. A clause could indicate that the parties agree to consider the options available.*)

Personal property and jointly owned property

18 On termination of this agreement, it is agreed that:

(i) all personal effects, chattels and other property solely owned by one of the parties in accordance with the terms of this agreement will be retained by that party and any party not remaining in the family home will remove all their personal effects on or before sale or transfer of the property.

(ii) all jointly owned property will be divided [equally (*or state appropriate proportions*)] by agreement between the parties. In default of agreement as to division of the goods, [all jointly owned items] [those jointly owned items which both parties wish to retain] will be sold, and the proceeds divided [equally (*or state appropriate proportions*)] between them.

Mediation/arbitration

19 In case of any dispute arising concerning the terms of this agreement, the parties agree that the dispute will be referred to (*insert name or organisation*) who will act as a [mediator][arbitrator] between the parties [without prejudice to either party's right to apply to the court for resolution of the dispute] [whose decision shall be binding upon both parties].

Maintenance and children

20 On termination of this agreement, [neither party shall be under any obligation to maintain the other.] [X will pay Y (*insert figure and amend order of parties as appropriate*) per month for (*specify fixed period if appropriate*).] [Where one party has reduced their income in order to undertake child care responsibilities any payments being made in accordance with clause 10(b) shall continue to be paid (*or indicate any other agreement which the parties wish to insert*).]

21 On termination of the agreement, the children shall live with [X or Y] (*or specify how children will divide their time*) who shall ensure that they have

regular contact with the other party and their family. Neither party shall change the child(ren)'s surname without the consent of the other party. (*This is of course subject to any orders made by the court.*)

22 This agreement shall be interpreted in accordance with the law of England and Wales. Any provision found by the court to be illegal, invalid or unenforceable may be severed from the agreement and the remaining provisions shall continue to have full force and effect.

Signed as a deed by X

in the presence of

Signed as a deed by Y

in the presence of

Schedule 1

Insert statement of the parties' respective assets, income and liabilities (see Recital 4).

Schedule 2

Insert statement of the parties' respective direct contributions at the date of the agreement (see clause 1(b)).

Note that additional Schedules may have been referred to in clauses 6 and 7 and the footnote to clause 1(b) (method of calculation).

Appendix II

DECLARATION OF TRUST FOR CO-OWNERS OF FREEHOLD PROPERTY WITH DEFERRED TENANCY IN COMMON AND SUBJECT TO ORDINARY REPAYMENT MORTGAGE

THIS DECLARATION OF TRUST is made this   day of   19

BETWEEN (*insert name*) of (*insert address*) (X) and

(*insert name*) of (*insert address*) (Y), hereinafter jointly called 'the co-owners'

IT IS HEREBY AGREED AND DECLARED THAT:

1 By a [conveyance][transfer] dated (*insert date*) and made between (*insert seller's name*) of the one part and the co-owners of the other part, the freehold property known as (*insert address of the family home*) [and registered at HM Land Registry under Title Number (*insert number*)] (hereinafter called 'the Family Home') was for a purchase price of £(*insert purchase price*) [conveyed][transferred] to the co-owners in fee simple TO HOLD as joint tenants in equity until severance of the equitable joint tenancy, whereupon they shall hold as tenants in common in equity in the shares specified in clause 5 below.

2 The co-owners purchased the Family Home to provide a joint home for themselves [and their children (*Add details where the children are not all the children of the relationship*). (*Note that this makes clear the purpose of the trust which may be important in the context of the Trusts of Land and Appointment of Trustees Act 1996.*) [The co-owners have entered into a Cohabitation Agreement dated (*insert date*) governing their occupation of the Family Home.] (*Where a cohabitation agreement is being entered into, the clauses governing the beneficial interests in the Family Home may be referred to or repeated in the declaration of trust. Advisers should ensure that the two documents are not inconsistent as regards the beneficial interests in the family home or indicate which is to prevail.*)

3 The Family Home has been purchased with the aid of a mortgage advance of £(*insert sum of advance*) from (*insert name of mortgagee*) plus capital contributions made by [each of the co-owners] (*or specify which co-owner if only one*) to the Total Purchase Price in the proportions referred to in Schedule 1 hereto.

4 The mortgage is an ordinary repayment mortgage and [subject to any agreed adjustment of contributions consequent upon reduction of a co-owner's income due to child care responsibilities and set out in the Cohabitation Agreement (*the relevant clause should be referred to or a similar clause added here where there is no cohabitation agreement*)] the co-owners covenant with each other to contribute [equally][in the following proportions] to the mortgage repayments [and upon sale or transfer of the Family Home, to redeem the

mortgage in those same proportions (*This should be used where the calculations of the shares are based upon the gross proceeds of sale and the co-owners agree to redeem their share of the mortgage redemption figure)]*—

[X (*insert proportion*)% and Y (*insert proportion*)%]

Fixed shares

5 Upon severance of the equitable joint tenancy and thereafter, the co-owners shall HOLD the Family Home as tenants in common in equity in [equal shares]

OR

[the shares specified below calculated with reference to the net proceeds of sale defined as (*insert definition agreed, eg the gross sale price less, sum required to redeem mortgage, estate agent's fees, legal expenses incurred in the sale*):

X (*insert percentage*) and

Y (*insert percentage*)]

regardless of the contributions actually made towards the purchase price, mortgage repayments and other outgoings.

OR

Floating shares

5(a)   Upon severance of the equitable joint tenancy and thereafter, the co-owners shall [subject to clause 6 below] HOLD the Family Home as tenants in common in equity in shares calculated by ascertaining in the first instance their respective proportions of direct contributions towards the purchase of the Family Home expressed as a percentage of the [gross] proceeds of sale (*define or adapt if legal or estate agency expenses are to be deducted prior to calculation of proportions*) but subject to deducting from each party's respective proportions, their individual mortgage redemption liability required to redeem their share of the mortgage redemption figure to be calculated in accordance with clause 4 as at the date of sale or transfer of the Family Home. The method of calculation of the co-owners' respective beneficial interests are set out in the Schedule hereto.

5(b)   For the avoidance of doubt, direct contributions to the purchase of the Family Home include (*specify as appropriate and indicate whether it is intended the list should be exhaustive*):

[capital contributions (including right to buy/acquire or other discount, incidental purchase costs) to the total purchase price]

[payment of mortgage instalments in accordance with clause 4 hereof]

[legal expenses incurred on purchase of the Family Home]

[AND DO NOT INCLUDE]

[contributions to the cost of repairs and/or improvements to the Family Home]

Failure to pay mortgage repayments

6 If, other than [by agreement of the co-owners in writing] [or] [by operation of the Separation Provisions of the Cohabitation Agreement made between the co-owners and dated (*insert date*)] [or] [by virtue of one of the co-owners having reduced their income in order to undertake child care on behalf of them both] [or] [by virtue of any practical arrangement whereby one co-owner undertakes instead to make a greater contribution than agreed to the payment of other outgoings [or debts] in respect of the Family Home on behalf of] [both co-owners][the other co-owner], one of them ('the co-owner in default') fails to make his/her agreed contributions to the mortgage repayments, it is hereby agreed that the calculation of the respective beneficial shares of the co-owner in default in the Family Home [shall not be thereby affected] *or* [shall be affected in so far as the consequent increased indebtedness to the mortgagee shall be added to the proportion of the mortgage redemption figure to be debited from the co-owner in default on sale or transfer of the Family Home. Any payment towards this debt made by the other co-owner to the mortgagee, unless otherwise agreed, shall be treated as a loan to the co-owner in default (*insert any terms with regard to interest*), which it is agreed may at the date of the sale or transfer be deducted from the co-owner in default's beneficial interest in the Family Home in so far as it has not been repaid and without prejudice to the other co-owner's right to recover any further balance of the loan debt.] (*This last option assumes instructions have been given that other than in specified situations, any default by one co-owner of the mortgage repayments is to remain that co-owner's debt and that any additional repayments made are to be treated as a loan to the co-owner in default.*)

General note: Carefully consider instructions on the issue of failure to pay and cross refer to any cohabitation agreement executed by the co-owners. Other relevant clauses included in the draft cohabitation agreement (see page 195) can be inserted instead in the declaration in the same form where no cohabitation agreement is to be executed. In particular, clauses in relation to sharing of outgoings, procedure and effect of payment for repairs and improvements, non-monetary contributions, lump sum repayment of mortgage.)

Signed as a deed by X

in the presence of

Signed as a deed by Y

in the presence of

Schedule 1

Method of calculation of shares of co-owners following severance of the equitable joint tenancy

1 Calculate the Total Purchase Price:

> **ADD**
>
>> Purchase Price +
>>
>> Legal Costs and Disbursements
>>
>> **TOTAL PURCHASE PRICE**

2 Calculate capital contribution of each co-owner

> **ADD**
>
>> Capital paid by X +
>>
>> Right to buy discount etc +
>>
>> Contribution to Legal Costs made by X
>>
>> **X'S TOTAL CAPITAL CONTRIBUTION**
>
> **DIVIDE** this by the TOTAL PURCHASE PRICE:
>
>> X'S TOTAL CAPITAL CONTRIBUTION   =**X's capital share%**
>> TOTAL PURCHASE PRICE
>
> **Repeat in relation to Y:**
>
>> Y'S TOTAL CAPITAL CONTRIBUTION   = **Y's capital share%**
>> TOTAL PURCHASE PRICE

3 Calculate the mortgage share of each co-owner

Total mortgage advance **x** (% payable by X in clause 4)= **X's mortgage share%**
> TOTAL PURCHASE PRICE

Total mortgage advance **x** (% payable by Y in clause 4) =**Y's mortgage share%**
> TOTAL PURCHASE PRICE

4 Calculate each co-owner's total share of the purchase price:

> **ADD**
>
>> X's capital share +
>>
>> <u>X's mortgage share</u>
>>
>> **<u>X's total share %</u>**

Then:

> **Repeat in relation to Y**

5 Calculate each co-owner's liability in respect of redemption of the mortgage

Multiply mortgage redemption figure **by** % payable by X in clause 4

Then:

> **Repeat in relation to Y**

6 Calculate final share of each co-owner on sale

Multiply

X's total share % **by** Gross Proceeds of Sale and **DEDUCT** X's redemption liability

> **Repeat in relation to Y**

Index

Armed forces
dismissal from, on grounds of
sexual orientation, 2.90, 2.94–
2.97, 2.101
homosexual conduct in, 1.20, 1.21,
1.27–1.29, 1.36
need for legislative reform, 8.17–
8.20

Assured periodic tenancy
notice to quit, 4.73
succession to, 4.75

Backroom sex see **Disorderly houses**

Breach of contract
sexual orientation, on grounds of,
2.99

Breastfeeding
European directive, 2.79

Brothels
condoms, use of, as evidence of
prostitution, 7.46
managing, 7.41–7.42
suppression, 1.04–1.06

Buggery see also **Homosexual acts**
arrest and punishment, 7.24–7.27
DPP's consent to prosecution
involving under-age party,
8.06
heterosexual, consensual, 1.20,
7.07
importuning, 7.29–7.33
maximum penalty, 7.27, 8.06
meaning, 7.07, 7.19
private, in, 7.07–7.18, 8.06
procuring, 7.28
time limits for bringing prosecution, 7.20–7.23, 8.06

Byelaws
indecent behaviour, regulating,
7.58–7.62

Capital gains tax
disadvantages for gay persons,
8.37

Capital gains tax—*contd*
exemption from, 5.18, 5.19
generally, 5.12
gifts not attracting tax, 5.14
liability to, 5.12
lifetime gift to avoid IHT, 5.13
main residence, disposal of, 5.18,
5.19

Care proceedings
young lesbians and gay men,
3.180, 3.181

Children
adoption see **Adoption**
care proceedings, where gay or
lesbian, 3.180, 3.181
creation see **In vitro fertilisation**;
Ova donation; **Surrogacy**
custody see **Custody, care and
control**
fostering see **Fostering**
knowledge of mother's lesbianism,
benefits from, 3.33–3.36
lesbian and gay man conceiving,
through sperm donation,
3.121
parenthood see **Parenthood**
teasing, likelihood of, 3.08, 3.09,
3.19

Codes of practice
anti-discriminatory, 2.103

Cohabitation agreement
absence of intention to create legal
relations, 4.13
advantages, 4.06, 4.07
contents, 4.09, 4.10
declaration of trust, in form of see
Declaration of trust
enforceability, 4.10, 4.11
generally, 4.04
illegal on grounds of public policy,
whether, 4.12
limitations of, 4.07
limited liability under, 4.06
need to review, 4.08
precedent, App I

Cohabitation agreement—*contd*
severance clause, need to include,
4.16
undue influence, voidable for, 4.15
validity, 4.05
void for uncertainty, where, 4.14
voidable, where, 4.15

Criminal law
acquittal statistics, 7.05
blasphemous libel, 7.186
brothels *see* **Brothels**
buggery *see* **Buggery**
byelaws, breach of, 7.59–7.62
caution and bind overs, 7.78–7.79
contradictions and inconsistencies
in, 8.06
decriminalised homosexual
activity–
generally, 7.07, 7.08
private nature of activities, 7.09,
7.11
disorderly houses *see* **Disorderly
houses**
drugs *see* **Drugs**
ecclesiastical law, 7.63–7.64
generally, 7.01–7.06
gross indecency *see* **Gross indecency**
importuning, 7.29–7.33
indecent assault, 7.91–7.93
kerb crawling, 7.43
new approach, need for, 8.07–8.09
outraging public decency, 7.47–
7.49
pimping, 7.38–7.40
policing strategy, shifts in, 7.65–
7.71
pornography *see* **Pornography**
private acts, 7.08, 7.09, 8.06
procuring, 7.28
prostitution, 7.34–7.35
public order offences, 7.50–7.54
rape, 7.90
sadomasochism *see* **Sadomasochism**
secondary legislation, need for
reform of, 8.10–8.11

Criminal law—*contd*
soliciting, 7.36–7.37, 8.06
Town Police Clauses Act 1847,
offence under, 7.55–7.57

Custody, care and control
expert evidence, importance of,
3.19–3.22, 3.30–3.41
generally *see* **Parenthood**
homosexuality, whether likely to
encourage, 3.19, 3.29
lesbian couple, 3.12–3.18, 3.23–3.29
militant lesbianism, 3.26, 3.27
non-militant lesbianism, 3.26
psychological stress, whether
likely, 3.24
severance from normal society,
whether likely, 3.24
teasing, likelihood of, 3.19
unhappiness etc, whether likely,
3.24

Death
inadequate provision in will—
generally, 5.55–5.62
iniquities of system, 5.61
limited nature of legislation,
5.62
person maintained by deceased:
meaning, 5.59
reasonable provision: meaning,
5.58
time limit for making
application, 5.60
intestacy, 5.55–5.62
tax planning for—
generally, 5.39–5.40
inheritance tax *see* **Inheritance
tax**
tax breaks, need to minimise, 5.65
will—
examples, 5.41–5.54
wisdom of making, 5.39, 5.40,
5.63, 5.64

Declaration of trust
deciding to share home of one
partner, 4.18
generally, 4.17

Political asylum—*contd*
generally, 6.36
HIV infection etc, whether
barrier to, 6.44–6.53
persecution, whether
prosecution amounting to,
6.43
'social group', whether sexuality
defining, 6.39–6.42
UK record on, 6.37

Pornography
carefully targeted audience, 7.134
child pornography, 7.163–7.173
'deprave and corrupt', attempts to
define, 7.129, 7.130
gay retail outlets, obtainable from,
whether readers likely to be
corrupted etc, 7.142, 7.143
generally, 7.123
importation, 7.152–7.153
indecent displays, 7.157–7.158
indecent material, control generally, 7.144
Internet, on the *see* **Internet pornography**
isolated items, viewing in context,
7.136
legislation to control, 7.125
obscene article: meaning, 7.127,
7.128
penalties, 7.126
permissible images, 7.131
possession of, 7.126
post, sending through, 7.154–7.155
'public good' defence, 7.137, 7.138,
7.139
public order offences, 7.159–7.162
publishing, 7.126
safer sex promotional material,
7.124, 7.133–7.139
seizure without prosecution, 7.140,
7.141
significant proportion of likely
readership, whether likely to
corrupt, 7.135
text, publication of, 7.130, 7.132
unsolicited material, 7.156
video recordings—
certification not a safeguard
from prosecution, 7.148

Pornography—*contd*
video recordings—*contd*
defences, 7.150
exemptions from control, 7.145
generally, 7.145–7.151
lending, 7.146
offences, 7.149
penalties, 7.149, 7.151
prosecution, preferred approach
to, 7.151
sex education, 7.147

Precedents
cohabitation agreement for owner
occupier, App I
declaration of trust for co-owners
of freehold property with
deferred tenancy in common,
App II

Pregnancy
European directive, 2.79

Property
disputes *see* **Family home** (ownership disputes)
purchasing–
good practice checklist, 4.46
see also **Declaration of trust; Joint
tenancy; Tenancy in
common**

Proprietary estoppel
generally 4.116–4.120

Prostitution
condoms, supply and use of, 7.44–
7.46
generally, 7.34–7.35
outreach work, 7.44
rent boy, 8.06

Rape
generally, 7.90

Redundancy
part-time worker's rights on, 2.76

Rent Act tenancy
succession to, 4.76–4.78, 8.24

Sadomasochism
branding not necessarily constituting, 7.103
depiction of such activities, 7.105
ECHR attitude towards, 7.101–
7.102
generally, 8.06
judicial condemnation, 7.99
justification for State interference,
7.98
Operation Spanner case, 7.94–
7.105
rubber and other fetish activities,
7.106–7.108

Self-employed women
European directive, 2.79

Settled land
abolition, 4.81

Sex discrimination
causing others to discriminate, 2.41
compensation, 2.46, 2.47
direct discrimination, 2.23–2.27,
2.31, 2.61, 2.62
directives, 2.77, 2.78, 2.79
dress codes, 2.27
educational provision, in, 2.24,
2.48
employment, in *see under* **Employment**
enforcement, 2.44
equal pay legislation, 2.21
exceptions on prohibition, 2.42–
2.43
gender reassignment, following,
2.85–2.89, 2.96
indirect discrimination, 2.28–2.29,
2.31
International Covenant for Civil
and Political Rights, 2.80
legislation, 2.19–2.32
like with like comparison, 2.22
maximum age limits, imposition of,
2.29
pregnancy discrimination, in, 2.26
questionnaire, service of, prior to
issue of proceedings, 2.32

Sex discrimination—*contd*
remedies, 2.45
sexual orientation, dismissal on
grounds of—
sex discrimination legislation,
whether available, 2.60–
2.72
see also under **Dismissal**
standard of proof, 2.31
time limits for issue of proceedings,
2.44
types, 2.20
victimisation, 2.30

Sexual harassment
acts outside the course of employment, 2.40
direct discrimination, as, 2.35
EC Recommendation, 2.36–2.38
employers' liability, 2.39, 2.40
generally, 2.34
homophobic behaviour of co-
worker, 2.65–2.72
single act constituting, 2.35
standard of behaviour constituting,
2.35

Soliciting
generally, 7.36–7.37, 8.06

Stonewall
Equality 2000 *see* **Equality 2000
campaign**
Immigration Group, 6.05
report into discrimination, 2.17

Surrogacy
commercial surrogacy arrangements, 3.124–3.126
commissioning party not donor,
3.123
disputes arising from surrogacy
arrangement, 3.127, 3.128
donor as commissioning party,
3.122
generally, 3.119
legal advice for payment to surrogate mother etc, provision of,
3.126
legislation governing, 3.119

Surrogacy—*contd*
  newspaper advertisement, prohibi-
    tion on, 3.125
  surrogacy arrangement: meaning,
    3.120, 121
  surrogate mother: meaning, 3.120

Tenancy
  assignment, restriction on, 4.73
  assured *see* **Assured periodic
    tenancy**
  joint *see* **Joint tenancy**
  Rent Act tenancy, succession to,
    4.76–4.78, 8.24
  succession to, on death, 1.34, 4.74,
    4.79, 8.24
  transfer, restriction on, 4.73

Tenancy in common
  creation, 4.36
  death of joint tenant, 4.34
  declaration of trust, need for, 4.43
  deferred ascertainment of benefi-
    cial interests, 4.36, 4.43
  drawbacks, 4.36
  express declaration—
    need for, 4.41
    variation, 4.43
  fixed shares, specifying, 4.43
  'floating shares' in, 4.43
  generally, 4.34, 4.45
  legal advice, appropriate, 4.42, 4.43
  negative equity, dealing with, 4.43
  registered land, 4.42
  severance, 4.34
  unequal contributions to purchase
    price, where, 4.40

Travel concessions
  same-sex partner's right to, 1.30,
    2.91–2.93

Trust of land
  constructive trust—
    generally, 4.95–4.96, 4.103,
      4.106, 4.108
    inferred, 4.101, 4.102
    judicial two-stage approach,
      4.110–4.113
  dispute resolution—
    caution or landcharge, lodging,
      4.84
    generally, 4.81
    orders, power to make, 4.81
    relevant circumstances, 4.82,
      4.83
  express trust, 4.87–4.90
  generally, 4.81
  introduction, 4.81
  resulting trust, 4.91–4.94, 4.102,
    4.104, 4.105, 4.106, 4.107
  rights under, 4.81

Trust for sale
  abolition, 4.81

Unfair dismissal *see* **Dismissal**

Will
  absence of, 5.55–5.62
  charitable bequests, 5.52–5.54
  children, gifts to, 5.43
  examples, generally, 5.41–5.54
  family bequests, 5.43–5.47
  gifts to others in addition to
    partner, 5.42
  inadequate provision in, 5.55–5.62
  married gay person, 5.48–5.51
  need for, 5.39, 5.40, 5.63, 5.64
  simple, 5.41

Wolfenden Report
  generally, 1.08–1.11
  publication, 1.07